THE STATE AND WORKING WOMEN

THE STATE AND WORKING WOMEN

A COMPARATIVE STUDY OF BRITAIN AND SWEDEN

MARY RUGGIE

PRINCETON UNIVERSITY PRESS
PRINCETON, NEW JERSEY

For John
  who helped make it possible
and Andreas
  who gave it a special meaning

CONTENTS

LIST OF TABLES

LIST OF FIGURES

PREFACE

As increasing numbers of women have entered the labor market in all advanced industrialized countries from the 1960s on, more attention has been paid by women's movements and social scientists to the issue of women and work. By and large, the concern has focused on women-specific factors that affect the status of women compared to men in the work force. That is to say, the emphasis has been on seeking to explain women's inequality on the basis of the deep-seatedness of traditional conceptions of women's roles and the pervasiveness of sex discrimination. My sense is that, as important as these factors are, they fail to explain fully the persistence of women's inferior status in the labor market. Moreover, they channel policy development in a direction that is as likely to perpetuate as to alleviate the condition of "separate and unequal." I contend that there are factors which are not gender-related that critically shape the relationship between social forces and women's position. Specifically, I argue that the issue of women and work must be placed within the broader context of the configuration of state/society relations.

In elaborating this thesis, I examine the different policies which have been developed by Britain and Sweden to facilitate women's employment and to equalize the status of women and men in the labor market. I first examine the relative importance of prevailing economic conditions and traditional conceptions of women's roles as explanations for the differences in policy responses. Neither is found to be compelling precisely because the state differentially mediates their effects in the two countries. The state in Britain has adopted what I call a liberal-welfare approach to social policy, in which intervention is hesitant and limited and programs are incremental and fragmented. The role of the state in Sweden resembles a societal corporatist model, whereby goals are determined by bargaining among the leading partners in the governing coalition of state, labor, and capital, for a clientele that is conceived in universalistic terms, and in which services are more integrated and holistic. The central argument of this study is that women in Sweden have achieved greater relative equality because the Swedish form of societal corporatism has allowed Sweden to develop a combination of general social and economic policies that also happen to benefit women. In contrast, the continued segmentation of state/society relations in Britain has prevented the kind of state intervention that would overcome the unmediated impact of economic constraints and traditional role conceptions on women's economic status. In sum, policies for women in these two countries cannot be explained directly in terms of factors that relate specifically and simply to women or to the economy. Rather, policies for women are a by-product of the broader configuration of state/society relations.

My thanks go, above all, to my husband, John, who gave me encouragement, support, and critical comments when they were most needed. Many people helped with the research. I want to thank officials at the various ministries in both London and Stockholm for giving generously of their time and expertise. Special thanks are owed to Peter Moss and the Thomas Coram Research Unit, University of London Institute of Education, for their assistance and hospitality during the initial phases of my research. An earlier draft of the manuscript was read by Philip Selznick, Guy E. Swanson, and Aaron Wildavsky; I am grateful for their advice and comments. Finally, a grant from the Institute on Western Europe at Columbia University made it possible for me to update the study and to undertake the happy task of turning a dissertation into a book, and a grant from Barnard College financed the typing of the manuscript.

MARY RUGGIE
New York City
June 1983

THE STATE AND WORKING WOMEN

CHAPTER 1

WOMEN, WORK, AND THE STATE: AN OVERVIEW

INTRODUCTION

In the past few decades, the number of women actively employed in the labor force has risen sharply. This phenomenon has occurred in almost every industrialized nation.[1] It has transformed the character of the work force, since the majority of new women workers are in the rapidly expanding white-collar and service sectors, and it has transformed the character of family life, since the major increase in women's employment has been among mothers with young children.

Demands are being made on the state not only to assist in some way in the provision of facilitative services for working women but also to guide the significant social changes involved. These demands do not only or necessarily come from women themselves. In fact, in many nations women's movements are weakly organized and far from forceful in voicing the concerns of working women.[2] Demands for state assistance are just as likely to stem from broader considerations concerning the economy as a whole and the proper use of the labor force within it. The capacity of states both to discern these requirements or demands and to respond to them is highly variable. In some cases, governments have taken the initiative to direct the changes

[1] Martha Darling, *The Role of Women in the Economy* (Paris: Organization for Economic Co-operation and Development, 1975).

[2] Carolyn Teich Adams and Kathryn Teich Winston, *Mothers at Work: Public Policies in the United States, Sweden, and China* (New York: Longman, 1980), Chapter 3.

involved. In other cases, "legislative measures and programmes [generally lag] behind the actual social, economic
and political changes they seek to institutionalize."[3] Differences such as these, especially when they occur among nations that are similar in other respects, are the stuff of
comparative analysis. The implications of such differences
in turn are important for social policy, concerning the future of women workers in particular and policy covering
social change more generally.

This study examines state responses to women's employment in two ostensibly similar nations: Britain and Sweden. Since Britain and Sweden are both forerunners in the
development of the modern welfare state, one might expect
similarity in ideology and even in substantive policies. The
following chapters show that this expectation is not borne
out. That it is not raises important questions about the role
of women as well as about the welfare state. The specific
questions asked in this study are: (1) What is the pattern
of differences in state responses toward working women
in Britain and Sweden, as seen in both policies and programs? (2) What accounts for these patterns? (3) What are
their implications for women workers?

POLICIES AND PROGRAMS

The policies examined in this study concern assistance
to women prior to and during employment, in particular,
labor market and child care policies. A number of specific
programs are included in each policy area. For example,
labor market policies which prepare women for employment include programs for training and job placement;
these are fashioned with an eye toward bottlenecks and
opportunities in the labor market. Another branch of labor
market policies pertains to the particular problems that
women face in employment, such as discrimination in
placement, promotion, and pay. Child care policies in gen-

[3] Darling, *The Role of Women*, p. 87.

eral are confined to the provision of facilities for preschool-aged children of working mothers. These programs may be organized through the public, private, or voluntary sectors, and may or may not be linked to other areas of policy, such as education.

In each of these policy areas the programs and measures in Britain are less facilitative of women's employment than are those in Sweden. For example, despite institutional changes in Britain's manpower programs, women's occupational segregation remains as persistent as ever. The vast majority of women trainees in public training programs are taking courses in commercial and clerical work, occupations in which their status is low and their opportunities for advancement are limited. Employment services can do little to assist women to find better positions if women are improperly trained. On top of that, the public employment exchanges in Britain are ineffective in filling vacancies. Formally, Britain has gone far in its measures to prevent sex discrimination in employment and pay. Legislation effective since 1975 has enabled women to enter occupations which are non-traditional for their sex, and to receive the same pay as men doing exactly the same work. However, women are neither encouraged to find nor assisted in finding non-traditional occupations; very few women do exactly the same work as men; and discrimination has turned out to be a formidable fact to prove. Chapter 3 presents these labor market policies for Britain and Chapter 4 for Sweden.

Child care policies in Britain are discussed in Chapter 5. In many ways child care policies in Britain are even less facilitative of mothers' endeavors to work than are labor market policies. This is because "normal" working mothers are excluded from public day care programs. These are services for welfare clients only, that is, mothers who have to work for financial reasons or who, for some other reasons, are recipients of public assistance. In principle, if these priority needs are met in a residential area, day nurseries can extend their services to "normal" working mothers for a small user fee. But lack of growth in provision has precluded this eventuality. In sum, child care policies have not kept pace with changes in women's employment in Britain. Labor market policies have changed, but have not effectively advanced the position of women in the labor market.

The contrast with Sweden could not be greater. In the 1960s, Sweden began to implement a new and far-reaching labor market policy. It includes programs for aptitude-testing, training, job placement, and analysis of labor market trends and related developments. Almost all of these services are conducted by the public sector to assure that all persons seeking work are provided with similar opportunities and that they have the best possible information available to them. Swedish labor market policies are organized on the basis of two goals: economic growth and full employment. The latter is believed to contribute to the former. Accordingly, all persons who want to work and can work, including mothers of young children and even the handicapped, are encouraged to work and assisted in doing so. Some special labor market programs exist for women, such as special courses for women re-entering the labor market after an absence.

Sweden's anti-discrimination legislation is not as strong as Britain's. Matters of sex discrimination are handled in two ways. The first is through positive incentives in labor market policies, encouraging employers to hire and train women for jobs that are non-traditional for their sex or stipulating hiring quotas in certain new jobs initiated by the public sector. Second, discrimination in on-the-job matters, such as hiring, promotion, and pay, is taken up by union representatives and management. If the matter cannot be settled at the decentralized level, labor courts act as arbitrators. The issue of pay, in particular, is the exclusive prerogative of collective bargaining. In the main, unions have readily adopted women's concerns in Sweden. But overall, the progress of women in the labor market is mixed. Women's pay as a proportion of men's is higher in Sweden than in most other western nations, but it is still not identical to men's. In some ways, women workers in Sweden are segregated to an even greater extent in fewer occupations than their cohorts in Britain. More women in Sweden are professionals than in Britain, but they are mostly in traditional and sex-typed professional occupations such as lower grade teaching and nursing. Despite these qualifications, we can say that labor market policies in Sweden are highly facilitative of women's employment.

The same is true of Swedish child care policies, which are treated in Chapter 6. In principle, all women who work are entitled to places for their preschool children in a public sector program. However, there are still too few places in child centers (the functional equivalent of day nurseries). Thus, many children are placed instead in family day homes (the functional equivalent of child-minders), which are organized and supervised by the public sector.

EXPLANATIONS FOR THE PATTERN OF RESPONSES

The study as a whole explores three major areas of explanation for these different patterns of policy responses to women's employment in Britain and Sweden. These are: (1) economic determinants or constraints, (2) sex dicrimination or related women-specific factors, and (3) the role of the state. Each chapter focuses on one area of explanation in particular, but the interplay between these three areas of explanation is stressed.

Economic Determinants. Perhaps the most obvious explanation for policy differences between Britain and Sweden regarding women's employment matters is the respective economic capacities of the two countries and the different demands for women workers in the two economies. Chapter 2 examines the effect of these economic factors. The respective economic capacities are analyzed through such aggregate variables as GNP, growth rates, structure of GDP and level of industrialization, and rates and sectors of employment and unemployment. Britain and Sweden do differ in their economic capacities, but not in such a way as to allow us to say anything conclusive about the effect of these differences on women's employment. The analysis is guided by the working hypothesis that greater economic capacity creates the conditions for higher rates of female labor force participation. In the 1950s, Sweden's economic capacity was somewhat higher than Britain's, but a smaller proportion of Swedish women were working at that time than in Britain. Employment rates among women in Sweden rose markedly in the 1960s. Sweden's economic capacity did advance significantly during this time period. However, a worldwide economic boom was taking place in the 1960s, which affected Britain as much as Sweden and it did not affect women's employment rates as much in Britain as in Sweden.

The reasons for this difference, I argue, lie in the form of the economic policies adopted by the two countries. In presenting these policies, I briefly note the nature of the economic constraints which prevented Britain from following an alternative course of action and enabled Sweden to adopt its chosen course. These include international as well as domestic factors, which are explored more fully in Chapter 7.

This argument suggests the necessity of looking more deeply into matters of policy, in short, at the role of the state and at the effect of state policies on economic factors. This conclusion is also underscored by the section in Chapter 2 that examines the differences in labor market "demand" for women workers. To analyze demand, I focus on women's occupational specializations and changes in the numbers employed and vacancies in these fields of employment. The findings are basically similar for Britain and Sweden: women in both countries are heavily employed in clerical and service occupations and by the public sector in health, education, and welfare-related occupations. Employment in these occupations increased significantly in the 1960s in both countries. During recessionary periods in the 1970s, however, women's unemployment rates increased in Britain much more than in Sweden. I argue that this rise and fall in "demand" for women workers is not a feature of the labor market alone, for government policies created the conditions for the changes in women's employment in each case. The rises in "demand" for women's employment occurred in part because of increases in public spending and corresponding expansion in the public sectors in both Britain and Sweden. The continuation of women's employment in Sweden despite the recession is directly related to the labor market policies discussed above. No comparable set of policies exists in Britain. Accordingly, women in Britain remain marginal workers subject to market forces.

The conclusion of Chapter 2 is that, while both economic factors (industrialization, growth) and women-specific issues (occupational segregation) do affect women's employment, the role of the state is a strong mediating factor in channeling these effects. In particular, the less active character of state intervention in Britain allows economic and sex-specific factors to have a greater impact on women workers; the state in Sweden has taken measures to mitigate the effect of these factors.

Women-specific Factors. Another area of explanation for policy differences in the two countries is in prevailing conceptions of the role of women. Chapter 3 presents a framework for analyzing these differences in conceptions of the role of women. Three models are proposed, depicting conceptions of the problems women face in employment related matters: individual, role-related, and social structural. In the individual model, women's employment problems are seen to stem from inadequacies in women themselves, such as personality disabilities or lack of training. In the role-related model, women's employment problems are seen to stem from women's dual roles at home and at work; since the two roles are in conflict, women's full and successful participation in the workplace is hindered. The social structural model focuses on factors in the labor market generally to understand the nature of the problems that women workers confront. Indeed, these problems are depicted as being not necessarily specific to women alone, but inclusive of all low status, low-paid workers. The existence of a "dual labor market" is taken to be responsible for the conditions of employment inequalities.

The substantive policies described in Chapters 3 and 4 are analyzed in terms of these three models so as to discern the differences between Britain and Sweden. Many of the policies in Britain appear to reflect the "individual" conception of the problem. For example, job training programs are oriented toward self-improvement for women to bring them up to the level of men. The British anti-discrimination and equal pay legislation is based on the premise that, to the extent that some women are capable of filling men's jobs, employers must only stop discriminating for equality to be achieved. This legislation misses the fact of inequalities in opportunities prior to employment that channel women into inferior jobs, including traditional sex-role training in the schools and lack of supportive systems for mothers. The Swedish policies appear to fall somewhere in between the role-related and social structural models. For example, there is a clear attempt in all the labor market policies to encourage women to enter occupations that are non-traditional for their sex, especially if labor shortages exist in these fields. Union efforts to narrow wage differentials between low- and high-paid workers also favor women. Even though these efforts are not specific to women, they are based on a recognition of the forces of duality in the labor market.

In sum, traditional conceptions of the role of women exist in both countries, but to a lesser extent in Sweden. Moreover, these conceptions have greater effect in shaping government policies for women in Britain than in Sweden. Why is this so? I have observed that the character of state intervention mediates the impact of women-specific factors and of economic factors in such a way that these factors are allowed to have a greater impact in Britain, whereas they are attenuated by the state in Sweden. Again, we must look at the role of the state for a deeper understanding of policies for women.

The Role of the State.   Britain and Sweden differ not only in the substance of government policy. More generally, the state in Britain intervenes weakly in altering the effects of the market and of tradition on women's employment, whereas the state in Sweden actively seeks to control market forces and to change traditional attitudes about women's roles. Why and how is this so? In Chapters 5 and 6, these differences in the character of state intervention are examined more intensely in the context of a single policy area: day care for children. The chapters show that Britain and Sweden differ fundamentally in both the form and the extent of state intervention in society, that is, in the balance of state/society relations. Chapter 7 demonstrates that these differences, in turn, are not themselves due to the issue-area of day care or the role of women in the economy, but capture an essential difference in the British and Swedish variants of the welfare state. Below, I sketch out what is meant by the term "welfare state," that is, what Britain and Sweden have in common, and I present two ideal-type variants of the welfare state, which I use to highlight how Britain and Sweden differ.

Among the many meanings of the term "welfare state," there is a core of agreement that it implies "a state commitment of some degree which modifies the play of market forces" in the attempt to achieve a greater measure of social equality.[4] The essence of this state/society nexus is generally expressed by the metaphor of intervention—that is, state intervention in the functioning of the market system. When fully spelled out, this becomes an extraordinarily powerful metaphor, as it contains within it the contours of a theory of social transformation. The metaphor of intervention first

---

[4] Dorothy Wedderburn, "Facts and Theories of the Welfare State," *The Socialist Register* (1965): 127-28.

of all implies the institutional separation of state and society that is characteristic of the modern liberal order. Moreover, it suggests that the state acts to intervene in social relationships in order initially to institute market relations and subsequently in response to the effects of market failure. Last, it implies that the state, as a result of so intervening, accumulates power over society that it increasingly comes to exercise in accordance with consumatory as opposed to instrumental norms and values. That is, the state begins to exhibit in its actions a "plan rationality" rather than a "market rationality."[5] Seen in this light, the development of the modern welfare state may be viewed as one subset of that broader class of social change that Karl Polanyi called "the great transformation"—a transformation in the balance of state/society relations that resulted from the protective measures that the state was compelled to undertake as a result of the dislocating and destructive social effects of "the commodity fiction" and the institution of the "self-regulating market" in land, labor, and capital.[6]

The modern welfare state may be differentiated from the other forms of state/society relations produced by "the great transformation" by virtue of its commitment to social equality and to democratic control. But of course not all welfare states are alike in all of these respects. How each welfare state goes about "intervening," that is, what frame of reference guides the timing, form, and extent of state action distinguishes one welfare state from another. These frames of reference for state intervention, then, form a basis for the comparative study of welfare states. I suggest now a simple typology of frames of reference for state intervention, consisting of two ideal types. I then locate the historical evolution of the welfare state in Britain and Sweden along the continuum produced by the two ideal types.

Within the genre of the welfare state, it is possible to

[5] Ralf Dahrendorf, "Market and Plan: Two Types of Rationality," in Ralf Dahrendorf, *Essays in the Theory of Society* (Stanford: Stanford University Press, 1968).

[6] Karl Polanyi, *The Great Transformation* (Boston: Beacon Press, 1944).

isolate two ideal types, one of which I shall call the liberal welfare model, and the other the corporatist welfare model. I shall depict them as polar opposites in terms of their frames of reference for state intervention. In the liberal welfare model, the proper sphere of state behavior is circumscribed by the functioning of market forces; inequalities produced by market forces become the occasion for state intervention. In the corporatist welfare model, the proper sphere of market forces is circumscribed by the state; the quest for social equality directly conditions the play of market forces. In the liberal welfare model, the instruments of state intervention are designed to compensate for market imperfections while remaining compatible with the basic principles of market organization. In the corporatist welfare model, the instruments of state intervention are designed to transform the market so as to avoid such imperfections. In the liberal welfare model, the state provides welfare in the amount deemed necessary to guarantee equality of opportunity. In the corporatist welfare model, equality of outcome is the proximate goal. In both cases, an "active state" will result, but in the liberal welfare model, the direct provision of services by the state, in an encapsulated state sector, will tend to be viewed, at any given time, as being the least disruptive of market mechanisms. As a result, however, an ever-growing state sector is a structural tendency of the liberal welfare model. In contrast, in the corporatist welfare model, the state, being more directive, ironically requires less institutional presence.

I elaborate these differences more fully by addressing three questions that encompass the entire cycle of state intervention, from initiation to implementation and institutionalization:

1. What determines state intervention? In a liberal welfare state, intervention is justified when a market dysfunction has created an unacceptably unequal social condition. In general, this condition is poverty. Poverty is identifiable

both as an inegalitarian social condition and as a consequence of market dysfunction. Other unequal social conditions which cannot be thusly identified do not warrant state intervention—for example, the psychologically debilitating effects of old age. This focus on problems in economic rather than social terms involves a particularistic segmentation of society into differential economic groups. In contrast, a corporatist welfare state intervenes to lead the market, not simply to forestall it, and to institutionalize social equality, not simply to compensate for inequality. The state determines the timing of intervention in accordance with its own agenda, rather than in response to market failures.

2. What form does state intervention take? Typically, state intervention at some point involves a public welfare program. Such a program has various dimensions which may be said to constitute its form. Two of these are its purpose and the extent of intervention it entails.

In a liberal welfare state the purpose of a public welfare program is to ameliorate or compensate for the consequences of market dysfunctions. There are various kinds of ameliorative measures, having a greater or lesser effect on "modifying the play of market forces." An example of a weak ameliorative intervention is financial compensation, as in workmen's compensation. A stronger measure would be legislation which neutralizes the consequences of market forces without actually altering them, such as in regulations for limiting the number of hours persons can work. The extent of intervention in a liberal welfare system is directly related to its limited purposes; overall, the depth of intervention in the market's structuring of social relations is low.

The purpose of a public welfare program in a corporatist welfare state is to redirect market forces and to institute equality. The program involves complete state control of the provision of services as well as in deciding who is to receive what kind of service and how much. The state thus supersedes market allocation. The depth of state intervention in restructuring social relations is considerable.

3. How does intervention become institutionalized? Since a liberal welfare state intervenes in an ad hoc fashion, in response to the consequences of market forces, it follows that institution-building is incremental. The institutional result is a fragmented structure whose parts are but weakly interrelated. The ability of such a system to develop a synoptic conception of problems is limited. Since the fundamental position of the market in structuring social relations is maintained, market-created social problems are forever reproduced. Ironically, while the intent of a liberal welfare state is to play as minimal a role as possible in intervening in the affairs of society, the structural reproduction of social problems necessitates a constant and ever-increasing state presence. Yet the system reinforces a basic division between state and society.

A corporatist welfare state begins as a dominant force in restructuring social relations toward greater egalitarianism. It therefore operates on the basis of an a priori synoptic vision which defines parameters for market forces. The state constructs a strong institutional system to implement its vision, but having determined the parameters of desirable social relations and outcomes, the state need not act directly to implement them, only to assure that they are implemented. Thus, in the end state/society distinctions become blurred, and a lesser institutional presence of the state may result as social equality becomes more broadly institutionalized.

In principle, both Britain and Sweden are attempting to achieve some measure of equality for women. The differences in how each state goes about this task loosely reflect the differences between a liberal and a corporatist welfare state, with attending implications for their respective commitments to the goal of equality for women.

In Britain, the primacy of the market is evident in determining the condition of inequality between men and women workers, as seen in the lower price paid for women's labor and the greater flux of women workers in and out of the labor market in tune with the business cycle. The state enters the picture after these conditions have been created and attempts to compensate for them through, for example, unemployment benefits and job placement services, which assure neither steady nor secure employment. Britain differs from the pure liberal welfare state model depicted above in that in certain areas the state has attempted to take an upper hand in instituting social change, the major examples being the Sex Discrimination and Equal Pay Acts. The question of why the state has taken a stronger role in certain areas than in others is difficult to answer in general terms because the variability itself reflects the ad hoc functioning typical of a liberal orientation.

In Sweden, the state alone is not the dominant actor depicted in the pure corporatist welfare model. For example, the labor market policies implemented in Sweden in the 1960s were actually developed by economists connected with Sweden's largest trade union organization. Day care policy was developed by a team of interest-group representatives and government officials, which constituted the Royal Commission on Child Centers. In general, the tripartite coalition (government, unions, employers) functions as a corporatist system. For this and related reasons I have called Sweden a societal corporatist welfare state. Moreover, the goal of equality is under greater pressure in Sweden than in the ideal type model. The representatives of capital in particular within the governing coalition put greater emphasis on economic than on social goals, though their presence also adds to the efficacy of governing mechanisms and reduces the need for the state to engage in direct institutionalized forms of intervention.

In sum, the depth of state intervention is lower in Britain than in Sweden. The role of the state in Britain is guided more by a "market rationality" and in Sweden by a "plan rationality." Because of the premises of these two systems, economic and sex-related factors have freer rein in Britain and are under greater control in Sweden. The role of the state thus has an independent significance in shaping policies for women workers, as well as playing the mediating role sketched out earlier.

IMPLICATIONS FOR WOMEN WORKERS

Throughout this study, the concerns of women workers are conceptualized both as being special, and therefore requiring selective treatment, and at the same time as being contained within a broader framework of social and economic considerations. A formulation suggested by Richard M. Titmuss has been most useful in developing this theme. In the context of social welfare, Titmuss speaks of the need to develop adequate "selective measures" which can differentiate and discriminate "positively, with the minimum risk of stigma, in favour of those whose needs are greatest."[7] However, this can only be done, he argues, if selective measures are placed *within* a "universal framework," and the real challenge is in constructing that universal framework.

This study suggests that Sweden has come closer than Britain to constructing such a "universal framework," and it is because of this framework that the interests of women workers have been more fully realized. The framework consists in the main of a labor market policy nexus which emphasizes national economic growth together with full employment. Within this framework everyone who can or is willing to work is encouraged to do so and any restrictions on participation in the work force or hindrances on worker satisfaction are removed. In contrast, the emphasis in British policies for women has been on selective measures *without* a universal framework. While some of these selective measures, such as the Sex Discrimination and Equal Pay Acts, have achieved some improvement for women workers, selective measures alone are limited in what they can do to institute equality. For they are premised on the conception that one group alone must change. The movement

---

[7] Richard M. Titmuss, *Commitment to Welfare* (London: Allen and Unwin, 1968), p. 135.

toward equality, however, is not such a simple one-way process.

The analysis of the place of women workers within a broader framework is more fully elaborated in the concluding chapter. The focus of that chapter is on labor/state relations in Britain and Sweden. It shows that the interests of labor in Britain are not on a par with other economic considerations. Whenever the Labour Party has been in office, it has been confronted with a set of inherited problems and policy frameworks which have incapacitated its responsiveness to labor and which its own policy initiatives have done little to mitigate. Moreover, the potential of the labor movement in Britain to advance its own concerns has been thwarted by labor's own internal divisions. Within this disunity, women workers are but another fragment, defined by their occupational niche as well as by their sex.

The contrast with Sweden is sharp. Labor has become strongly integrated into the governing coalition in Sweden. The interests of labor are at the heart of Sweden's labor market policy (secure employment, free choice of occupation, available jobs for all who want to work). Moreover, the representatives of organized labor are firmly integrated as equal partners in the tripartite system upon which Sweden's societal corporatist welfare state has been built. This process of the integration of labor developed over many years and through many experiments. As far as women are concerned it crystallized, in a manner of speaking, sometime in the 1960s. At this point, when labor as a whole had acquired a position of significance within the dominant governing coalition and within the framework of national economic goals, new employment measures for women as workers began to be introduced in Sweden.

In sum, this study looks not only at what states do to facilitate women's employment and women's equality in the labor force but also at how states act within contexts that are not wholly of their making, contexts which are inherited, which consist of social groupings and the relations among these, and which include extranational factors.

Americans tend to look to Sweden for insights and examples of what can be done in their own country. Insight we will find, and creative examples, but not ones we can necessarily use unless we are fully aware of what might happen to these practices when they are taken out of context. At the same time, much of what we see in Britain is familiar to Americans, since the ideological heritage of these two countries is similar. Certain of the constraints facing Britain, however, are peculiar to that country and have little relevance to the United States. Still, one generalization which we would expect to carry over into the American context as well is that, ultimately, progress for women in the economy depends less on appeals to human rights or social cost accounting than it does on a material base, specifically the role and status of labor in society and within the state.

Alternative Explanations

The explanation in this study for differences in British and Swedish policies for women is grounded in a theory of state/society relations. The argument is that the extent to which factors such as economic constraints and sex discrimination, which exist in varying degrees in any society, are allowed to be acted out depends on the broader character of state/society relations. The nature of these relations varies according to the particular state formation. Some states, such as Britain, remain strongly embedded in a liberal paradigm which limits the extent and shapes the character of state intervention. Hence, we can expect that, in these states, factors such as economic constraints and traditional conceptions of women's roles would determine policy outcomes for women. Other states, such as Sweden, have never been as strongly based in liberalism and, accordingly, have developed a more active orientation to state policy. Hence, we would expect to find greater state control over the direction of social forces such as market and tradition, producing as a by-product a more favorable outcome for women.

This is certainly not the only possible explanation for the role of the state in social change as it concerns the position of women in the advanced capitalist societies. While there is no single prevailing model against which I am arguing, one can derive several alternative models from the literature which touch upon my concerns. I briefly describe three models and then indicate my reasons for not adopting them. (1) Policy-analytic studies imply a rationalist-voluntarist conception of the state, as an agency that is capable of moving progressively toward optimality in defining and implementing goals. (2) Feminist interpretations imply a conception of the state as being epiphenomenal, a mere expression of patriarchy. (3) Neo-Marxist theories of the state explicate a conception of the relative autonomy of the state from the economic base of society, but suggest that this relative autonomy is ultimately illusory.

Most policy-analytic studies on comparative policies for women are not framed within any explicit theoretical perspective at all. Their purpose is more directly task-oriented: to analyze specific problems in women's employment and to find appropriate policy solutions. The accumulation of studies on the variety of programs and regulations that have been developed in different nations has produced an increasingly refined survey of policies that do and do not achieve equality for women. We now know what constitutes the "best" policies that have improved the situation of women in different countries; we also know which policies are inadequate and perpetuate women's inferior employment position in other countries.[8] It is important to know such facts.

---

[8] Among the more commonly cited differences between best and inadequate policies are: degree of coordination between related policy areas, such as family and labor market policies, and degree of integration among the phases of policy development and implementation. Cf. Sheila B. Kamerman and Alfred J. Kahn (eds.), *Family Policy: Government and Families in Fourteen Countries* (New York: Columbia University Press, 1978); Ronnie

However, implicit in the policy-analytic approach is a conception of the role of the state that we might call rationalist or voluntarist. It appears to be premised on the assumption that state actors have free rein over the policy process, from diagnosis to decision making to implementation. As Rosabeth Moss Kanter puts it, "the effectiveness of any intervention strategy is inextricably bound up with how adequately one diagnoses the problem."[9] Hence, this model perforce would explain differences in policies for women in Britain and Sweden in terms of such factors as adequate information and political will. State actors in Sweden presumably have more fully and accurately diagnosed the problems in women's employment, more methodically developed appropriate solutions, and displayed a greater willingness to change the condition of women than have state actors in Britain. But such an explanation of the differences between Britain and Sweden would not be entirely correct. We cannot charge state actors in Britain with ignorance about the problems of women workers, nor with a lack of will to achieve equality for women. The fact of the matter is that state actors in Britain are more constrained than in Sweden in their capacity both to develop and to implement public policy, including policies for women. My study attempts to identify the character of these constraints, and to demonstrate their consequences.

A rationalist-voluntarist model does not take state action itself to be problematical. In the introduction to a recent edited volume, Ronnie Steinberg Ratner says that "the papers [in this volume] do not dwell on the idiosyncracies of each country's policies. Rather, they address issues that transcend the more narrow concerns peculiar to any country."[10] As my study shows, however, while the problems of women workers may well transcend particular country-level

Steinberg Ratner (ed.), *Equal Employment Policy for Women: Strategies for Implementation in the United States, Canada, and Western Europe* (Philadelphia: Temple University Press, 1980).

[9] Quoted in Ratner, *Equal Employment Policy*, p. 437.
[10] Ibid., p. xviii.

factors, the solutions to these problems do not. Policy cannot be predicted from the diagnoses of a particular problem at hand; nor does repeated state intervention necessarily indicate an ability on the part of the state to handle problems as knowledge develops.

Thus, my analysis begins where the rationalist-voluntarist model leaves off, by asking why it is that the "best" policies, even when known, are not adopted; and why it is that even when the "best" policies are in effect, systematic shortcomings appear in the achievement of goals. My own explanation situates policy "choices" and policy limitations within particular characteristics of state/society relations. Furthermore, I show in Chapter 7 that these relations are historically contingent within a national context.

In contrast to the wide degree of freedom of the state implicit in policy-analytic studies, a second body of literature, feminist interpretations, suggest a pessimism with regard to the possibility that the state can improve women's conditions. Both radical and socialist feminists have identified capitalist patriarchy as their problematic. Each of these two groups understands patriarchy differently, but this does not affect their conceptions of the role of the state.[11]

Radical feminists take patriarchy to mean the law of the father. Following Juliet Mitchell's reading of Freud, patriarchy is seen as the primal structuration of social relations.[12] This means that patriarchy is universal, even though it can take different manifestations in different types of society. In this analysis, patriarchy is the first moment of

---

[11] This summary grants more unity to feminist thought than actually exists. For a discussion of the varieties of feminism and other theories of women's work see Natalie J. Sokoloff, *Between Money and Love: The Dialectics of Women's Home and Market Work* (New York: Praeger, 1980). The common underlying features of feminism which I assume are its conception of the state as epiphenomenal and its over-riding emphasis on women-specific factors.

[12] Juliet Mitchell, *Psychoanalysis and Feminism* (New York: Penguin Books, 1975). See also the penetrating critiques of Mitchell in Annette Kuhn and AnnMarie Wolpe (eds.), *Feminism and Materialism: Women and Modes of Production* (London: Routledge and Kegan Paul, 1978).

social structuration. It is thereby reflected in all social forms, including the state. Accordingly, state action ultimately reflects, or is an epiphenomenon produced by, the patriarchal base of society.

Socialist feminists take patriarchy to mean the hierarchical sexual division of labor. Socialist feminists are not united in their understanding of the universality or extent of patriarchy outside of capitalism, but there is agreement that under capitalism patriarchy takes a form that is more oppressive to women than under any other socioeconomic system. The site of patriarchy in capitalist society is the nuclear family, where women are confined to unpaid domestic labor. Women's condition in the work force reflects this familial base, for women are relegated to inferior positions and paid less than men. Moreover, this hierarchical division of labor based on sex feeds the needs of capitalism, providing a constant pool of consumption and a reserve of labor.[13] Socialist feminists adopt the classical Marxist conception of the relationship of the state to capitalism. The state is the handmaiden of capitalism. Therefore, state policies reinforce and maintain the subservient position of women.[14] State action ultimately reflects the capitalist-patriarchal base of society.

To feminists, then, the state is an epiphenomenal expression of patriarchy. Be this as it may, the fact is that patriarchy as an independent variable does not adequately account for the differences that are evident in policies for women in Britain and Sweden. There simply is not sufficient variance between the two countries along any "patriarchy" dimension. And what variance there is, suggesting a declining manifestation of its effects in Sweden, needs to be

[13] Batya Weinbaum and Amy Bridges, "The Other Side of the Paycheck: Monopoly Capital and the Structure of Consumption," and Heidi Hartmann, "Capitalism, Patriarchy, and Job Segregation by Sex," in Zillah R. Eisenstein (ed.), *Capitalist Patriarchy and the Case for Socialist Feminism* (New York: Monthly Review Press, 1979).

[14] Mary McIntosh, "The State and the Oppression of Women," in Kuhn and Wolpe, *Feminism and Materialism*.

explained with respect to some other independent variable. The feminist framework cannot account for the change that has taken place in Sweden. Radical feminism might be reconstructed so as to address this issue. But to do so, it would have to draw upon other explanatory logics in neo-Marxism which speak more directly to theories of the state.

The neo-Marxist literature on theories of the state does not yet include an explanation of the role of women in advanced capitalism. However, one can readily construct such an explanation. Among neo-Marxists, the work of Nicos Poulantzas is most relevant to my purposes. Poulantzas developed the concept of the relative autonomy of the capitalist state to show that a theory of political phenomena as such could be formulated within the broader realm of the capitalist mode of production. His theory allows that the capitalist state can acquire purposes of its own (that is, purposes outside of its basic necessity of contributing to capitalist accumulation and reproduction). Above all, "the state has the particular function of constituting the factor of cohesion between the levels of a social formation."[15] As Poulantzas elaborates, social equilibrium is an achievement of the state—it is not given by the economic imperative. This achievement benefits the state (as apart from the economy), for it fashions the state as the nodal point of social cohesion as well as societal transformation.

In this sense, the state becomes the arena for the structuration of the class struggle. This struggle can be said to occur at the level of the state and in accordance with rules set by the state, and not strictly within the confines of the economy or the mode of production. The role of the state in the class struggle is first to mask it, presenting itself as above the class struggle, but ultimately to maintain the economic competition on which class struggle is based. The state appears to represent the unity of all classes through

[15] Nicos Poulantzas, *Political Power and Social Classes* (New York: New Left Books, 1973), p. 44. See also the lucid exposition of Poulantzas by Amy Beth Bridges, "Nicos Poulantzas and the Marxist Theory of the State," *Politics and Society*, 4 (Winter 1974).

universal suffrage. Accordingly, all classes support the state, including the working class which is organized to make demands on the state and is granted concessions by the state. But in supporting the state and its policies, all classes are supporting the dominant class. For what the state actually represents is society as a united bourgeois mass.[16] In the last instance, the interest of the state corresponds to the interest of the dominant capitalist class. Notwithstanding this conclusion, the weight of Poulantzas's argument focuses on the long detour prior to the last instance, discussing political phenomena in their own right.

This way of formulating the role of the state, as a source of its own power and as being relatively autonomous from economic forces, comes closer to my own conceptualization than do the two perspectives presented above. However, in this particular neo-Marxist perspective the concept of the relative autonomy of the state is closely tied to an intellectual and ideological baggage that limits its usefulness to my study. Were I to apply the framework I could argue, for example, that the Swedish state appears to exercise a greater measure of relative autonomy in its management of society than does the British state. But the framework does not explain the difference. Differences in class configuration are part of the explanation, to be sure. In contrast to the neo-Marxist presumption, however, the "relative autonomy" of the state in Sweden is based on a more effective integration of the state into a governing coalition along with labor and capital than exists in Britain.

In sum, while my study draws upon aspects of all three of these perspectives, I reject the conception of the role of the state that each either implies or holds. In contrast to the policy-analytic studies, which give free rein to state actors in formulating and implementing optimal policies, my case studies show that state action is more constrained within

[16] See also the analysis by Claus Offe, "The Theory of the Capitalist State and the Problem of Policy Formation," in Leon Lindberg (ed.), *Stress and Contradiction in Modern Capitalism* (Lexington, Mass.: Lexington Books, 1975).

specific parameters, and different states are differently constrained. In contrast to feminist interpretations, which give little freedom to the state to act over and above its societal base, I show that the state in Sweden has effectively changed the expression and consequences of society's patriarchal heritage although not necessarily for women-specific reasons. In contrast to the neo-Marxist perspective, which surrounds the concept of the relative autonomy of the state in deception of the working class, I show that the state can be composed of a viable coalition of class actors and that, so structured, the state can act within historically conditioned limits to the mutual benefit of all social classes.

CHAPTER 2

THE ROLE OF WOMEN IN THE ECONOMY

INTRODUCTION

The focus of this study is the difference in policies for working women in Britain and Sweden and the consequence of those differences for women. This chapter looks at perhaps the most obvious explanation for these differences, namely, economic determinants in general and, specifically, the different "demand" for women workers in the two economies. Demand for women workers is a function of two sorts of economic factors: aggregate factors, such as level of economic development and rate of economic growth; and more discrete factors, such as an increase in the service sector or a decline in a specific industry. These two factors are related, for as an economy grows and reaches higher levels of development, the service sector expands and the proportionate contribution of agriculture and industry to the economy declines. These economic changes affect women and draw them into the labor market for two reasons. One, women constitute a readily available national labor source to be tapped when labor shortages exist in an expanding economy. Second, women traditionally work in the service sector, either in lower level professional occupations, such as nurse or teacher, lower level manual jobs, such as cook or cleaner, or as clerical workers.

This chapter shows first that aggregate economic conditions in Britain and Sweden, though they differ, in and of themselves do not explain the variance either in the labor force participation and integration of women or in policies for women. The aggregate differences that existed throughout the 1950s would lead us to expect a greater

)ortion of women workers in Sweden than in Britain,
... in fact the reverse was the case. In Sweden, major
changes both in women's labor force participation rates and
in government policies toward working women occurred
in the 1960s. While these changes were related to the worldwide economic boom that was taking place at the time, that
boom did not have a significantly greater impact on Sweden
than on Britain. However, the Swedish government responded to these economic conditions differently than did
the British government. The Swedish approach to economic planning was becoming more finely tuned, coordinating macroeconomic measures with microeconomic intervention, that is, with selective techniques targeted for
differential impact on economic factors. In this scheme, the
role of women workers was directly linked with changes in
the economy as a whole. Thus, the character of state intervention is a powerful mediating variable for the consequences that changing economic conditions have on women
workers. In fact, I conclude that the role of the state ac-
quires the force of an independent variable in the case of
Sweden. This is not so in Britain, except in the negative
sense. Although economic planning developed in Britain,
it took a different form from the one in Sweden. Moreover,
British plans for economic growth were plagued throughout the 1950s and 1960s by a number of mostly political
international and domestic crises, including the pressure
on sterling and the tensions between government and labor
over the choice of means for dealing with the inflation-
unemployment dilemma. As a consequence, women workers in Britain remained in a secondary position, both in
their status in the labor market and as a focus of concern
in economic policies and economic planning.

The consequences of changing economic factors on women
workers are further analyzed by looking at sectoral or oc-
cupation-specific changes in demand. This reinforces the
conclusion that objective economic conditions are mediated
and, in fact, shaped by state intervention. To elaborate this,
I focus on the events of the 1960s. At that time, the gov-

ernments of both Britain and Sweden were responding to certain changing economic circumstances by increasing public spending. The immediate effect on women was similar in both Britain and Sweden, in that more women were drawn into the labor market by the creation of jobs in health, education, and social work. But the eventual effect on women of expanding job opportunities in the public service sector differed profoundly in the two countries. Women in Britain remained marginal workers; in Sweden they became more integrated into the labor market as permanent workers. This difference is directly related to differences in the role of the state in taking control over the direction of economic forces. This analysis suggests that economic factors in and of themselves are less significant than the character of state intervention in conditioning the labor force participation of women and in explaining the differences in policy toward women workers. In other words, women's employment situation is a by-product of the role of the state. Women workers in Sweden are in a better position than elsewhere (with certain qualifications) because the state intervenes not for the sake of women alone, but for the sake of the economy and the labor market as a whole. Women in Sweden are becoming part of a universal category of workers, not a separate and marginal group as in Britain.

DEMAND FOR WOMEN WORKERS

The Economy and Women's Labor Force Participation

Cross-national studies consistently find a positive relationship between economic development and women's labor force participation.[1] While the relationship is most evident when comparing developing and developed countries,

[1] Harold L. Wilensky, "Women's Work: Economic Growth, Ideology, and Structure," *Industrial Relations*, 7 (May 1968); Ester Boserup, *Woman's Role in Economic Development* (London: Allen and Unwin, 1970); Naomi Black and Ann Baker Cottrell (eds.), *Women and World Change: Equity Issues in Development* (Beverly Hills: Sage, 1981).

it still holds among countries within each group.[2] The differences among developed countries, which is the concern here, are due both to the different patterns of development experienced by each country as well as the level of overall development each has reached. Historically, as western countries industrialized, the increase in jobs available in factories drew women workers from rural areas. Britain is the prime example. Earlier in this century there were more women in the labor force in Britain than elsewhere. In certain other countries, which experienced a contraction of the agricultural sector only in this century, the labor force participation rates of women actually fell with economic development. As husbands' occupations changed from farmer to factory worker, women's occupations changed from "employed" family helper to unpaid housewife. Belgium, Finland, and Italy are examples.[3] In these countries, women were not drawn into industry because, for one, industry was able to exploit already existing technology and to develop rapidly without requiring much additional labor. Certain other countries, which underwent late and rapid industrialization, proceeded immediately thereafter to expand their service sectors. Unlike the ambiguous relationship between industrialization and women's labor force participation, there is clear evidence that an expansion of the service sector attracts women workers. In fact, the size of the service sector seems to account even more than national wealth for the participation rates of women workers in advanced nations. Wealth alone does not signify, as does expansion of the service sector, that an increase is occurring in the sorts of jobs in which women specialize[4]—jobs in public services, such as health, education, and social work; domestic-type work, such as in restaurants; and jobs in

[2] Rosemary Santana Cooney, "Female Professional Work Opportunities: A Cross-National Study," *Demography*, 12 (February 1975).

[3] Martha Darling, *The Role of Women in the Economy* (Paris: Organization for Economic Co-operation and Development, 1975), p. 20.

[4] This is especially true of Germany, which has one of the highest GNP's, but a lower service sector than other advanced industrial nations.

luxury services such as hairdressing. Within the last two decades, in France, Japan, and Sweden in particular, the number of women workers in agriculture has declined markedly, while the number in the service sector has increased substantially.[5]

An expanding service sector indicates that the character of an economy which has reached an "advanced industrial" stage is changing, and new jobs of a different sort are being generated, drawing women into the labor force. Another factor that contributes to women's increasing labor force participation is a high level of economic growth. The rate of growth has been found to be more important than the level of economic development in augmenting work opportunities for women.[6] When an expanding service sector and high level of growth are combined, women are drawn into the labor force not only because of an increase in the sorts of jobs in which they specialize but also because the expansion in job opportunities is likely to outstrip the number of men available and qualified to fill them.

An important link between all of these factors—level of economic development, rate of growth, expansion of service sector, and labor force participation of women—is increasing female enrollment in higher education, which has been positively associated with each of these factors. The reason for the link is the change in attitudes toward working women that accompanies expansion of higher education, a change that goes beyond the participating women themselves. In addition, an expansion of services, in particular professional, cultural, and social services, requires an expansion of the qualified labor force. Whether or not women will fill the newly created positions depends, among

[5] Darling, *The Role of Women*, p. 21. Nevertheless, in France and Japan (as well as Belgium and Italy) there has been a decline in the total proportion of working women compared to the level earlier in this century. The service sector still does not occupy women to the extent that agriculture once did in these countries.

[6] Cooney, "Female Professional Work Opportunities"; Boserup, *Woman's Role*.

other factors, on the availability of qualified men. Where
the male enrollment in higher education has increased more
than female enrollment, women's labor force participation
rate, in the professions specifically, has remained stable
rather than increasing (because qualified men were occupying professional positions).[7]

Let us look more closely now at the differences between
Britain and Sweden in aggregate economic factors. Table
2.1 summarizes the essential points of discussion. Taking
GNP per capita as an indicator of wealth, Sweden is and
has been for some time wealthier than Britain. Taking growth
of GNP as an indicator of economic activity, Sweden is and
has been for some time developing its economy at a faster
rate than Britain. This would lead us to expect that the size
of the service sector is proportionately larger in Sweden
than in Britain, and, indeed, such became the case by 1970.
This, in turn, leads us to expect further that the labor force
participation rate of women in Sweden is and has been for
some time greater than in Britain. We can include other
indicators to increase this expectation, such as the participation rate of women in higher education, which is and
has always been greater in Sweden than in Britain. However, we can see that these expectations are wrong when
we look at Figure 2.1, comparing labor force participation
rates of women in Britain and Sweden from 1930. It is
surprising that even in 1960 virtually the same proportion
of women in Britain and Sweden were working, and in
Britain an even greater proportion of married women were
working in 1960 than in Sweden. The figures for labor
force participation rates begin to shift in the mid-1960s
when the proportion of Swedish working women (total and
married) exceeds the British. We cannot claim that this is
due to changes in aggregate economic factors alone, as has
just been shown. Indeed, as the data in Table 2.1 indicate,
after 1965 the growth rate in Sweden's GNP began to slow
down considerably. Employment in the service sector in

[7] Cooney, "Female Professional Work Opportunities," p. 109.

TABLE 2.1   Economic and Social Indicators

| | GNP ($ billion) | | GDP ($ billion) | |
	1955	1965	1975	1980
Britain	53.83	99.59	227.0	513.9
Sweden	8.97	19.73	67.3	124.6

| | GNP/Capita | | GDP/Capita | |
	1960	1970	1975	1980
Britain	1,380	2,170	3,370	7,170
Sweden	1,680	4,050	6,880	12,820

| | Growth Rates | | | | | |
| | GNP | | | | GDP | |
	55/60	60/65	65/70	75/76	79/80	60/80
Britain	6.1	3.3	2.4	1.5	− 2.25	2.3
Sweden	7.0	5.3	3.9	1.5	2.25	3.3

| | Structure of GDP | | | | | |
| | Agriculture | | Industry | | Other | |
	1970	1980	1970	1980	1970	1980
Britain	2.9	2.2	44.4	40.2	53.8	58.6
Sweden	4.0	3.3	36.8	32.3	59.5	65.5

| | % Total Civilian Employment | | | | | |
| | Agriculture | | Industry | | Other | |
	1965	1980	1965	1980	1965	1980
Britain	3.5	2.6	47.5	39.0	49.0	58.4
Sweden	11.5	5.8	42.6	32.5	45.9	61.7

| | Total Public Expenditure (% GDP at current prices) | | |
	1955-57	1967-69	1974-76
Britain	32.0	38.2	44.5
Sweden	16.5	41.5	51.8

| | Changes in Public Expenditure (% GDP in current prices) | | | | | | | |
| | Education | | Income Mainte-nance | | Health | | Total "Welfare" | |
	early 60s	mid 70s	early 60s	mid 70s	early 60s	mid 70s	early 60s	mid 70s
Britain	3.7	4.4	4.4	7.7	3.2	4.6	12.6	16.7
Sweden	4.0	5.9	6.0	9.3	3.6	6.7	13.6	21.9

TABLE 2.1 (continued)

| | | Enrollment in Higher Education | | |
		1960	1970	1979
Britain	Men	101,820	401,500	509,543
	Women	48,927	199,800	289,919
Sweden	Men	24,560	83,180	108,425
	Women	12,352	61,074	90,373

Adapted from: Organization for Economic Co-operation and Development, *Main Economic Indicators* (Paris: OECD, various issues, 1955-79); Organization for Economic Co-operation and Development, *The OECD Observer* (Paris: OECD, various issues, 1962-82); Organization for Economic Co-operation and Development, *Quarterly Economic Review of the United Kingdom 1980/81* (Paris: OECD, 1982); Organization for Economic Co-operation and Development, *Quarterly Economic Review of Sweden 1980/81* (Paris: OECD, 1982); Organization for Economic Co-operation and Development, *The OECD Observer*, No. 92 (Paris: OECD, May 1978), pp. 8, 10; United Nations Educational, Scientific and Cultural Organization, *Statistical Yearbook* (Paris: UNESCO, various issues, 1962-82).

Sweden increased during the decade of the 1960s, because of the influx of women workers. To see what changes were occurring in the service sectors of both countries (and more so in Sweden) and attracting women workers, we must shift our focus from aggregate economic factors to specific ones.

The Labor Market

Aggregate economic variables constitute only one indicator of possible demand for women workers. Another kind of indicator looks at demand as a function of specific features of the labor market. Labor market demand itself consists of both aggregate and specific factors: aggregate "manpower," or the total level of employment, unemployment, and vacancies within specific sectors or occupations. The differences between Britain and Sweden in each of these dimensions are examined below.

Manpower.   Large changes in population, through birth, immigration, or emigration, affect a nation's supply of available manpower. Population changes in Sweden have

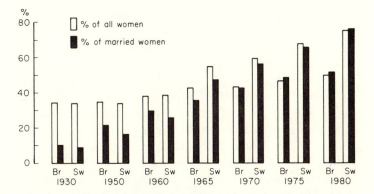

2.1. Labor Force Participation Rates, Historical. Adapted from: *Censuses of Population: Great Britain*, as cited in Department of Employment, *Women and Work: A Statistical Survey* (London: HMSO, 1974), p. 44. Equal Opportunities Commission, *Fifth Annual Report, 1980* (London: HMSO, 1980), pp. 60-61. Arbetsmarknadens Kvinnonämnd, *Woman in Sweden: In the Light of Statistics* (Stockholm: AKN, 1973), p. 37. National Labour Market Board, *Equality in the Labour Market, Statistics* (Stockholm: AMS, 1980), p. 8. Prior to 1963, Swedish data are based on household censuses which underestimate actual participation. After 1963 they are based on labor force sample surveys.

a greater impact on labor supply than in Britain because Sweden's population is smaller (8 million compared to 56 million in Britain). In the 1930s Sweden experienced a critical population decline. It occurred in part because of emigration during the Depression and, more importantly, because of lower birth rates, reflecting the expense of raising children.[8] However, women's labor force participation

[8] Rita Liljeström, "Sweden" in Sheila B. Kamerman and Alfred J. Kahn (eds.), *Family Policy: Government and Families in Fourteen Countries* (New York: Columbia University Press, 1978), p. 26. A 1935 Population Committee attributed declining birth rates to the lower standard of living of families with young children. The Myrdals contributed greatly to the recognition of the relationship between population and poverty. Policies that followed helped improve the standard of living of families with children, but did not change the birth rate. The birth rate rose briefly in the

was not affected by the labor shortage in the 1930s because there was also a job shortage, as elsewhere. Britain experienced large population changes during both world wars, which created labor shortages that did affect women's labor force participation. Other than this, Britain's population has been affected primarily by ebbs and flows in migration, but to no greater proportionate extent than Sweden. In fact, greater immigration into Sweden, particularly in the decade of the 1960s, might lead us to expect, falsely, a tighter labor market in Sweden. For the year 1960, net migration in Britain was +69 (thousands), in Sweden it was +11. But for 1970, net migration in Britain was −46, in Sweden it was +49. Overall, during the decade of the 1960s, the population in Sweden increased more than in Britain (0.75% compared to 0.60%).[9]

And yet, during the 1960s Sweden began to experience a labor shortage and Britain's labor market began to experience a surplus with rising unemployment. Neither of these developments was related to population changes. The proportion of working age men (15-64) within the population as a whole has remained fairly constant in both countries for decades.[10] However, in both countries the absolute number of men in active civilian employment began to decline after the mid-1960s due to changes in the structure

---

1940s from a low of 1.4 to a high of 1.9. By 1980 it was down again at 1.16 (compared to 1.31 for Britain).

[9] These are OECD figures: *The OECD Observer* (Paris: OECD, 1972) and *Labour Force Statistics 1959-70* (Paris: OECD, 1972). Immigrants are a slightly larger proportion of the population in Sweden than in Britain. In 1975 foreign subjects (non-naturalized residents) were 5% of the population in Sweden and 4.5% in Britain. The commonly held view that a greater proportion and inflow of immigrants depresses demand for women workers does not hold here, at least for Sweden.

[10] The figure has been steadily declining in both countries because of a rising number of elderly persons. In 1970 the proportion of men aged 15-64 within the total population was 31.9% in Britain and 32.7% in Sweden. The difference might suggest a slightly greater demand for women workers in Britain, which is not the case. These figures are based on OECD data.

of the labor market. Figure 2.2 vividly illustrates one dimension of the change. In Britain unemployment rose considerably in 1966 and remained high, while job vacancies decreased and remained low. In Sweden unemployment remained steady while job vacancies increased. The situation in Sweden spelled a labor shortage, and would lead us

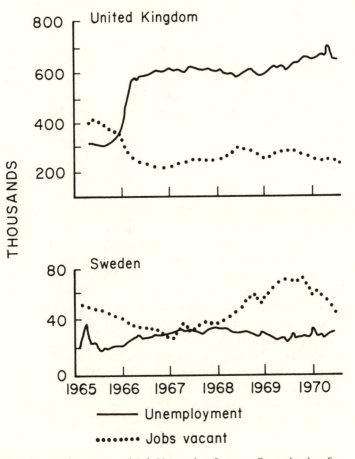

2.2. Unemployment and Job Vacancies. Source: Organization for Economic Co-operation and Development, *Main Economic Indicators* (Paris: OECD, 1971), p. 13.

to expect women to be drawn into the labor market. Indeed, from the early 1960s, the number of women in active civilian employment steadily increased in Sweden.[11] But the same was happening in Britain, and from a much earlier time. As Figure 2.1 indicates, women's labor force participation in Britain has been slowly but steadily increasing, and the rates for married women have risen substantially.

Clearly, there was a different kind of demand for women workers in both countries that does not show up in these aggregate data. Shortages of labor supply requiring the participation of women in the labor force have in the past resulted from vast population changes (emigration or war) and from changes in the total number of jobs (increase because of industrialization or economic booms). But more important than these factors for the significant change in women's employment that took place in the 1960s was an increase in the *kinds* of jobs available, jobs which required women because of their traditional specialization. Let us compare these changes in Britain and Sweden.

Occupations.   The most basic fact in the study of labor market demand for women is occupational specialization. Table 2.2 shows the occupational distribution of men and women in Britain from 1966 to 1979. Table 2.3 gives the same information for Sweden from 1965 to 1980. Looking first at the distribution of women workers in Britain, we see a strong concentration in two types of occupations, clerical workers (31%) and service, sports, and recreation workers (23%). The first category includes secretaries, machine operators, and cashiers; the second includes domestic workers, restaurant workers, cleaners, launderers, and hairdressers. The proportion of women who are professional or technical workers is roughly similar to the proportion who do manufacturing or related manual work (about 15%).

---

[11] Prior to 1960 the increase in women's employment was intermittent although it was definitely occurring. This discussion is based on data in OECD, *Labour Force Statistics 1959-70* (1972).

Another 9% of women work in sales. The lack of change in the distribution of women workers in Britain over the last two decades is remarkable. Women in Sweden are concentrated in three occupational groups: professional and technical workers including medical (47%), service workers (23%), and clerical workers (22%). The increasing proportion of professional women since 1965 is noteworthy. In both countries, male workers are more evenly distributed among the occupations. Where they are concentrated, the proportion is not nearly as high as for women.

Now let us look more closely at the distribution of women in the professions, because these are the kinds of jobs that increased in the 1960s. Table 2.4 shows the proportion of women in selected professions in 1971. In Britain, 40% of all professionals were women at that time; the corresponding figure for Sweden was 42.5%. In both countries there was and still is a strong concentration of women in three professions: nursing, teaching (non-university level), and social welfare work. Within these three professions, women are by far the majority of workers.

The occupational concentration of women, particularly in the professions, is important when we look at job increases in the 1960s. Table 2.5 shows employment increases in Britain between 1961 and 1974 in selected service sector occupational categories. The greatest increases were in those occupations in which women are concentrated: education (where women are lower-level teachers), insurance and banking (where women are clerical workers), and health (where they are nurses). Table 2.6 presents the data for selected occupational categories in Britain, so that we may compare this increase in total employment with the increase in employment by sex.

The substantial increase in female employment in insurance, banking, finance, and business services is accounted for primarily by an increase in clerical work, and over 70% of all clerical workers are women. We can speculate that much of the increase in female employment in public administration was also due to an increase in clerical work.

TABLE 2.2 Britain: Occupational Structure of the Labor Force (annual average, age 16-74)

	Men (thousands)	Women (thousands)	Women as % of total in occupat.	% of all women in occupat.
Professional, Technical Workers, Artists				
1966	—	854	—	10.4
1971	1,490	995	40.0	11.9
1979	2,398	1,488	38.3	15.8
Administrators, managers				
1966	—	57	—	0.7
1971	849	79	8.5	0.9
1979	1,571	406	20.1	4.3
Clerical Workers				
1966	—	2,231	—	27.1
1971	1,041	2,430	70.0	29.1
1979	1,110	2,926	72.5	31.1
Selling				
1966	—	976	—	11.8
1971	830	896	51.9	10.7
1979	582	870	59.9	9.2
Farmers, Foresters, Fishermen				
1966	—	72	—	0.9
1971	387	67	14.7	0.8
1979	310	48	13.4	0.5
Transport and Communications				
1966	—	158	—	1.9
1971	1,140	146	11.3	1.7
1979	1,566	90	5.4	1.0

	Manufacturing, Other Laborers				Service, Sports, Recreation			
1966	—	2,129	—	25.8	—	1,980	—	24.0
1971	6,821	1,680	19.8	20.1	707	1,932	73.2	23.2
1979	5,780	1,327	18.7	14.1	806	2,129	72.5	22.6

	Total[a]		
	Men	Women	Women as % of Total
1966	—	8,239	—
1971	13,548	8,344	38.1
1979	14,706	9,420	39

Adapted from: Department of Employment, *Women and Work: A Statistical Survey* (London: HMSO, 1974), pp. 55-56; Department of Employment, *Labour Force Survey 1979* (London: HMSO, 1980), pp. 31-32.

[a] *Includes armed forces, inadequately described occupations.*

TABLE 2.3 Sweden: Occupational Structure of the Labor Force
(annual average, age 16-74)

	Men (thousands)	Women (thousands)	Women as % of total in occupat.	% of all women in occupat.
	Technical, Scientific, Sociological, Humanistic and Artistic			
1965	339	237	41.1	17.2
1971	440	354	44.6	22.3
1975	474	443	48.3	25.2
1980	528	585	52.6	30.7
	Administrative Work			
1965	59	8	11.9	0.6
1971	71	8	10.1	0.5
1975	73	9	11.0	0.5
1980	82	16	16.3	0.8
	Commercial Work			
1965	156	181	53.7	13.1
1971	174	176	50.3	11.1
1975	184	170	48.0	9.7
1980	178	165	48.1	8.7

	Men (thousands)	Women (thousands)	Women as % of total in occupat.	% of all women in occupat.
	Medical and Health Services (included in technical, etc.)			
1965	11	132	92.3	9.6
1971	15	196	92.9	12.3
1975	20	243	92.4	13.8
1980	31	305	90.8	16.0
	Accounting and Clerical Work			
1965	93	265	74.0	19.0
1971	100	347	77.6	21.8
1975	106	386	78.5	22.0
1980	105	412	79.7	21.6
	Agriculture, Forestry, Fishing			
1965	326	95	22.6	6.9
1971	236	67	22.1	4.2
1975	205	67	24.6	3.0
1980	178	57	24.3	3.0

Table: Employment by sector, by sex (thousands), Sweden 1965–1980

	Transport and Communications				Manufacturing, Machine Maintenance, etc.			
	Women	Men			Men	Women		
1965	46	214	17.7	3.3	1,087	217	16.6	15.7
1971	50	198	20.2	3.1	1,043	183	14.9	11.5
1975	56	195	22.3	3.2	1,015	203	16.6	11.6
1980	62	195	24.1	3.3	925	174	15.8	9.1

	Services				Total		
	Women	Men			Men	Women	Women as % of Total
1965	89	326	78.6	23.7	2,364	1,378	36.8
1971	110	404	78.6	25.4	2,371	1,590	40.1
1975	118	423	78.2	24.1	2,373	1,756	42.5
1980	137	434	76.0	22.8	2,326	1,906	45.0

Adapted from: National Labour Market Board, *Equality in the Labour Market, Statistics* (Stockholm: AMS, 1980), pp. 4-5.

TABLE 2.4   Women in the Professions, 1971

	% of All Women Professionals		Women as % of Total in Occupation	
	Britain	Sweden	Britain	Sweden
Nurse	38.4	55.2	91.6	92.6
Teacher	36.4	24.6	57.0	59.2
primary			75.0	75.0
secondary				
university			10.0	10.0
Social Welfare work	3.5	9.5	61.9	95.0
Laboratory assistant,				
technician	4.8	1.1	38.9	7.0
Other	16.9		13.4	

Adapted from: Department of Employment, *Women and Work: A Statistical Survey* (London: HMSO, 1974), p. 57; Arbetsmarknadens Kvinnonämnd, *Woman in Sweden: In the Light of Statistics* (Stockholm: AKN, 1973), pp. 49-50.

The increase in the professions is accounted for by the aforementioned increase in education and health care. Overall, the increase in female employment between 1961 and 1971 in Britain was 6.2%. Given the large increases in specific occupational-industrial categories, we can see that a great deal of occupational channeling occurred. Let us look more closely at the demand side of the picture.

One measure of occupational demand is the number of vacancies listed at employment offices.[12] When we compare this number with the number of unemployed persons in the field, we have some idea of persisting labor shortages in particular occupations. Using the data in Table 2.7 as a sample, we can see that in Britain the largest number of vacancies are reported for manufacturing work, personal services, clerical work, and administration and management.

When we look at number of vacancies as a proportion of number unemployed by occupation, we see that the

[12] Not all vacancies are listed with employment offices in Britain; therefore, this measure underestimates demand.

TABLE 2.5   Britain: Numbers Employed in Selected Service
Categories (thousands)

	1961	1970	1974	% increase 1961-1974
Total employment	21,789	21,993	22,297	
Transport	1,649	1,549	1,483	− 10.1
Distribution	3,356	3,238	3,312	− 1.3
Insurance, banking, etc.	985	1,324	1,532	55.5
Education services	960	1,412	1,693	76.4
Medical services	779	1,007	1,130	45.1
Leisure	897	950	1,067	19.0
Public administration	1,280	1,446	1,551	21.2

Adapted from: Robert Bacon and Walter Eltis, *Britain's Economic Problem: Too Few Producers* (London: Macmillan Press, 1976), p. 168, as drawn from *Department of Employment Gazette*, various issues, 1961-1974.

TABLE 2.6   Britain: Increase in Employment by Industry and Sex

	1971 Total (thousands)		1961-1971 % increase	
	Men	Women	Men	Women
Professional, scientific	943.2	1,960.6	35.1	42.6
Public administration, defense	945.0	471.3	8.4	29.9
Insurance, banking, finance	458.2	513.1	25.2	61.9
Distributive trades	1,127.4	1,454.8	− 12.5	− 0.8
Transport, communication	1,280.2	283.8	− 9.6	8.8
Miscellaneous services	800.5	993.5	5.3	− 8.4
All manufacturing industries	5,855.3	2,574.3	− 3.2	− 11.0
Agriculture	278.4	66.1	− 41.9	− 26.1

Adapted from: Department of Employment, *Women and Work: A Statistical Survey* (London: HMSO, 1974), p. 50.

greatest labor shortages occur, respectively, in health, science and engineering, miscellaneous labor, welfare administration and management, personal services, and selling. Only one of these occupations is exclusively "men's work": miscellaneous labor. Men predominate in two others: science and engineering and administration and management, but because both of these are occupations which

TABLE 2.7   Britain: Vacancies and Unemployment, 1976

	Number of Vacancies	Number of Unemployed	Proportion of Vacancies to Unemployed
Professional in science, engineering	4,538	15,335	30%
Health	2,366	5,987	40
Education	375	5,573	7
Welfare	469	2,160	22
Literary, artistic	445	11,200	4
Administration, management (incl. legal)	11,932	2,667	22
Clerical	16,195	157,949	10
Selling	9,157	55,449	17
Agricultural	1,015	13,904	7
Manufacturing, making, repairing	28,338	152,631	5
Construction, mining	3,939	74,019	5
Transport	4,916	97,242	2
Miscellaneous labor	8,676	482,737	29
Personal services	18,246	62,170	19

Adapted from: *Department of Employment Gazette* (August 1976).

women are fully capable of performing with proper training, women are gradually taking them up. Vacancies constitute demand for labor, especially when they exceed the number of unemployed. Demand is greatest in those (combined) occupations in which women specialize; and it extends to those non-manual occupations which women could perform with proper training.

We can compare this with demand for women workers in Sweden by looking again at the increase in employment by occupation and sex. Table 2.8 shows that between 1963 and 1971 female employment in the professions, and in health care in particular, increased substantially. The next highest increase occurred in clerical work. (The large percentage increase in administrative work is due to the small number of women in the field to begin with.) These occupational increases are the reverse of those in Britain, but the proportions are as large as the increases in female employment in Britain. Overall, female employment in Swe-

TABLE 2.8   Sweden: Increase in Employment by
            Occupation and Sex

	1971 Total (thousands)		1963-1971 % increase	
	Men	Women	Men	Women
All professions	440	354	40.6	63.1
Health	15	196	36.4	64.7
Administration	61	8	10.9	60.0
Clerical	100	347	−11.5	39.9
Commercial	174	176	−7.4	−3.8
Agriculture	236	67	−34.6	−41.2
Transport, communications	198	50	1.0	4.2
Manufacturing	1,043	183	2.4	−10.3
Services	110	404	11.1	16.1

Adapted from: National Labour Market Board, *Equality in the Labour Market, Statistics* (Stockholm: AMS, 1976).

den increased by 15.8% between 1963 and 1971, a greater increase than the 6% for women in Britain, but one that shows greater occupational channeling than in Britain.

We can see how these employment increases are related to demand for women workers, measured by vacancies in specific occupations, if we take as our sample the data in Table 2.9, which presents the statistics as calculated by the Swedish National Labor Market Board, Arbetsmarknadensstylresen (AMS).[13] The persistently large number of vacancies reported in traditional female occupations (health care, education, and other professional work, as well as services and office work) is overwhelming. Given the occupational structure based on sex, demand for women workers in Sweden is clear.

Conclusion. Two sorts of economic determinants of demand for women workers have been examined here: aggregate variables, such as national wealth, economic structure, and rate of development; and microeconomic factors specific to the labor market and particular occupations. In

[13] All vacancies must be reported to employment offices in Sweden.

TABLE 2.9   Sweden: Vacancies Reported at the Employment Office (per 100 jobseekers)

	October 1975	March 1976	January 1980	January 1981
Technology, etc.	57	96	217	154
Public health, sick care	131	309	337	245
Educational services	228	237	393	233
Legal, social science, artistic work, etc.	185	128	441	378
Administration	57	88	299	253
Accounting, general office work	44	103	139	92
Commercial work	51	57	89	66
Agricultural, forestry, fishery	28	28	47	41
Mining and quarrying	60	58	26	44
Transport, communication	69	85	107	68
Manufacturing (excluding construction, stock)	74	72	159	77
Construction, engineering	88	32	59	28
Stevedoring, stock, misc.	34	37	132	69
Services	88	127	205	141

Source: National Labour Market Board, *Swedish Employment Policy: Annual Report 1975/76, 1980/81* (Stockholm: AMS, 1976, 1981).

the mid-1960s these two sets of determinants combined to create a situation of greater demand for women workers, and much more so in Sweden than in Britain. For example, total civilian employment in the service sector in Sweden for the first time exceeded total employment in agriculture and industry, and, as a result, the size of Sweden's service sector exceeded Britain's. This, together with Sweden's higher level and rate of development, created new jobs that attracted women workers. The increased demand for women workers in Sweden was reflected in the greatly accelerated rate of female participation in the labor market.

But there was also a substantial demand for women workers in Britain, and for the same reasons as in Sweden. The structure of employment in Britain also shifted in favor of the non-industrial and non-agricultural sector at about the same time as in Sweden (mid-1960s). Although the magnitude of the change was not as great as in Sweden, it still signaled an increase in the sorts of jobs in which women specialize. The resulting demand for women workers was reflected, as in Sweden, in a rise in female employment, although again the magnitude of this change was more limited than in Sweden.

This analysis establishes a connection between changes in the economy and changes in women's labor force participation. But the connection is not always clear or direct. There are links between changes in the economy and women's employment that are masked by this sort of analysis. Why did all these changes occur so suddenly in the mid-1960s in Sweden? Why was there suddenly (and still) such a great need for nurses in Sweden? Since health care is a public sector function in both Britain and Sweden, this particular link can be found in differences in public policy. That is, the government in Sweden must have decided to expand public sector health care at a rapid pace. As I argue below, the link between women's employment and changes in the economy is to be found in the nature of public policy in each nation. A major difference that will be elaborated is that in Sweden public policy preceded changes in women's employment and shaped it, whereas in Britain public policy initiatives for women followed by many years changes in the economy and the effects of economic changes on women's employment. These differences have had critical consequences for the situation of women workers in the two countries.

The Role of the State

This discussion of the role of the state will focus on public policy, in particular economic policy. In the 1960s both Britain and Sweden (and a number of other advanced industrial nations) once again found themselves in the situation where they needed to come to terms with immense changes in the world economy. The reasons for the need and responses were different in each nation. I present sep-

arately the unique sets of constraints and possibilities that
confronted Britain and Sweden at the time, and effects on
employment that resulted.

Britain and the Legacy of the "Tried and No Longer True"

Throughout the 1950s Britain's economic climate was
almost as comfortable as elsewhere—growth was low but
steady, and it was combined with low unemployment. A
worldwide economic boom was taking shape by the 1960s.
This, in turn, increased aggregate consumer demand. Governments have to make two different kinds of responses
to two different aspects of increased demand. One concerns
the pressure on productivity, which has to be stepped up
to meet the demand. The other concerns the pressure on
inflation that can result from increased demand. The response of successive British governments to both of these
pressures has been called "tinkering" in one recent, after-
the-fact analysis.[14] (As Bacon and Eltis put it, "Tinkerers
believe that a country's economic ills can be cured by ad-
justing demand, the exchange rate, or the money supply,
and by persuading workers to accept periods of wage restraint."[15]) The pressures, and the failure of tinkering to
deal with them satisfactorily, revealed fundamental structural problems in the British economy which required
structural responses. However, just what these structural
problems are, and what suitable responses should be made,
is still a matter of dispute.[16]

One of Britain's greatest economic weaknesses has been

[14] Robert Bacon and Walter Eltis, *Britain's Economic Problem: Too Few
Producers* (London: Macmillan Press, 1976). See also F. T. Blackaby (ed.),
British Economic Policy 1960-74: Demand Management (London: Cambridge
University Press, 1978); Douglas E. Ashford, *Policy and Politics in Britain:
The Limits of Consensus* (Philadelphia: Temple University Press, 1981).

[15] Bacon and Eltis, *Britain's Economic Problem*, p. 1.

[16] On the left, Tony Benn emphasizes nationalization and a greater role
for Britain's declining industrial base; on the right, Margaret Thatcher
emphasizes a greater role for market forces in controlling the economy.

in industrial production. In the first few years of the 1960s industrial output did not grow at all. On the other hand, productivity, which is a measure of efficiency, did grow. Thus, limited growth in output indicated slack in the system and the possibility of unemployment unless something was done.[17] To stimulate growth in production output, the Chancellor of the Exchequer followed the advice of the newly created National Economic Development Council (NEDC) to increase aggregate demand through increased investment in the public sector at a very high rate (25% in fifteen months). There was nothing unusual in this decision, except that it was a large amount coming from a Conservative government. The measure immediately had the desired effect—it saved some jobs and created new ones in the public sector, supplying more disposable income to be spent on consumer goods and thus increased orders to industry. But the effect was short-lived. The events that followed revealed a penchant in British policy making for single-targeted measures without adequate support and without adequate appreciation of the full range of consequences.

For example, the NEDC had forecast that employment in the public sector would increase by about 1.5% per annum in relation to industrial employment. As it turned out, the increase in non-industrial employment was much greater. The relative annual increase was 5.7% between 1961 and 1964, and for the remainder of the decade non-industrial employment increased at least twice as much as expected. Meanwhile, total employment, and industrial employment in particular, fell, directly nullifying the whole intent of stimulating demand (which was to increase production through increased employment in industry). The consequence, of course, was that industrial production did not increase and, because industry could not keep up with

[17] Productivity refers to the number of workers needed to staff machines. This discussion is based on Bacon and Eltis, *Britain's Economic Problems*, Chapter 2. See also, Wilfred Beckerman (ed.), *Slow Growth in Britain: Causes and Consequences* (Oxford: Clarendon Press, 1979).

growing domestic demand, imports increased, thereby leading to a deficit in the balance of payments. During this period, the pressure to devalue the pound was intense. Devaluation came about only in 1967 after massive borrowing by the government to support the value of the pound, but the British economy could be shored up only temporarily.

There are numerous arguments as to why all this happened in Britain, and I will briefly review a few before presenting some additional considerations of my own. Resistance to devaluation of the pound prevented Britain from taking full advantage of the possibilities offered by worldwide increased demand until it was too late.[18] However, as has been suggested, devaluation may have been one of those marginal measures that could only have patched up, temporarily, deeper structural problems in British industry. Analyses of what these structural problems were have ranged from the role of unions (and management-worker relations),[19] to the organization of work,[20] to matters beyond the plant itself and in the sphere of wider economic policy.[21] With regard to this last issue, it is argued that the nature of British economic planning represents a critical failure in realizing what planning entails. For example, the decision to stimulate industrial production through increased demand was not immediately backed up by in-

[18] Throughout the post-World War II era, Britain has adhered to principles inappropriate to its resources that locked the country into a situation of economic stagnation. See Stephen Blank, "Britain: The Politics of Foreign Economic Policy, the Domestic Economy, and the Problem of Pluralistic Stagnation," *International Organization*, 31 (Autumn 1977).

[19] M. S. Joseph, "Trade Unions in Western European Politics," in Jack Hayward and R. N. Berki (eds.), *State and Society in Contemporary Europe* (New York: St. Martin's Press, 1979); Brian Burkitt and David Bowers, *Trade Unions and the Economy* (London: Macmillan Press, 1979).

[20] Still a classic is Ronald Dore, *British Factory, Japanese Factory* (London: Allen and Unwin, 1973).

[21] Andrew Martin, "Is Democratic Control of Capitalist Economies Possible?" in Leon N. Lindberg (ed.), *Stress and Contradiction in Modern Capitalism* (Lexington, Mass.: Lexington Books, 1975).

creased investment in industry to expand plant and equipment to meet demand and increase jobs.[22] Such investment required changes in taxation policy and in the system of incentives; by the time renewed investment took place, it was too little and too late. Each of these arguments is valid, and, no doubt, a confluence of factors offers the most viable explanation for "what went wrong in Britain." In presenting an alternative consideration, my intention is to supplement these facts with one that is persistently overlooked in British economic policy, namely, the role of women workers in the economy.

Two significant characteristics of women's role in the economy in Britain are their occupational specializations and their employment marginality (that is, the fluctuation of women workers in and out of the labor market in response to changes in the business cycle). We have seen that women workers in Britain (and elsewhere) are segregated into a limited number of occupations: clerical, service, and lower-level professional. These were precisely the sorts of jobs that increased in Britain in the 1960s. The greatest increase occurred in local government jobs (as Table 2.10 shows). These were jobs in health, education, and welfare, specifically for school teachers, nurses, social workers, and related white-collar workers. In other words, because of

TABLE 2.10 Britain: Increase in Employment 1961-1974

| | Numbers Employed (thousands) | | |
	1961	1974	% Change
Central Administration	524	575	9.4
Local Government	1,755	2,697	53.7
Other Services	7,898	8,944	13.2

Source: Robert Bacon and Walter Eltis, *Britain's Economic Problem: Too Few Producers* (London: Macmillan Press, 1976), p. 167, as drawn from *Department of Employment Gazette*, various issues, 1961-1975; and *British Labour Statistics: Historical Abstract 1886-1968*.

[22] This is the basic argument in Bacon and Eltis, *Britain's Economic Problem*.

increased government expenditures, jobs for women and women's labor force participation rates increased. Many of the women were new entrants to the labor force, attracted by the availability of jobs. Many were married women. As more women entered the labor force, the proportion of working men fell. More importantly, the absolute number of working men also began to fall, for the new jobs were being taken up by women, and men were becoming un-employed as the occupational/industrial structure began to shift. By 1967 male unemployment was at a record high level. Thus, the measures taken in the 1960s to stimulate the economy and offset structural unemployment failed because the creation of new jobs in the public sector (in health and education) had nothing to do with the kind of structural unemployment that was occurring (industrial de-cline). Moreover, because the new jobs were being taken up by women, and in particular married women, overall unemployment became severe once recession set in, for women in Britain are marginal workers. I will elaborate the meaning of this concept and its applicability to Britain below. The important point now is that when recession came in the late 1960s and early 1970s, women were forced out of the labor market *en masse*, since they were in jobs peripheral to the economic survival of firms and other or-ganizations and in jobs dependent on a high level of public spending. Female unemployment, combined with pre-ex-isting male unemployment, made the overall rate of un-employment rise drastically.

By the late 1960s, British governments had to contend not only with rising unemployment and consequent pres-sures from unions for positive measures to deal with it but also with the fact that unemployment and inflation were rising together. With a determination that acquired a force of its own, the Labour government (and later the Conser-vative) fell back on a favorite remedy for inflation: wage restraint.[23] The measure (a "tinkering" one) was inappro-

[23] Harold Wilson felt that the special relationship between the Labour

priate to the magnitude of the problem. Both unemployment and inflation continued to rise, and repeated efforts
to impose an incomes policy indicated that, in the trade-
off between inflation and unemployment, unemployment
was allowed to rise more. Largely ignored again was the
fact that women bore the brunt of unemployment; they
were the last to come and the first to go. What significance
does this have for the economy? Women work in the lower-
paid jobs in each occupational category. These were the
kinds of jobs lost to inflation. As a result, there were still
enough workers working in higher-paid jobs who could
keep up with inflation, up to a point. The failure to dampen
their demand continued to fuel the trend of rising prices.

The purpose of interjecting here the role of women
workers in the economy is to point to one of the many
factors that need to be taken into account in economic
planning and policy making, and one that is given exceed-
ingly short shrift in Britain. The fact that women function
as they do in the labor market had a fundamental effect
on the economy. First, the occupational specialization of
women workers diverted the intended consequences of
government measures to ease the structural shift in unemployment. (To repeat, the intention was that aggregate
unemployment, mostly male and industrial, would be absorbed in newly created public sector jobs, thereby increasing overall demand and eventually increasing orders to and
employment in industry. The new jobs were in fact taken
by women.) Second, the marginality of women workers
exacerbated the effects on unemployment once recession
set in. Government policies first attracted, then repelled,
women workers without full consideration of the implications.

Aside from this substantive omission, two other shortcomings of British policy making are apparent. First, the

---

Party and the unions would see him and his government through, despite
wage restraint. It did not. See Andrew Martin, "Labor Movement Parties
and Inflation: Contrasting Responses in Britain and Sweden," *Polity*, 7
(1975).

measure taken to improve the economy (namely, increased public spending) was many steps removed from the intended consequence (which was to increase industrial production and industrial employment). Much faith was put in the ability of the market to shape processes along the best path for the nation, and in the ability of planners to forecast how the market would operate. Second, the policy and its intended consequence focused on the macroeconomic or aggregate level. The labor market was conceptualized basically as a whole, at most consisting of industrial and non-industrial sectors. Although everyone is aware that machine operators in industry do not become typists in public offices (certainly not without retraining, at the least), any acknowledgment of this fact was not obvious in the plans for structural shifts in employment. Just as the role of women workers was insufficiently considered, there was also insufficient consideration of the functioning of most other microeconomic dimensions of the labor market.

These considerations on perspective and planning will be emphasized in describing the role taken by the state in Sweden. Faced with the same international economic situation and similar domestic employment and industrial structures, Sweden's initial response to economic imperatives in the 1960s was similar to Britain's—public spending was increased. What was different was the system of supports to guide this measure toward its intended consequence, and the consideration given to microeconomic factors, including the role of women workers, in achieving national goals.

Sweden: Planned Innovation

Before Keynes published his ideas on managing economic recessions through increased public expenditure, Sweden was experimenting with its own version of countercyclical financing. Sweden's economic program in the 1930s attempted to "transform capitalist society" through a type of planning that was "modest in scope."[24] The purpose of the program was to achieve full and efficient employment, and it was organized by increasing levels of public expenditure and taxation.[25] Labor efficiency was expected to lead to increased production and this was expected eventually to help finance the social welfare measures of social democracy. Sweden's economic recovery from the Depression surpassed other governments' attempts at economic control (for example, the New Deal in the United States under Roosevelt). The same basic program continued in Sweden through the post-World War II era, and brought about the full development of Sweden's welfare state. But by the late 1950s the tendency of full employment combined with expansionary fiscal policies to stimulate inflation was becoming manifest. Social Democratic government leaders and their cohorts in the trade union movement recognized that something more was required to offset this tendency. What developed was not so much a shift in policy as a consolidation of existing fundamentals.

An Economic Planning Council was set up in 1962. The heart of Swedish economic planning became an active manpower policy.[26] This was facilitated by earlier decisions, such as the focus on efficient and full employment and the rejection of such measures as wage restraint and a low level of unemployment to dampen overheated economic situations. Sweden's active manpower policy came to full bloom in the 1960s when rising demand presented the possibility of industrial expansion at the same time as it threatened

[24] Especially compared to French indicative planning. Timothy A. Tilton, "A Swedish Road to Socialism: Ernst Wigforss and the Ideological Foundations of Swedish Social Democracy," *American Political Science Review*, 73 (June 1979), p. 509.

[25] The introduction of planning as a tool of economic management, even if "modest," was not an easy achievement. See M. Donald Hancock, *Sweden: The Politics of Postindustrial Change* (Hinsdale, Ill.: The Dryden Press, 1972), pp. 208-14.

[26] I discuss manpower policy more fully in Chapter 4. It is a very broad and far-reaching policy framework and has implications for a number of issue areas.

prosperity with possible inflation. (Such an interpretation of what was being offered by the economic situation in the 1960s contrasts notably with Britain's lack of foresight about the consequences of government actions on economic conditions.) When the onset of an economic boom became apparent in the 1960s, Sweden was in a better position to take advantage of the opportunities offered by increased international demand than Britain.[27] One reason was that Sweden's economy was more export-oriented than Britain's, and it was not plagued by the same considerations and constraints imposed on Britain by virtue of its position in the international community. In addition, by the 1960s, and even earlier, Sweden's labor force was already operating at close to full capacity. This was as much a function of the favorable economic conditions of the 1950s as of the Swedish government's commitment to the policy of full employment.[28] The earnestness of that commitment did not become clear until the decade of the 1960s and thereafter. The most important aspect of Sweden's response to changing economic conditions in the 1960s was the realization that in a situation of full employment, increased production to take full advantage of increased demand required both greater technological efficiency and an expanded labor force. The first required investment; the latter meant that women, the most readily available source of new labor, had to be encourged to enter the labor market.[29]

When demand increases, new jobs open up in industry.

[27] Martin, "Is Democratic Control . . . Possible?" p. 47, and *passim*.

[28] In the 1960s most nations had "full employment," meaning, for the most part, low unemployment.

[29] At the same time, Sweden was allowing a large number of new immigrants to enter the country, a policy which was soon to change. As I argue elsewhere, these two types of labor, immigrant and female, are not necessarily interchangeable. That is, women workers were not tapped only after the problems of vast immigration were recognized. The variety of methods used to encourage women to enter the labor market are examined throughout this study. They include job opportunities, new and expanded training programs, changes in taxation, and day care facilities for children.

This is somewhat of a direct cause-effect relationship, but in Sweden a special measure is taken to make sure the cause has its intended effect. This is the system of the Investment Reserve Fund. By law, certain firms can avoid taxes on profits if they place some of their profits in the special Fund. However, the government controls the money in the Fund. The most common use of the Fund is for investment in industry when an economic downturn occurs. By the 1960s the government had become quite skilled at this sort of economic management.[30] Therefore, it was becoming increasingly capable of exercising even greater control, and used the Fund to direct the economic upturn as well. Releasing investment funds even when there was a high level of demand assured that production would continue to expand, that new and better equipment could be procured, and that the labor force would have to be increased to the extent necessary to keep up with demand. Employment in industry did increase in the early 1960s, continuing a trend that had been building since 1945. Later in the decade the government also stipulated that a certain proportion of the new employees in certain industries be women.[31]

By the mid-1960s, however, another change was occurring in the economy and the structure of employment, also under the direction of the government. With increased technological efficiency, the absolute number of persons employed in industry stabilized, and then fell. Sweden's commitment to the policy of full employment became particularly manifest at this time. As in Britain, the Swedish government increased public spending at a higher than usual rate, creating new jobs in the public sector. The measure was also intended, as in Britain, to offset structural unemployment and to keep up aggregate demand. But whereas in Britain employment was to be achieved through increased aggregate demand, in Sweden the focus was on

---

[30] Andrew Shonfield, *Modern Capitalism: The Changing Balance of Public and Private Power* (London: Oxford University Press, 1965), p. 202.

[31] Sex quotas and regional industrial development policies are described more fully in Chapter 4.

labor itself. A new labor market policy was formulated with the express purpose of maintaining full employment through an expanding economy.

New jobs, such as those created in the public sector in the 1960s, loosen up the labor market if labor is mobile. Two types of Swedish measures aim to assure labor mobility. One consists of grants and other assistance for rehousing and for income maintenance during job changes. The other is a highly developed and well-thought-out program of retraining. Any person who is willing to train for a job in which a labor shortage exists can enroll in the program and be paid at a rate slightly higher than that received through unemployment benefits. The National Labor Market Board keeps close tab on trends in the labor market. Such monitoring, together with a career counseling service, guides trainees into secure employment positions. In this way labor market policy eases the burden on individuals of the shift in the occupational structure, and the burden on the economy is eased through such measures as continuing investment in industry to assure that industry can keep up with growing demand and the economy can continue to expand.

Conclusion

The Swedish response to the economic conditions of the 1960s seized the opportunities that were being offered, but recognized that opportunity had to be helped along to result in long-term advantage. The form of help amounted to precisely what was lacking in Britain, namely a back-up system. Such a system eases the structural shift in employment that accompanies economic development; at the same time, it facilitates that development by maintaining full employment and aggregate demand. With a policy framework that includes investment, both countercyclical and expansionary, as well as effective use of a mobile labor force, economic efficiency is more likely. The support that the Swedish policies receive from the country's largest trade union organization, the Swedish Trade Union Confederation, Landsorganisationen (LO), indicates that the policies are beneficial for labor.[32] The LO tolerates the short-term unemployment that results, for example, from phasing out inefficient industries because the long-term effect improves wages. In contrast, British unions cling to job maintenance, fearing the consequences of unemployment. Labor inefficiency is one result.

In sum, the basic difference between Britain and Sweden has been in their perspectives. In Britain change has occurred one step at a time, as the government intervened in an ad hoc fashion, and the outcome is largely unpredictable. In Sweden all the factors that shape the economy as a whole have been subject to government manipulation, with the result that both the process and the direction of change have been more certain.

Have these differences in policy perspectives and approaches made any difference for women workers? In some ways, the differences for women in the two countries may not have been so great. Women's labor force participation increased in both countries, although much more in Sweden. However, occupational segregation remains as high, if not higher, in Sweden than in Britain, so the value of the quantitative improvement is diminished by considerations of status. In addition, women in both Britain and Sweden were drawn into the labor market to perform similar economic functions—to keep up and perhaps increase aggregate demand, that is, in their capacity as *consumers*, not producers, since they perform "non-productive" jobs.[33] This suggests that the marginality of women workers may not have been altered by policy differences in Britain and

[32] Furniss and Tilton claim that such measures mean that newly unemployed workers need not fear for their livelihood, and, therefore, that more efficiency in the use of labor can be achieved. Norman Furniss and Timothy Tilton, *The Case for the Welfare State: From Social Security to Social Equality* (Bloomington: Indiana University Press, 1977), p. 136.

[33] John Kenneth Galbraith, *Economics and the Public Purpose* (Boston: Houghton Mifflin, 1973), Chapter IV.

Sweden. I turn now to examine this proposition more fully and elaborate the dimensions of the marginality of women workers.

CONSEQUENCES FOR WOMEN

Thus far, my analysis of women's role in the economy has rested on the single most important fact in women's employment: occupational specialization. As economies advance beyond the stage of industrialization, more jobs become available in those occupations in which women specialize. We now must ask a central question about the future of the labor market: what is so peculiarly exclusive about women's work, and is it permanent? Women's occupational specialization does not occur, as some have suggested, because the jobs are somehow biologically suited to the female sex, nor because they are closely associated with household duties, nor because they require "sex appeal."[34] In the nineteenth century and early in the twentieth, men were the majority of elementary school teachers and office workers—until women entered the labor force and occupied these positions.[35] Once this happened, the ideological underpinnings of occupational prestige underwent a transformation. So did the structure of pay. Clerical work, for example, quickly plunged from being relatively well paid to one of the lowest-paid categories of work today.[36] We

[34] Wilensky, "Women's Work."

[35] Women first took up these positions, if they were qualified, because the work was clean and suitable for a "lady." Very few women were qualified to do any other work at a more professional level. Most women who worked at the turn of the century were manual workers in Britain, agricultural workers in Sweden.

[36] Braverman cites British and American evidence. He also notes that the change accompanied an increase in the volume of production, requiring an increase in the "accounting of value." Harry Braverman, *Labor and Monopoly Capital: The Degradation of Work in the Twentieth Century* (New York: Monthly Review Press, 1974), pp. 296-97, 302. See also Margery Davies, "Woman's Place is at the Typewriter: The Feminization of the Clerical Labor Force," in Richard C. Edwards, Michael Reich, David M.

come, then, to a second characteristic of women's role in the economy: women workers function in a marginal capacity, occupying the lower-status, lower-paying positions in all categories and levels of work.

In the next section I will analyze how and to what extent women workers constitute an "underclass" in the modern, contemporary settings of Britain and Sweden. The purpose of the analysis is to show that this concept has differential relevance in the two countries. As was suggested above, in both Britain and Sweden women were drawn into the labor force to stimulate aggregate *demand*, that is, to fulfill a consumer, not a producer, purpose. To the extent that women workers perform this role, their employment is marginal and fluctuates with economic cycles. We will see, however, that this is the point at which differences in government approaches to women workers and the economy have had the greatest impact. The underclass position of women workers in Britain is an economic fact, that is, women's employment is dependent on the economy in a number of ways. The underclass position of women workers in Sweden is a political fact, and it is undergoing transformation within the framework of union policies (and strength) on the one hand, and government policies on the other.

The Marginality of Women Workers

When women worked on farms earlier in this century and in the last, in all western countries, their work was part of their role of housewife. They performed the more menial tasks, which men did not do, and not the essential productive work.[37] The view is still dominant in many ad-

---

Gordon (eds.), *Labor Market Segmentation* (Lexington, Mass.: D. C. Heath, 1975).

[37] This is true of Sweden, too. Rita Liljeström, Gunilla Fürst Mellström, Gillan Liljeström Svensson, *Sex Roles in Transition: A Report on a Pilot Program in Sweden* (Stockholm: The Swedish Institute, 1975). Other comparative studies on the development of labor in pre-industrial agricultural societies find the same distinction between the tasks of women and men.

vanced industrial societies that women who work outside
the home continue to be marginal workers by virtue of
their traditional roles as housewives;[38] that is, women's ties
to the labor market are looser than men's because women
have household duties and women take their home responsibilities more seriously than men do when considering
work outside the home. An alternative explanation for the
marginality of women workers is that the work they do
when in paid employment is insufficiently rewarding to
encourage greater commitment.[39] It can also be argued that
women's home duties are more likely to affect their exit
from and re-entry into the labor market in connection with
their child-rearing responsibilities, as well as the number
of hours they work. Furthermore, women's status in the
labor market is more likely to affect rates of job turnover
and unemployment.

One additional explanation for the marginality of women
workers, taking into account all of these factors, is that
women's employment is dependent on the business cycles
of capitalist economies. A traditional ideology emphasizing
family duties allows women to function as a labor reserve,
prepared to enter the labor force when needed, and willing
to return to (or stay at) home when job opportunities are
not available.[40] The analysis in this chapter relates most
directly to such an explanation, for, as we have seen, women
were drawn into the labor market in both Britain and Swe-

[38] This view prevails in economic studies of the costs incurred by job-
taking and job-leaving. For a critique, see Cynthia B. Lloyd and Beth
Niemi, "Sex Differences in Labor Supply Elasticity: The Implications of
Sectoral Shifts in Demand," and Claire Vickery, Barbara Bergmann, and
Katherine Swartz, "Unemployment Rate Targets and Anti-Inflation Policy
as More Women Enter the Workforce," *American Economic Review*, 68 (May
1978).

[39] Harriet Zellner, "The Determinants of Occupational Segregation" in
Cynthia B. Lloyd (ed.), *Sex, Discrimination and the Division of Labor* (New
York: Columbia University Press, 1975).

[40] Eleanor Burke Leacock, "Introduction," in Heleieth I. B. Saffioti,
Women in Class Society (New York: Monthly Review Press, 1978), p. x. Wars
create the same situation of need for female labor as business cycles.

den during periods of economic boom. The explanation can be tested by looking at what happened to women when the boom dissipated. My argument is that the subsequent differences between women workers in Britain and Sweden are not due to different economic conditions, for both countries experienced recessions, but to differences in government policies for working women. I look first at the general indicators of marginality for women workers in Britain and Sweden, specifically, at job status and pay, employment cycles, and rates of unemployment.

Status and Pay.   In the study of occupations, status has two connotations: prestige and position. Prestige is a social attribution. It is the basis for deference/derogation and for occupational desirability.[41] Position is a structural attribute. It refers to the varying degrees of inferiority and superiority on a scale of tasks. Women are commonly found in occupations with lesser prestige and lower position than men. While studies of occupational status attempt to inform us about occupations irrespective of holder, when women are involved we learn more about the occupation because of the holder. The transformation in the status of such occupations as teacher and clerical worker are cases in point.

Earlier, we began to examine the occupational concentration of women workers in Britain and Sweden. In Britain in 1971 the highest concentration of women workers was in clerical work, which includes secretarial work (typing, shorthand), office machine operation, bookkeeping, and cash work. The second highest concentration was in service work, which includes domestic workers, launderers, restaurant workers, and hairdressers. In 1971 (indeed, since 1961) over half of all women workers were in these two

---

[41] In 1961 Otis Dudley Duncan published an index of socioeconomic status of occupations in the United States which is still widely used, even abroad. Since it was developed for males, its direct applicability for women has been questioned. See David L. Featherman and Robert M. Hauser, "Sexual Inequalities and Socioeconomic Achievement in the U.S., 1962-1973," *American Sociological Review*, 41 (June 1976).

categories of occupations. The same was true in 1980. Moreover, within the clerical and service occupations, women constitute a disproportionate majority of the workers (about 75%). We need not dwell on the low prestige of these occupations. The analysis of occupational prestige and position is more significant within another occupational category, namely, the professional.

The proportion of British women in the professions has been gradually increasing. It is interesting to note that earlier in this century proportionately more women were professionals; later they became clerical workers (see Table 2.11). However, within the category of professional worker, women dominate the lower ranks. In 1971 38.4% of professional women workers in Britain were nurses, another 31.2% were primary and secondary school teachers. About 18% of all doctors in Britain were women, 10% of university

TABLE 2.11   Women Workers in Britain: Percentage in Major Occupational Groups

Occupational Groups	1911	1921	1931	1951	1961	1971
Employers, proprietors	18.8	20.5	19.8	20.0	20.4	24.9
White-collar workers	29.8	37.6	35.8	42.3	44.5	47.9
Managers and Administrators	19.8	17.0	13.0	15.2	15.5	21.6
Higher professionals	6.0	5.1	7.5	8.3	9.7	9.9
Lower professionals and technicians	62.9	59.4	58.8	53.5	50.8	52.1
Foremen and inspectors	4.2	6.5	8.7	13.4	10.3	13.1
Clerks	21.4	44.6	46.0	60.2	65.2	73.2
Salesmen and shop assistants	35.2	43.6	37.2	51.6	54.9	59.8
All manual workers	30.5	27.9	28.8	26.1	26.0	29.4
Skilled	24.0	21.0	21.3	15.7	13.8	13.5
Semi-skilled	40.4	40.3	42.9	38.1	39.3	46.5
Unskilled	15.5	16.8	15.0	20.3	22.4	37.2
Percentage of women in total working population	29.6	29.5	29.8	30.8	32.4	36.5

Source: Catherine Hakim, "Job Segregation: Trends in the 1970's," *Department of Employment Gazette* (December 1981), p. 525.

professors, 6% of all barristers, and 8.5% of all managerial positions were held by women.[42] The increase in British women's labor force participation rate to the present has not been accompanied by a change in women's occupational segregation, neither within the professional field nor overall.[43]

Changes in the occupational structure in the Swedish labor force were presented in Table 2.3. By 1980 about 40% of women workers in Sweden were professionals (technical, etc., and medical), the category of greatest increase. However, within this occupational group, women are in the lowest ranks. For example, among workers in the health field, women dominate as nurses; among workers in the educational field, women dominate as preschool and primary school teachers (see Table 2.12). Furthermore, when one compares level of task performed, women tend to dominate the lower ranks. Table 2.13 shows the unequal distribution of level of task for male and female members of the Swedish Central Organization of Salaried Employees, Tjänstemännens centralorganisation (TCO), which is the major white-collar union in Sweden. Finally, the most common occupational category of women workers in Sweden is in the secretarial field, as Table 2.12 shows. Thus, while proportionately more women in Sweden work in the professions than in Britain (and proportionately fewer in clerical and service work), their status within these higher occupations does not place their lot significantly above women in Britain.

Perhaps the best indicator of the lower status of women workers is the consistently lower rate of pay of women compared to men. For centuries, differential earnings be-

[42] Department of Employment, *Women and Work: A Statistical Survey* (London: HMSO, 1974); Nancy Seear, "The Economic Position of Women in the United Kingdom," *American Economic Review*, 66 (May 1976); Darling, *The Role of Women*; Marjorie Galenson, *Women and Work: An International Comparison* (Ithaca: Cornell University Press, 1973).

[43] Catherine Hakim, "Job Segregation: Trends in the 1970's," *Department of Employment Gazette* (December 1981), pp. 521-29.

TABLE 2.12   Women Workers in Sweden: Most Common
              Occupations, 1975

Occupation	Number	Relative Distribution (%)	Proportion of Women in Occupation (%)
Secretary, typist, special clerks	219,446	16.0	86.9
Nurse's assistants	115,630	8.4	94.7
Shop assistants, etc.	107,352	7.8	78.5
Charwomen	66,481	4.8	88.4
Children's nurses	50,405	3.7	98.0
Kitchen maids	37,804	2.8	93.7
Registered nurses	36,289	2.6	96.6
Class teachers (grades 1-6)	36,027	2.6	78.7
Bookkeepers and cashiers	35,389	2.6	74.6
Domestic helpers, etc.	29,969	2.2	99.2
Farm hands, livestock workers	24,571	1.8	55.8
Headwaiters, waitresses	24,106	1.8	84.5
Tailors, seamstresses	22,372	1.6	93.8
Counter clerks, restaurant cashiers	19,170	1.4	97.6
Preschool teachers	18,116	1.3	96.2
Total	843,127	61.4	
All other occupations	529,506	38.6	
Total	1,372,633	100.0	

Note: Half of all working women are in public service. Twelve percent of the men are in public service. Within the group "engineering" the situation is reversed; 43% of the men work there and only 10% of the women.

Source: "Figures on Men and Women in the Labor Market," *Current Sweden* 4, No. 260 (November 1980), p. 7.

tween categories of work has been justified on the basis of the quality of the work. One would think that Adam Smith's dictum still holds:

Wages would vary too with the ease or hardship, the cleanliness or dirtiness, the honourableness or dishonourableness of the employment; with the easiness

TABLE 2.13   Members of the Swedish Industrial Salaried
Employees Association by Level of Occupation,
1968 and 1977 (%)

Level of Occupation	1968		1977	
	Men	Women	Men	Women
Managers, directors, certain specialists	0.4	0.0	0.6	0.0
Leading executive positions	3.6	0.1	4.6	0.1
Independent work	14.2	0.5	17.8	1.2
Fairly independent work	30.1	3.7	37.0	6.8
Less independent work	31.0	13.9	28.2	24.4
Fairly routine tasks	17.9	44.9	10.3	51.4
Routine tasks	2.8	36.9	1.5	16.2

Source: "Figures on Men and Women in the Labor Market," *Current Sweden*, No. 260 (November 1980), p. 8.

and cheapness or the difficulty or expense of its learning; with its constancy or inconstancy; with the small or great trust which is reposed in the workers and with the probability or improbability of success in the employment.[44]

Over the years, however, the work that some women do has become cleaner, more honorable, requiring more learning, and so on, without being compensated by higher pay, equal to men's in the same occupations. One reason for this is the lower-status positions of women workers. Women are clerks or assistants and not managers, primary school teachers and not professors, nurses and not doctors, and this is reflected in pay.

In 1970 Britain passed an Equal Pay Act to make amends for wage discrimination based on sex. The act came into full effect in 1976. Women doing exactly the same work as men must now be paid at the same rate. (The Act and its implementation are elaborated in the next chapter.) There remains, however, a great deal of unevenness in the

[44] Quoted in John F. Burton, Jr., et al. (eds.), *Readings in Labor Market Analysis* (New York: Holt, Rinehart and Winston, 1971), p. 38.

achievement of equal pay among different occupational and industrial groups. For example, in 1976 women were still receiving about 80% of men's hourly rates of pay in certain industries,[45] and the weekly rates for women manual workers and for women in the private sector are consistently lower than men's. In general, weekly wages are much lower than hourly rates, as shown in Figure 2.3, reflecting the fact that women work either part-time or at least not overtime. However, even the average hourly rates, excluding the effects of overtime, are much lower for women than men. The difference reflects the difficulty of defining and measuring equal work, as well as the valuation given to the work women do.

In 1960 the Swedish Employers' Confederation, Svenska arbetsgivareföreningen (SAF), together with Sweden's largest trade union organization, LO, agreed to abolish lower wages for women.[46] The dramatic and steady rise in women's average hourly and monthly rates of pay compared to men's in industry is also shown in Figure 2.3. Although the relative percentage is much higher in Sweden than Britain, the differential between women's and men's pay still reflects occupational status. A 1973 study by the major white-collar union in Sweden, TCO, found that the main factor accounting for salary differences between women and men in white-collar jobs was the different kinds of jobs that women and men hold and not wage discrimination (different pay for same work) or seniority differences.[47]

In sum, when we look at status and pay as indicators of the marginality of women workers in Britain and Sweden, the major difference between the two countries centers on equal pay. More women in Sweden are professionals, but

---

[45] These were hosiery, timber container, baking, knitwear, gloves, and agriculture. In addition, no plans for further progress were reported for electrical engineering and clothing and footwear. "Further Progress Towards Equal Pay," *Department of Employment Gazette* (August 1975).

[46] Only after did Sweden sign the ILO Convention.

[47] Elisabet Sandberg, *Equality is the Goal* (Stockholm: The Swedish Institute, 1975).

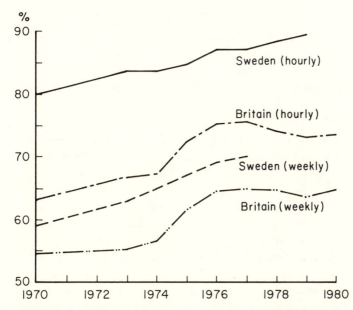

2.3. Women's Pay as a Proportion of Men's, 1970-1980, Britain and Sweden. Adapted from: Equal Opportunities Commission, *Fifth Annual Report, 1980* (London: HMSO, 1980), pp. 70-71. Swedish Trade Union Confederation, *This Is How We Work for Equality between Men and Women in Working Life and in the Trade Unions* (Stockholm: LO, 1980), p. 6. "Figures on Men and Women in the Labor Market," *Current Sweden*, No. 260 (November 1980), p. 9.

there is greater occupational segregation in Sweden. However, the rate of pay for women compared to men is much higher in Sweden than in Britain, even in the industrial sector alone. Interestingly, the state in Britain has intervened to a greater extent than in Sweden to achieve equal pay. Sweden still relies primarily on wage agreements reached in collective bargaining, whereas Britain has passed legislation to institute equal pay. Yet state intervention in Britain has been less effective for women than has the Swedish method. As I noted above and elaborate again in subsequent chapters, when the state in Britain intervenes, its measures are more single-targeted, circumscribed, and ad hoc than in Sweden. Much is left to market forces to complete the intention of limited government intervention. The consequences for women are detrimental.

Employment Cycles. Besides the conditions that women find in the labor market, it is also claimed that their household responsibilities encourage employment marginality. Home and family are said to affect women's employment in two ways. First, women quit work with the birth of their first child and re-enter only when their youngest child begins school. Second, many women, especially if they are mothers, work part-time, either until their children are grown or for the remainder of their work lives. The first pattern, known as the M-curve, is illustrated in Figure 2.4 for women in Britain and Sweden in 1971 (the only year for which comparable data are available). At that time the dimensions of the M-curve were certainly sharper in Britain than in Sweden. The difference between the two countries became even more pronounced as the decade wore on, for women in Sweden became increasingly less likely to quit work during the childbearing and childrearing years. Figure 2.5 illustrates more directly the effect of preschool-age children on women's employment rates in Britain and Sweden. The figure is so graphic as to require no further elaboration.

The presence of children encourages women to work part-time. Data reveal that part-time employment is as prevalent in Sweden as in Britain. In Britain in 1971 34% of all employed women worked part-time, which in Britain is considered to be less than 30 hours per week. (Another 13.6% worked less than 35 hours per week.) By 1976 the figure had risen to 40%.[48] In Sweden in 1971 about 35% of employed women worked less than 35 hours per week.

[48] Based on data in J.A.S. Robertson and J. M. Briggs, "Part-time Working in Great Britain," *Department of Employment Gazette* (July 1979).

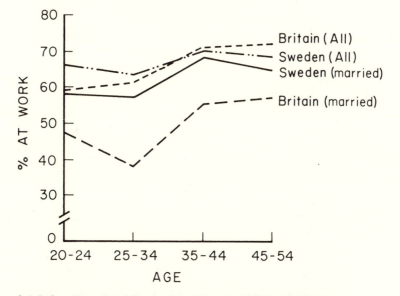

2.4. Labor Force Participation Rates, by Age, 1971. Adapted from: Department of Employment, *Women and Work: A Statistical Survey* (London: HMSO, 1974), p. 45. Arbetsmarknadens Kvinnonämnd, *Woman in Sweden: In the Light of Statistics* (Stockholm: AKN, 1973), p. 37.

By 1980 the figure had increased to 46%.[49] In both countries about 10% of employed men work part-time. Table 2.14 compares the effect of children on the number of hours women work in Britain and Sweden (comparable data are available only for 1971). Women with children of any age are much less likely to work and to work full-time in Britain than in Sweden, and the ages of children affect the number of hours worked by women in Sweden much less than in Britain. Working less than full-time, in and of itself, is not necessarily a good indicator of employment marginality. Ideally, such an indicator should include other

[49] Based on data in National Labour Market Board, *Equality in the Labour Market, Statistics* (Stockholm: AMS, 1980).

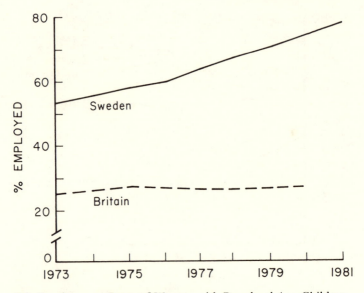

2.5. Employment Rates of Women with Preschool Age Children. Adapted from: Office of Population Censuses and Surveys, *General Household Survey* (London: HMSO, 1980), p. 11; National Labour Market Board, *Swedish Employment Policy: Annual Report 1980/81* (Stockholm: AMS, 1981), p. 6.

factors, such as the nature of the work, whether or not it is seasonal, and so on. However, we do know that in general part-time work can be less rewarding than full-time work in that it is likely to involve less productive work and the benefits and opportunities for promotion are lower. It is these factors, and not simply the number of hours worked, that lead to employment marginality in the sense of both job commitment and employment fluctuation.

Employment turnover is a better indicator of marginality, for it reveals either job dissatisfaction on the part of the employed or shows who is most prone to layoffs. Unfortunately, information is available only for Britain. There is strong evidence that the turnover rate for women workers in Britain is much higher than for men. For example,

TABLE 2.14   Hours Worked by Women with Children, 1971 (%)

| Britain | | Youngest Child Aged | |
Number of Hours	0-4	5-10	11-15
Under 18	35	31	25
18-36	36	44	54
Over 36	23	21	26
Sweden		Youngest Child Aged	
Number of Hours	0-4	5-10	11-15
Under 20	28	26	20
20-34	32	31	36
Over 34	41	43	44

Adapted from: Office of Population Censuses and Surveys, *Census 1971, England and Wales, Household Composition Tables, Part III* (10% sample) (London: HMSO, 1975), pp. 242-244; Arbetsmarknadens Kvinnonämnd, *Woman in Sweden: In the Light of Statistics* (Stockholm: AKN, 1973), p. 46.

in 1972, in all manufacturing industries, the rates of hiring and discharging women were much higher than for men (45.8 women per 100 employees were hired, compared to 25.7 men; 40.1 women per 100 employees were discharged, compared to 26.0 men).[50] The data for job tenure in other occupations are of a different nature, but show the same situation of lower attachment to jobs among women than among men. For example, a 1971 survey of full-time employees showed that, in nearly every occupational group, a far greater percentage of women than men had been with their current employers for less than a year.[51] Moreover, women of every age group were much more subject than men to this kind of job instability, and the situation was significantly worse for part-time working women. Well over half of the part-time working women under age 30 had been with their current employers for less than a year.

We would not be able to put the same interpretation on job turnover in Sweden, were data available, because much

[50] Department of Employment, *Women and Work*, p. 66.
[51] *New Earnings Survey 1971*, cited in ibid.

of the unemployment that results due to job loss or from workers wishing to change jobs is taken up in labor market training programs. Women constitute about half of the new trainees in these programs. Since many of the women are new entrants or returnees to the labor force, rather than already employed job changers, we cannot impute anything about job turnover. After completion of a training course women are as successful as men in obtaining jobs.[52]

Thus, a comparison of the employment cycles of women workers in Britain and Sweden shows some evidence that women in Sweden are becoming less marginal to the labor force. In Britain women's employment is still subject to the dependencies of children, which affects not only rates of employment but also hours of work and job turnover. Once women in Sweden enter the labor force, they appear more likely to remain in employment or in training for re-employment. This conclusion is verified when we look at the obverse of employment, namely rates of unemployment.

Unemployment. In Britain the rate of female unemployment is generally lower than the male rate. In Sweden the opposite case exists—the rate of female unemployment is higher than the male rate, but the difference is so small as not to warrant much discussion (see Table 2.15). Male unemployment in Britain is highest in manual occupations (manufacturing, miscellaneous labor). Men become unemployed because of redundancies (layoffs when industrial profits are low). The discrepancies in unemployment among regions is enormous. Unemployment in Britain is largely structural—it is related to the shift in the occupational base from predominantly industrial to predominantly non-industrial (and non-agricultural), and it represents an imbalance between skills and demands. Britain's lackluster manpower program has ill-served the changing labor requirements of the nation. It might seem from all

---

[52] Data in Arbetsmarknadens Kvinnonämnd, *Woman in Sweden: In the Light of Statistics* (Stockholm: AKN, 1973), p. 63; also, personal interview (National Labour Market Board, May 1982).

TABLE 2.15   Unemployment Rates

	Britain		Sweden	
	Men	Women	Men	Women
1960	1.4	1.1	1.3	1.7[a]
1965	1.3	0.7	0.8	1.7
1970	2.9	0.9	1.4	1.7
1975	4.4	1.6	1.3	2.1
1977	6.5	4.0	1.5	2.2
1980	8.7	5.7	1.7	2.3

Adapted from: Organization for Economic Co-operation and Development, *Labour Force Statistics* (Paris: OECD, various issues, 1960-1977); *Department of Employment Gazette* (March 1981); National Labour Market Board, *Equality in the Labour Market, Statistics* (Stockholm: AMS, 1980).
[a] Information is for 1962.

of this that men in Britain are likely to be more of a traditional "industrial reserve army" than women, and that men are more subject to the ups and downs of the economic cycles. However, this is not quite true. Male unemployment in Britain is more subject to the secular shift from industrial to non-industrial employment, but women's unemployment is more subject to the exigencies of the business cycle. To see this we can compare unemployment rates as presented in Table 2.15. From 1960 to 1970 (which is when the major occupational shift occurred), the male unemployment rate in Britain increased by 107% and the female rate decreased by 18%. However, between 1975 and 1977 Britain underwent a major recession. During this period the male unemployment rate increased by 48% and the female rate by 150%. The difference is clearly illustrated in Figure 2.6.

In Sweden the changes in rates of unemployment are remarkably small. Male unemployment suffered most from 1965 to 1968 (increasing by 188%), when the shift in dominance from industrial to non-industrial employment occurred in Sweden; but the rate quickly restabilized. Most intriguing is the minimal change in the female rate of unemployment, even during the recessionary period which began in 1975, as illustrated in Figure 2.6. Sweden's active manpower program is behind these low rates. As soon as

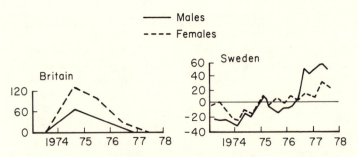

2.6. Rates of Change in Unemployment. Source: Organization for Economic Co-operation and Development, *Labor Force Statistics* (Paris: OECD, 1978).

unemployment begins to increase, labor market programs also increase. These programs include relief work, training programs, and subsidies to employers to avoid more lay-offs. Throughout the 1970s, while the registered unemployment rate in Sweden hovered around 2% of the labor force, the various labor market programs absorbed another 5% of the labor force.[53] The low unemployment rate in Sweden also indicated a reduction in the marginalization of women workers. I will now look more closely at the impact of the recession on women workers in Britain and Sweden in order to outline the dimensions of this change in both countries.

Unemployment and Recession

The recession which began in the mid-1970s has been the most severe in the post-World War II period, and in some dimensions, the most severe in this century. In Britain, the general weakening of the economy began in about mid-1974 with a hesitation in consumer spending on both goods and services, a drop in private investments, and a slowing of exports. By 1975 GDP had declined 2.9%; there-

[53] Bo Jangenäs, "Employment and Labor Market Policy in Sweden during the Recession of the Late 1970's," *Current Sweden*, No. 266 (February 1981), p. 5.

after a slight upturn resumed, but it was not immediately reflected in the labor market. The impact of this recession on the labor market was deep. In 1974 the unemployment rate was 2.5%. By 1975 it had risen to 4.5%, and it has continued to rise to its highest ever rate (13% in 1982). Besides unemployment, the labor market was also forced to adjust to the recession through a sharp drop in the number of working hours and work days and through an increase in other part-time arrangements. At first the disproportionate burden of this labor market slump fell on women workers.[54] Nearly half of the increase in total female unemployment was found among the youngest age group of new job seekers, and another one-third among women aged 20 to 29. Moreover, unemployment among young women under 18 increased ten times over the two-year period between 1974 and 1976, whereas it increased four times among young men under 20. Overall, the number of women workers who registered as unemployed during this period more than tripled (rising 96% in 1974-1975, 70% in 1975-1976), compared to a doubling in the number of men registered as unemployed (a rise of 56% in 1974-1975, 33% in 1975-1976). However, by the 1980s the difference in unemployment rates between men and women began to widen considerably, in favor of women! The explanation for both phenomena rests on the marginal nature of women's employment.

The recession in 1974 had a greater effect on women's unemployment for two reasons. Because they are less integrated into the labor market, women are the last hired and first fired. The sorts of jobs that women do are least essential to the survival of firms in an economic crunch. We can see how these factors operated by examining increases in unemployment in different occupational sectors.

When the recession began in Britain, the greatest losses in employment were in the manufacturing and construc-

---

[54] This discussion is based on Diane Werneke, "The Impact of the Recent Economic Slowdown on the Employment Opportunities of Women," *World Employment Programme Research* (Geneva: International Labour Organisation, WEP 2-32/WP 4, May 1977).

tion industries. Women lost more jobs than men in these industries, both those in which fewer women than men were employed and those in which women were the majority of workers (textiles and clothing). Women's employment in industry is more vulnerable than men's because women predominate in the least skilled occupations, and are the first to be laid off. In addition, many companies have last-in first-out agreements with trade unions, which disadvantages women more than men in all sectors of employment. But the proportion of women in manufacturing is small, and, in fact, the greatest unemployment among women occurred in those occupations in which women are concentrated: distributive trades and clerical work. The number of women employed in retail sales is only somewhat greater than men, but the number of women who register as unemployed in this occupation is much greater than the number of men, especially in the assistant category.[55] Job losses in clerical work would affect, of course, women primarily.

These job losses during the recession in the 1970s were mostly among full-time workers. The recession had the opposite effect on opportunities for part-time workers. Because most part-time workers are women, their unemployment pattern began to look better than men's as the recession progressed into the early 1980s. Part-time employment actually increased throughout the 1970s, especially in sales. In fact, since 1971 virtually all of the increase in women's labor force participation is accounted for by an increase in part-time work. Marginality in this sense buffers women's employment. However, we cannot say that being able to work part-time has had a positive effect on women workers, and certainly not in terms of their marginalization. Women who take on part-time jobs (especially in sales) during a recession do so to supplement family income.[56] Their work is secondary to them and peripheral to the economy. More-

[55] *Department of Employment Gazette* (August 1976).
[56] This has been called the "added worker" syndrome. See William G. Bowen and T. Aldrich Finegan, *The Economics of Labor Force Participation* (Princeton, N.J.: Princeton University Press, 1969), especially Chapter 6.

over, the proportion of married women among unemployed women in Britain has risen (from about 35% in 1977 to about 45% in 1982).

This information indicates that the impact of the recession in Britain appears to have been just as bad for women as for men, if not more so. Making matters still worse, the data on unemployment for women in Britain were underestimated for much of the 1970s because of a peculiar feature of the Social Security Act, which allowed women workers to "opt out" of paying full social security contributions while in employment. Since they therefore did not receive unemployment benefits, they had no incentive to register at unemployment offices, especially during recessions when job opportunities were low. The number of "discouraged" women workers who "opted out" of the labor force during the 1970s was probably higher than normal.[57] (Generally, about 75% of working women took advantage of their right to exemption.) The exemption was abolished with the passage of the Sex Discrimination Act in 1975, but there was a phase-out period for those women who had used it in the past.

Sweden's economy may be strong in its own right, but it is heavily dependent on the international economic situation. Any decline in demand for Swedish goods abroad severely affects its GNP, one-third of which is represented by the value of exports. Thus, the global recession that started in 1974 began to be felt in Sweden by 1975. The domestic economic policies that had developed over the years were not enough to offset Sweden's vulnerable dependence on trade. During 1974 exports fell by 816%, and growth in GNP slowed considerably. Domestic activity also slowed and was reflected in a decline in industrial production and a decrease in investment which eventually became a decline. By 1976 exports began to increase again but the other economic indicators remained sluggish. Throughout the 1970s, however, consumption and government spend-

[57] Bowen and Finegan find that the "discouraged worker" syndrome is greater among women during recessions. Ibid.

ing continued to rise, the latter assisted in part by government borrowing abroad.

And yet the impact of the recession on the labor market was minimal. Between 1975 and 1976, one of the worst periods of the recession, total employment in Sweden actually grew. Over the decade of the 1970s, the labor force increased by over 9%. Most of the increase was in women's employment, and most of it in part-time work. As in Britain, the steady increase in women's part-time employment no doubt indicates that women workers are being affected more negatively than men, for part-time work in Sweden is also usually of low occupational status, lower paying, and less secure than full-time work. In addition, the fact that much of the increase in employment was in part-time work suggests that some Swedish housewives may also have taken on temporary extra work to supplement the family's budget.

The recession reduced the demand for labor in industry. The decline in exports in 1975 was felt throughout the manufacturing industries to different degrees and at different times. The job losses that occurred in manufacturing affected women more severely than men. Women incurred about 70% of the total losses, primarily in textiles, electrical work, and woodwork, which are sectors where women who are in manufacturing are concentrated. At first, men were most severely affected by losses in heavy manufacturing and machine and motor maintenance, but their losses overall were more limited than those of women, and in the long run male losses were spread more evenly among the occupational sectors.

These job losses indicated that one of the tools of labor market policy, namely the attempt to contain layoffs by subsidizing employment through grants to companies, was not working well, particularly as the recession grew longer and deeper.[58] To offset job losses in the private sector, the government began to increase employment in the public

[58] Another subsidization measure is relief work in the private sector. In general, after the subsidization period is over, three-quarters of the men and two-thirds of the women remain in employment with the same employer.

sector as another labor market measure. As in the past, women once again benefited from this increase. Table 2.16 shows the increase in public sector employment in Sweden from 1960 to 1979. Women now constitute two-thirds of the public sector employees. More women are employed in the local than national level of government, and at the local level women far outnumber men. Forty-five percent of all the women who are government employees work part-time.[59]

TABLE 2.16   Sweden: Government Employees and Employees in Local Authorities

	1960	1970	% Increase 1960-1970	1979	% Increase 1970-1979
General Civil Service and Defense					
Men	76,824	105,149	36.9	134,696	28.1
Women	43,789	63,497	45	105,264	65.8
State Business Enterprises					
Men	81,168	87,819	8.2	99,423	13.2
Women	33,063	40,188	21.5	56,537	40.7
State Subsidized Activities					
Men	31,322	45,933	46.6	60,313	31.3
Women	30,905	60,678	96.3	103,761	71.0
Employees in County Councils					
Men		24,949		53,561	114.7
Women		146,359		282,698	93.2
Employees in Primary Local Authorities					
Men		80,873		110,392	36.5
Women		220,758		353,113	60.0
Total					
Men		344,723		458,385	33.0
Women		531,480		901,373	70.0

Adapted from: *Statistisk Årsbok 1981* (Stockholm: Sveriges Officiella Statistik, Statistiska Centralbyrån, 1981), p. 243.

[59] Table 2.16 indicates that only a small proportion of the increase in employment was in "state subsidized activities," that is, relief work in the public sector. It should be noted that women have benefited more than men from this measure, although 42% of them work part-time.

In sum, the impact of the recession on employment in Sweden was minimal, especially in comparison with Britain. Compared to the consequences of the recession on women as well as men in Britain, Swedish women on the whole were not much more negatively affected than men. With some qualification, especially regarding increased part-time employment, we can say that women in Sweden are becoming more integrated into the labor market as permanent workers.[60] The fact that they continue to be drawn into the labor market in greater numbers than men even in a recession, and that they remain employed even during a recession, is an indication of the government's commitment to a full employment policy, and one that includes women. It is also an indication that Sweden's labor market programs are working. (These will be discussed in more detail in Chapter 4.) The role taken by the Swedish state to offset the severity of recession is different in important ways from the role of the state in Britain. Government actions in Britain basically allowed un/employment to fluctuate with the demands of the market, a process that has a harsher effect on women because of their great marginality. The government in Sweden adopted new mechanisms of microeconomic intervention through the labor market, with ramifications for both workers and the economy. At the same time, however, the government has continued its macroeconomic concern with maintaining as high a level of demand as possible in the recession, with positive implications for the labor force participation of women. The different policies and positions of the state in Britain and Sweden are clearly evidenced in the different patterns of employment fluctuation of women workers in the two countries.

[60] My negative assessment of part-time employment requires some modification here. Part-time employment in Sweden is receiving more social approval and is being encouraged in public policies for working parents. Parents with small children are allowed shortened working hours and time off to care for sick children or to tend to their other needs with little loss of pay. Fathers are expected to participate as much as mothers. Employees in the public sector are more likely to be the forerunners in realizing these policies.

The differences in the impact of the recession allow us to say that women in Britain continue to function as marginal workers and that women in Sweden are becoming less marginal, both to the economy and to the social concerns of the nation.

CONCLUSION

This analysis has shown that women's employment is dependent on much more than the objective economic conditions precipitating demand for women workers. In examining the aggregate economic differences between Britain and Sweden, we found that these differences do not adequately explain the labor force participation of women. The higher economic development and economic activity of Sweden should have been reflected in a higher proportion of women workers throughout the postwar years. But not until the mid-1960s did proportionately more women work in Sweden than in Britain; curiously, this was at a time when Sweden's economic growth was beginning to slow down. Focusing on expansion of the service sector as an explanation for women's labor force participation rates yielded a similar inconclusiveness: both Britain and Sweden underwent an expansion of their service sectors in the 1960s and in both countries women were drawn into the labor force as a result. But the proportion of new women workers in Sweden was much larger than in Britain, and this difference cannot be accounted for simply in terms of the expanded service sector, which was not that much greater in Sweden than in Britain. The specific event that led to the increase in women workers in both countries was actually an act of government: an increase in public sector spending that increased the number of public sector jobs. Government expenditure as a percent of GNP became much greater in Sweden than in Britain, affecting, thereby, the structure of employment in the public sector. Thus, rather than relying on economic variables and the magnitude of change in them as explanations for women's work, the analysis at this point turned to an apparent difference underlying the economic situations of Britain and Sweden: differences in the role of the state.

I have suggested that a change in the economic policy framework occurred in Sweden and not in Britain and that this difference accounted for differences in women's labor force participation. In the 1960s Sweden developed more refined mechanisms for microeconomic intervention, which included a manpower policy with programs for (re-)training, labor mobility, labor market analysis, and career guidance. The program not only signaled a change in attitude toward women workers, it also created the security of employment that complements availability of jobs. Together, these factors drew large numbers of women into the labor force and, most importantly, kept them there. In contrast, the lack of British policies for the labor market, let alone a policy framework that included women, allowed the conditions of employment for both women and men to be determined by free market forces. The single act of increasing demand through increased government expenditures did not have positive long-term consequences on employment in Britain because it was not followed up by a support system. The impact of the recession was thus more severe in Britain than in Sweden. But while both women and men were badly affected by economic deterioration in Britain, women fared worse than men, for continuing to allow the market to be the main determinant of employment meant that women continue to function as marginal workers, a necessary reserve of labor in a capitalist economy that undergoes fluctuations in demand. British policies for social security payments reinforced this aspect of the marginality of women workers. It is clear that if women are to become less marginalized in the economy as well as society, their employment dependence on the market must be reduced. At this point, it appears that any change in women's dependence rests on an active state. In the 1970s, the government in Britain began to make some changes in its policies for women. These and their correlates in Sweden are the subject of the next two chapters. The analyses there show that change is related not only to what the government does but also how it acts.

One final implication of the analysis in this chapter concerns the interpretation of "demand" for women workers. Labor demand is commonly accepted as an objective economic condition, or at least one that is solely determined by the market. I have shown that demand for women workers is influenced by government actions, whether or not governments are fully aware of the consequences of their actions. For example, when governments increase employment in the public sector, women are attracted to the newly created female occupations—in health care, education, social work, and clerical work. There is an inherent paradox in these events, particularly apparent in the case of Sweden. State actions enhance women's opportunities to work, thus contributing to one aspect of social equality for women; but this occurs through the reinforcement of a type of segregation that has resulted from past inequities in market processes. A more generalized example of the role of the state in influencing labor demand is the way in which economic policy and planning keep the economy functioning at a high level of activity, thereby creating the sort of labor "shortage" that we see in Sweden. To the extent that expansion of the public sector is a major means of economic revitalization, labor "shortages" are created which women tend to fill—because of the persistence of occupational segregation. Irony is to be found in this contradictory consequence of public sector employment for the status of women workers. In sum, labor demand is as much a product of governmental actions as it is of objective market forces. Differences among countries even when they face similar economic circumstances therefore stem from the extent and character of state intervention to control economic and social forces.

CHAPTER 3

BRITAIN:
EQUAL EMPLOYMENT
OPPORTUNITY

INTRODUCTION

The last chapter on the role of women in the economy focused on economic explanations for the differences between Britain and Sweden in policies for working women. The conclusion drawn was that economic explanations alone are inadequate to account for the variance, for a clear difference emerges between Britain and Sweden in the role of the state in shaping economic factors which thereby affect the social status of women. This chapter and the next examine more closely differences in the role of the state in facilitating the employment situation of women.

These chapters have two purposes. First, they present the substantive differences between Britain and Sweden in labor market policies that affect working women. The policies examined are those in the "manpower" field (training programs and placement services); as well as measures to prevent sex discrimination and to achieve equal pay for women. The second purpose of these chapters is to suggest what underlies the differences in policy between Britain and Sweden. The explanation has two components. The first concerns different conceptions of the problem in women's employment. These conceptions are institutionalized in state policy toward women. The second component concerns different conceptions of how deeply the state ought to intervene in the private affairs of the market in order to overcome employment problems. These conceptions are institutionalized in state policy toward society. I will elaborate the substance of these two components before suggesting how they are interrelated.

The Problem in Women's Employment

Rosabeth Moss Kanter has suggested three basic models depicting conceptions of the problems women face in the world of employment: individual, role-related, and social structural.[1] These three models correspond to three levels of explanation for the determinants of social life. As Kanter says, which of these models most informs policy makers has "radically different implications for the level of intervention, the assumptions about women, the scope of change, and the effectiveness of change."[2] In examining labor market policies, we will see that this is indeed the case. The following outline is informed by Kanter's three models.[3]

The individual model focuses on women's personalities and capabilities. The inferior positions in which most women find themselves at work as well as at home is explained as stemming from basic differences between men and women in character, temperament, attitudes, self-esteem, language, gestures, and interpersonal orientations.[4] Whether these differences are attributed to biological and social natures, to socialization patterns that exaggerate or create predilections, or to both, they are the factors that are assumed to keep women in their inferior positions in the aggressive world of work. The model allows for change, but it places the burden of change wholly on women and their abilities to contend with the requirements for success.

[1] Rosabeth Moss Kanter, "The Policy Issues: Presentation VI," in Martha Blaxall and Barbara Reagan (eds.), *Women and the Workplace: The Implications of Occupational Segregation* (Chicago: University of Chicago Press, 1976).

[2] Ibid., p. 282.

[3] I place some examples in different categories from Kanter and make more of the social structural and less of the role-related models than she.

[4] Margaret Henning and Ann Jardim, *The Managerial Woman* (Garden City, N.Y.: Anchor Press, 1977), take this approach.

The model suggests the use of compensatory measures to help women overcome their deficiencies. For example, programs in management or in assertiveness training have been developed especially for women. They have helped some women to climb promotional ladders or at least to engage in self-promotion. But, of course, only a few jobs lend themselves to upward mobility. Other compensatory measures reach back to the preconditions of women's own attitudes toward work and success generated through the educational system. Along this line, girls may be encouraged to take courses in woodworking or mechanics, and boys in typing or cooking. Insofar as all of these measures assume that women have been insufficiently prepared for certain occupational positions, they are within the tenets of the "individual" model. This model aptly identifies some of the employment problems women encounter, but use of this model in and of itself can have pernicious implications for sex discrimination. In addition, the extent and scope of change contained in the model is very limited; in fact, it is limited to those women whose personalities and capabilities differ from the stereotypical assumptions of the model. The consequence of any change leaves intact the structure of segregation and inequality in the labor market, while enabling some women to better adapt themselves to that structure.[5]

The role-related model focuses on the "dual" roles handled by women who work, thus assuming that most working women have families and homes to take care of.[6] In this model the traditional homemaker role of women is the major constraint on their full and successful participation

---

[5] David M. Gordon notes that the crudeness of a "blame the victim" approach has been refined by "human capital" explanations, which extend causes of differences in productivity to many more intangibles—learning opportunities, on-the-job experience and training, preferences about risk. "The Policy Issues: Presentation III," in Blaxall and Reagan, *Women and the Workplace.*

[6] The concept of dual roles was first presented by Alva Myrdal and Viola Klein, *Women's Two Roles: Home and Work* (London: Routledge and Kegan Paul, 1956).

in the workplace. Women suffer from divided loyalties and multiple demands on time and energy. They are restricted in the sorts of jobs they can accept, often basing their choice on such non-work-related criteria as location and hours. All of these considerations hinder women's work commitment and chances of promotion. Day care is certainly a measure that relieves one of the major worries of women with small children, but day care itself does not affect the duality of roles. For example, in the Soviet Union, where public provisions and public attitudes facilitate women's employment, women work a full day outside the home and a full evening in the home.[7] In the same way measures which increase the opportunities for women to work part-time or according to various "flexible time" schemes enable women to work, and to work with reduced worries and personal demands, but in and of themselves they do not necessarily deal with the fact that it is women alone who have dual roles.[8] (Measures that would extend these work schedule opportunities to men do recognize duality in responsibilities, and in doing so bridge the role-related and social structural models.) The role-related model suggests entirely different sorts of possibilities for change than the individual model, since the focus extends beyond women themselves to the broader system of supports and services that make it easier for women to work. But the emphasis is on *permitting* women the opportunity to participate in the labor force, without full recognition of the limited effectiveness of participation alone for women's secondary position both at work and at home.

The explanations for women's employment problems

[7] See studies by Gail Lapidus; for example, "Occupational Segregation and Public Policy: A Comparative Analysis of American and Soviet Patterns," in Blaxall and Reagan, *Women and the Workplace*.

[8] In one OECD study, it is concluded that "By and large, then, when wives take on paid employment, their husbands' minimal contribution to the work of the household remains unchanged. . . . In addition, the total work load of these two-job women surpasses that of either single-job holders." Martha Darling, *The Role of Women in the Economy* (Paris: Organization for Economic Co-operation and Development, 1975), p. 67.

contained in the social structural model are more complex than those in the first two models. One major difference is that, whereas the individual and role-related models focus on problems on the supply side of employment, that is, problems with women workers themselves, the social structural model focuses on the demand side of employment. One factor in particular is emphasized in this model, namely, that employment-related inequalities between men and women in opportunity, status, pay, benefits, and promotion have developed into a "dual labor market," both at the aggregate level and within specific occupational sectors. A social structural approach aims at identifying factors contributing to the perpetuation of duality in the labor market. For example, it clarifies how occupational segregation and questionable evaluations of entirely different jobs (e.g., between nurses aides and sanitation workers) are both factors which lead to differential pay. Measures emanating from this model seek to eradicate specific imbalances in the conditions of work between women and men in general, and between women and men in the same occupation. But the implications of the social structural model go beyond the labor market itself. For example, discrimination on the part of employers has closed women's entry to certain jobs and led to "crowding" in certain other jobs.[9] But "blaming the employer" and legislating that "he" stop discriminating may not result in the sort of equality that holders of the social structural approach are seeking. If it can be shown that sex discrimination is based on factors that occur outside the work environment, and more generally in the hierarchical relationship between men and women, then measures aimed only at the "employer" will fail in the long run to achieve social equality. Thus, the social structural model also iden-

---

[9] Barbara Bergmann and Kenneth Arrow are generally acknowledged as the first proponents of the "crowding hypothesis" (having developed their ideas separately). The hypothesis states that employers hire women for certain occupations because of stereotypes of women's capabilities. Most employers tend to have the same stereotypes based on women's domestic roles.

tifies the configuration of supporting social structures on which the dual labor market is built. In this way, it subsumes the individual and role-related models. It treats as problems the fact that women hold dual roles and the fact that women, men, and employers alike hold conceptions of female inadequacies. In short, the ramifications of this approach are potentially far-reaching, for they strike at a basic structural parameter: the hierarchy of sex-based inequality in society at large.[10]

The normative bias distinguishing these three models is self-evident. Only the social structural model rises above sex-based discrimination and allows full perception of the multiple dimensions of the problems women workers face. Nevertheless, a social structural model informs public policy without invalidating the significant ideas in the individual and role-related models. Each of the models suggests certain kinds of policies and measures to overcome the problems identified. For example, training programs fulfill the tenets of the individual model; day care programs are closely associated with the role-related model. These programs and others are important measures facilitating women's employment, but they do not necessarily contribute to women's quest for social equality. The potential to do this is realized only through the approach suggested by the social structural model.

All labor market policies have the potential to aim at social structural change as conceptualized within the paradigm of the social structural model. That is, a program for training need not be confined simply to self-improve-

[10] My presentation of the social structural model in particular differs from Kanter's analysis. Since Kanter is interested in organizational structures and the organization of work within institutions, her model is institutional not broadly societal. However, the variables that she says are important determinants of organizational behavior are also important determinants of the broader employment situation: opportunity structures, internal labor markets, dominance structures, and sex ratios within and across hierarchical levels. Kanter in Blaxall and Reagan, *Women and the Workplace*, p. 287. See also, Rosabeth Moss Kanter, *Men and Women of the Corporation* (New York: Basic Books, 1977), Chapter 9.

ment. Within a social structural approach, it becomes a measure to break down sex-role stereotyping in choice of occupation on the part of women and in hiring on the part of employers. When analyzed in this way, the social structural model is akin to what Richard M. Titmuss called, in another context, a "universal framework" within which "selective" measures can "discriminate positively, with the minimum risk of stigma, in favour of those whose needs are greatest."[11] The crucial ingredient is the universal framework, which incorporates and attempts to change the attitudes and behaviors of all the relevant actors—women, men, employers, and so on. Moreover, a universal framework places the particular concerns of women within the broader picture of the economy as a whole, and accordingly can speak to the concerns of other low-status social groups. Without the scope of a universal framework, selective measures by themselves simply discriminate and further isolate those who have been differentiated. This sort of formulation suggests that individual and role-related conceptions of the problem in women's employment are associated with selective measures which are inadequate to change the economic situation of women and that only a structural conception of the problem can lead to a balanced integration of selective measures within a universal framework. Only the combination can produce social change. The universal framework is the harder to develop and institutionalize, as we will see.

In the following chapters labor market policies in Britain and Sweden are analyzed to reveal which conception of the problem in women's employment most informs the policy framework. The individual model predominates in Britain, whereas Swedish policy approaches the social structural model. The implications of this difference are discussed within the context of the composite policy nexus of each nation.

[11] Richard M. Titmuss, *Commitment to Welfare* (London: Allen and Unwin, 1968), p. 135.

State Intervention: Depth and Scope

In addition to revealing a distinctive conception of the problem in women's employment, labor market policies also reveal a conception of how deeply and broadly the state ought to intervene in society. In particular, labor market policies intervene in the freedom of the market to match supply and demand for labor. This is as true of policies that aim at full and secure employment as of policies that train individuals in occupations for which a future labor shortage is anticipated. It is not simply intervention as such that distinguishes labor market policies in different countries, that is, in how many dimensions of the labor market the state intervenes; the more important difference among nations is the depth of state intervention.

By depth of intervention in the labor market I mean the extent of departure from the liberal principle that, left to its own devices, the market can take care of divergences between demand and supply and between wages and prices. To elaborate, I offer two examples in which the depth of intervention is contrasted. The first example describes the target of intervention, the second the means. Both contrast intervention which is close to the liberal principle with intervention which is more removed from it.

One distinction to be made about state intervention is whether it is confined to the public sector or includes the private sector as well. The public sector itself has become a huge enterprise in advanced industrial societies, employing a substantial share of the labor force—in Britain 55%, in Sweden 40%. Therefore, certain measures can be confined to the public sector and still have a desired impact on the entire economy. For example, an increase in public sector jobs can reduce total unemployment or stimulate aggregate demand. Other measures, such as restricting wage increases or providing for employment benefits, can serve as examples for negotiators in the private sector and thereby set the pace for policy or for change. Measures that are confined to the public sector have a great impact on women

workers, whether or not they are so intended, simply because women are disproportionately employed in the public sector. In both Britain and Sweden, almost 75% of women
workers are public sector employees. When public sector
spending increased so dramatically in the 1960s, a large
number of women workers were drawn into the labor force,
many for the first time, in positions in health, education,
and social services.[12] Nevertheless, labor market policies
that are confined to the public sector represent a lower
level of intervention than those that include the private
sector as well. They are so confined because of a disincli-
nation on the part of the state to intervene in the affairs
of the private sector. They are underpinned by a belief that
the free market ought to function in the private sector at
least. Labor market policies that extend to the private sector
as well affect more workers, of course. Because they also
represent a greater depth of intervention in the economy,
they are a greater departure from the principle of freedom
for the market.

Another example of a contrast in depth of intervention
focuses on means. The most basic distinction commonly
made about the means of state intervention in the economy
is whether the measures are macroeconomic or microeconomic. Macroeconomic measures affect the economy as a
whole, manipulating aggregate variables, such as money
supply or government deficits, to create desired effects.
Microeconomic measures are targeted at particular economic actors or sectors, and thus have a differential impact
among the components of the economy. Wage and price
policies are an example of microeconomic manipulation of
the economy. Microeconomic measures constitute a greater
depth of state intervention than macroeconomic measures,
for macroeconomic measures set the boundaries within which
individual economic units or actors operate without directly
coercing their compliance to the standards involved. In
contrast, microeconomic measures isolate specific actors and

---

[12] This is analyzed in greater detail in Chapter 2.

sectors, and thus directly shape economic maneuverings. The former upholds the domain of private authority traditionally exercised by business interests; the latter requires a greater wielding of state authority. Macro and micro measures are two approaches to manipulating the economy, and they represent different depths of intervention in the economy. When directed at the labor market, macro and micro measures also represent different depths of intervention. To elaborate this, we must begin with the fact that the labor market is segmented, in various ways. For one, there is a horizontal segmentation into a dual labor market based on sex (others on education, race, and so on).[13] For another, there is vertical segmentation into internal labor markets at the level of the sector and firm.[14] Both dual and internal labor markets contain primary and secondary segments. The primary segment is characterized by such factors as higher pay and better opportunities for advancement than the secondary segment. The rules of behavior for each segment of dual and internal labor markets differ from each other, and the rules for any single segment differ from those of the aggregate labor market because of factors such as training, entry criteria, and promotion.

A macro approach does not take into account the existence of dual or internal labor markets. The *consequences* of macroeconomic measures on these labor market segments are ignored in a macro approach. For example, anti-inflationary fiscal and monetary policies that reduce real wages aim to lower overall demand by creating greater unemployment. The unemployment that results is not evenly

[13] Michael Reich, David M. Gordon, Richard C. Edwards, "Dual Labor Markets: A Theory of Labor Market Segmentation," *Annals of the American Economic Association*, 63 (May 1973); Peter B. Doeringer, *Low Pay, Labor Market Dualism, and Industrial Relations Systems*, (mimeo., 1973).

[14] Peter Doeringer and Michael Piore, *Internal Labor Markets and Manpower Analysis* (Lexington, Mass.: Lexington Books, 1971); Richard C. Edwards, Michael Reich, David M. Gordon, *Labor Market Segmentation* (Lexington, Mass.: D. C. Heath, 1975).

distributed within the labor market. The differential impact of macroeconomic policies can reduce their effectiveness. For instance, unemployment may be largely confined to secondary segments, leaving the primary segment with as much buying power as ever. In fact, some primary segments may be able to offset anti-inflationary fiscal and monetary measures by, for example, raising their own wages to keep up with inflation. If this occurs, inflation continues to rise—and so does unemployment. This is not to suggest that macroeconomic measures are totally inadequate in organizing labor market policies and in contributing to social equality for women. Macro measures constitute a universal framework setting the parameters of social change. However, macro measures are not designed to institutionalize social change. Without the support of selective micro measures, a universal framework alone is an empty shell.

A micro approach takes into account the existence and functioning of labor market segments and is sensitive to the different consequences of economic policies on these segments. Micro measures can manipulate specific labor markets to lessen the severity of unemployment. For example, labor and other resources may be purposely shifted to more productive and efficient industries and coordinated with supporting measures such as special retraining programs. Or a similar policy may become part of regional development programs. This certainly does not assure a positive effect on inflation, but recession, at any rate, is avoided. The use of these macroeconomic measures suggests not only a greater wielding of state authority but also a more concrete understanding of the way the economy and labor markets work. The importance of macroeconomic measures is that they are targeted and selective. They can treat each specific internal labor market according to its peculiar set of circumstances and its special relationship to other market factors. Micro measures represent a greater depth of intervention in the labor market than macro measures because micro measures affect the composition of the basic units of the economy. However, as was suggested above, micro measures in and of themselves are selective and can lead to the sort of discrimination and stigma that further isolates women workers from genuine integration. Whether or not they can overcome this tendency and affect the actual structural relationship among the units depends on the scope they are given by the universal framework of macro measures. As Titmuss notes:

> The challenge that faces us is not the choice between universalist and selective social services. The real challenge resides in the question: what particular infrastructure of universalist services is needed in order to provide a framework of values and opportunity bases within and around which can be developed socially acceptable selective services aiming to discriminate positively, with the minimum risk of stigma, in favour of those whose needs are greatest.[15]

Since either macro- or microeconomic measures can distort equality if used alone, we can surmise that they are most effective in unison. Both types of measures are necessary in the construction and implementation of labor market policies. But what constitutes the most effective relationship between them? The case of Britain offers an important paradox to consider. The previous chapter demonstrated that economic measures in Britain tend to be macro, displaying a characteristic hesitancy on the part of the state to intervene in the free market. We will see in this chapter that Britain has developed certain highly selective, and therefore micro, measures to affect women's position in the labor market, in particular the Sex Discrimination Act. However, the mere coexistence of macro and micro measures is not a combination. In Britain the former does not constitute a universal framework for the latter. The consequence is that in Britain economic policies and antidiscrimination employment measures each function in their

---

[15] Titmuss, *Commitment to Welfare*, p. 135.

own separate spheres, neither influenced by the other, and the result for women is less than the sum of the parts.

The question, then, of what constitutes the most effective relationship between macro and micro measures, of what constitutes the particular infrastructure of universal measures within which selective measures can discriminate positively, is an empirical question. I will attempt to answer it in terms of both the short-comings and potentialities that are evident in the labor market policies of Britain and Sweden.

Conception and Intervention: Their Interrelationship

The conception of the problem in women's employment is one-half of what goes into the development of policies for women. The other half is based on a conception of how deeply the state ought to intervene in general economic and specific labor market forces. To relate these two halves, we can recall that an individual-level conception of the problem elicits a low depth of state intervention. That is, labor market measures informed by the "individual" conception tend to be selective, affecting certain women with certain problems, but not women as a whole. The accumulation of selective measures for women has a limited impact on equal employment. In contrast, a social structural conception of the problem in women's employment goes together with a broader-based intervention which affects labor as a whole and a deeper intervention into the functioning of the economy. What factors differentiate each of these two kinds of association between conception and intervention?

The "individual" conception (as well as some features of the role-related conception) is the traditional mode of conceptualizing the problem in women's employment. Historically, this approach first informed attitudes and public policies for women in both Britain and Sweden and elsewhere. Traditional conceptions of any issue prevail until something happens to change them. What happened in Sweden, and did not happen in Britain, was a long process of sustained change, not in the conception of women's roles, but in the allowable depth and sphere of state intervention. Over decades Sweden has evolved out of the liberal mode of state/society relations; Britain has not. This evolution has enabled Swedish policy makers to develop new approaches to economic and social issues. The persistence of liberalism in Britain has prevented conceptual and policy changes and has reinforced the persistence of tradition.

This and the next chapter begin to present the outlines of this explanation by focusing on how policies in Britain and Sweden reveal the association between certain conceptions of the problem and the allowable depth of state intervention to handle the problem in women's employment. The full explanation of the relationship between conception and intervention and the differences between Britain and Sweden must await the analysis of changes in state/society relations presented in Chapter 7.

LABOR MARKET POLICIES

Training Programs

Manpower policies seek to match labor resources with the market's need for labor. In Britain this is done in two ways: through a training program and an employment service. The training program has been in operation since 1973. To fully appreciate what a bold step it is for Britain we will look first and briefly at its predecessor.

In the 1960s, Britain's publicly sponsored adult training was conducted by Government Training Centres under the jurisdiction of the Department of Labour, as it was then called. The capacity and extent of training in these centers was extremely limited. In 1970 17,000 persons at most were enrolled in the programs, and few of the centers scattered throughout the country operated at more than 60% capacity.[16] The trainees were almost entirely men (97%) preparing for employment in the skilled trades in the manufacturing and construction industries. These training programs cannot be said to have done much for employability, for in general about half of the recruits were already employed when they first entered the centers. Nor did they do a great deal to match labor resources with the need for labor, for there was no assessment of the latter. The program simply assisted a few individuals to become better skilled or re-skilled, at the individual's own discretion. Thus, prior to 1973, there was no publicly sponsored training component of manpower policy to speak of in Britain. Instead, training for the job market was the responsibility of the educational system and of the private training programs conducted by industries. Both of these still exist and are examined in relevant sections below.

In the 1970s the Department of Labour was reorganized. Its new name, the Department of Employment, was intended to reflect a renewed purpose in achieving full employment, which had been severely battered in an earlier recessionary period, by means of a revitalized "active" employment policy. An Employment and Training Act in 1973 created the Manpower Services Commission with its two branches, the Training Services Agency (TSA) and the Employment Services Agency (ESA). This represented the first explicit statement of a manpower policy for Britain, and training was placed at its core.

For the first time too, women were consciously included in the training component of manpower policy. In 1974, the first year of operation, over 17,000 women were enrolled in training courses (37.6% of total trainees), a vast increase over the 620 women enrolled in 1970. By 1980 the number of women completing training opportunities

[16] A. P. Thirlwall, "Government Manpower Policies in Great Britain: Their Rationale and Benefits," *British Journal of Industrial Relations* (1972): 178.

courses was over 34,000 (43% of the total).[17] The numbers are commendable. However, when we look at the sorts of courses in which women were enrolled, we see that in the first two years of operation about 80% of all the women were taking low-level commercial and clerical courses. By 1980 the figure had dropped to 73.5%, but this is still a large proportion (see Table 3.1).

There are at least two problems with this kind of concentration in women's training. First, clerical work is the only occupation for which young women are already well enough prepared by the educational system.[18] Second, clerical work is the one occupation in which women workers are particularly segregated and which, in addition, has low status, is low paying, and offers few opportunities for advancement. Thus, the range of employment possibilities for British women has not been expanded by the TSA. The initial determination of courses to be offered was based on the existing occupational structure. In its first and only report, the TSA presented the usual data and charts on the occupational distribution of women workers as a justification for its courses.[19] Furthermore, that so many women are taking clerical courses has suggested to the TSA that there is a continued client demand for these courses. Accordingly, on the basis of existing occupational structure and apparent client demand, the agency continues to expand the number of places in clerical courses. No attempt has been made to verify the assumption that occupational concentration in, and client demand for, clerical courses means that jobs are available. As a result, in a rather myopic assessment of its early "success," the first report says "this

[17] Equal Opportunity Commission, *Fifth Annual Report, 1980* (London: HMSO, 1980), p. 57. The figures before and after 1978 are not exactly comparable, since the earlier ones included 18-year-olds and the more recent figures exclude persons under 19 years of age.

[18] The schools also emphasize general liberal arts courses for girls, but this does not offer an immediate employment outlet.

[19] Training Services Agency, *Training Opportunities for Women* (London: Manpower Services Commission, 1975).

TABLE 3.1   Women Completing Training Courses

	Number		Women as % of Adult Completers	
	1978/79	1980/81	1978/79	1980/81
Management	607	658	16	18
Management services	601	1,096	23	25
Education, health, etc.	714	439	59	56
Science and technology	94	111	10	8
Clerical	7,427	5,589	84	88
Shorthand and typing	13,785	11,311	98	97
Office machine operating	902	1,018	70	63
Selling	42	29	25	27
Food preparation/serving	1,330	1,351	68	72
Hairdressing/cleaning, etc.	284	269	65	74
Farming, fishing	67	106	13	21
Material processing excluding metal	65	59	49	37
Metal making/engineering	145	189	1	1
Welding	13	10	0.5	0.5
Electrical making/repair	51	60	2	2
Other making/repair	724	614	58	57
Carpentry and joinery	17	49	1	2
Assembling/inspecting	8	6	4	3
Construction	24	10	1	0.5
HGV driving	64	52	2	1.5
Miscellaneous	1,368	2,155	30	40
Total	28,332	25,181	40	38

Sources: Economic Opportunities Commission, *Fourth Annual Report, 1979* (London: HMSO, 1979), p. 68; private communication, Manpower Services Commission, 1982.

growth is expected to continue, though there is at present some concern about the placement rate."[20] Time has proven this assessment correct.

Other courses are available and are certainly open to women. In its explanation of why so few women are taking other courses, the TSA's conception of the problem in women's employment becomes apparent. The decision to take any course is entirely up to the individual. The TSA offers no counseling (but realizes that it probably ought

[20] Ibid., p. 19.

to). It suggests that schools ought to improve their vocational guidance programs. The future guidance programs that the TSA is proposing seem not to be designed to encourage women to enter non-traditional careers (although the TSA recognizes that "more should be done in this direction"). The emphasis of guidance is rather on assisting in "self-presentation" and "self-development" to "help women to participate later with men in standard programmes of career development."[21] Special courses are also suggested for "mature people who have been out of employment for some time and are liable to suffer from lack of confidence which adds to their difficulty in getting work."[22] But none of these courses on self-presentation and self-development, for women of any age, is available yet on a systematic basis.

Nothing in the TSA's assessments of women's employment situation suggests a conception of a problem on the demand side of employment (let alone at the level of social structure). The fact that many women have home responsibilities is recognized as a barrier preventing them from re-entering competitive careers as well as precluding their opportunities to take training courses. To help such women the TSA is experimenting with part-time training programs—in clerical and commercial courses. Although limited to about 160 persons at any one time throughout the country, the programs have been successful. Of those completing part-time courses in 1974, 20% entered part-time work and 19% entered full-time work in the training occupation; another 3% entered part-time work outside the training occupation; and 25% "failed to gain employment." The report noted that "for the moment the economic situation has caused a reduction in vacancies for part-time employment," adding that there is a "need for local labour market research to establish those occupations which have the capacity to absorb trainees from part-time courses and which will attract sufficient demand from women for part-

---

[21] Ibid., p. 23.
[22] Ibid., p. 22.

time training."[23] Unfortunately, its programs are still not informed by such research. The deterioration of the economic situation in the late 1970s brought with it a reduced concern with women's employment (part- or full-time) and instead a greater emphasis on training the alarming number of unemployed youth.[24]

In sum, the TSA exhibits bafflement about women's "unwillingness to accept responsibility" to change their life chances.[25] In presenting a "case" for training women, the TSA report notes legislative consideration first: that is, the Sex Discrimination Act makes it "lawful" to provide special training opportunities for women. A second reason for training programs is economic considerations (wasted manpower); and, third, social considerations (women ought not remain "second-class citizens").[26] More numerous than the reasons why training programs should be provided, however, are the "practical limitations on expanding women's training." These are economic (women do not work as much as men, thereby reducing the return on training), educational (schools do not prepare girls adequately, in fact, many discourage them from most careers, especially those involving scientific, technical, or mathematical knowledge), and social-psychological (with a long list of the differences between men and women). It is clear that the conception of the problem in women's employment embodied in the provision of training opportunities is at the individual level of analysis—within women themselves, who hold the "deep-rooted attitudes about their place at work and in society" to the same extent that others do.[27]

Let us now turn to examine training programs from another angle to determine what they tell us about state intervention. The program we have discussed thus far is pro-

---

[23] Ibid., pp. 22-23.

[24] See Manpower Services Commission, *A New Training Initiative* (May 1981) and *Youth Task Group Report* (April 1982).

[25] TSA, *Training Opportunities*, p. 4.

[26] Ibid., p. 12.

[27] Ibid., p. 14.

vided by the public sector. There are also a number of training programs organized by various industries in the private sector. Before the creation of the Manpower Services Commission, the major part of training was undertaken by these private-sector Industrial Training Boards, as they are called. The Boards were officially set up by the Industrial Training Act in 1964. In fact, the Act legislated what already existed; nevertheless, its passage represented a major breakthrough in the role of the state in industrial relations. For decades governments had "felt that it was somehow indecent for outsiders to presume to offer guidance to industry about what it ought to do to train the manpower it so badly needed."[28]

In the 1964 Act the state for the first time required all industries to contribute to the new type of Industrial Training Boards. The government would provide additional funds if necessary. In addition, government representatives were to sit on the Boards. However, the power to levy contributions would reside with the industrial representatives on the Boards, that is, with an equal number of representatives from trade unions and employers. The state made no assumptions or conditions in providing its grants. This is the extent of the state's intervention in private sector training. When it comes to industrial training, governments continue to believe that industry knows its own needs better than public sector experts do. As for trade unions, governments continue to allow union requirements for rather long apprenticeships. Unions, too, apparently know best the prerequisites for certain skilled trades. Thus, this form of intervention hardly intervenes at all.[29]

The new training courses offered by the Manpower Services Commission can be thought of as supplements to the

[28] Andrew Shonfield, *Modern Capitalism: The Changing Balance of Public and Private Power* (London: Oxford University Press, 1965), p. 117.

[29] Industrial Training Boards arouse expected ideological differences between political parties. The Labour government had begun to phase them out in the 1970s, and Thatcher's Conservative government had phased many back in by 1982.

training courses offered by Industrial Training Boards. For one, there is some evidence that the Industrial Training Boards continue to provide the major part of training in Britain. This is difficult to substantiate because the Boards are not required to publish any of their reports and the full extent of their training is not well known. For another, since the courses offered by the TSA are based on immediate demands for labor, they tend to provide a service for the overflow from Industrial Training Board courses. TSA trainees are not assured a job after taking a course—it is assumed, instead, that the market will take over. This single-act approach of the TSA (indeed, of manpower policy) carries a risk for the trainees. In contrast, acceptance in an Industrial Training Board course includes prior acceptance to a position in the industry. In sum, state intervention is basically confined to the public sector.

Since the private sector has a significant role in training, what can be said about the concern for women workers in the private sector? Very little. The Department of Employment did manage to estimate that in 1970 there were about 110 women apprentices in skilled craft occupations in the private sector, compared with over 112,000 men, and that about 420 women were receiving other systematic training, compared to 17,000 men. The differences between men and women in training opportunities were not as wide in semi-skilled occupations, but an estimate could not be made. A government assessment of the Industrial Training Boards admitted that "most of them have not in the past considered it their function to make special efforts in favour of women and girls."[30]

The Training Opportunities Scheme provides for some small parceling out of training to "employers' establishments." In 1980 6% of the women in TSA training programs were within an employer's establishment.[31] The only other way of analyzing private sector training or provision

---

[30] TSA, *Training Opportunities*, p. 11.
[31] EOC, *Fifth Annual Report*, p. 57.

for further education of women workers is through the number of 16-18-year-olds who are receiving "day release" by their employers. While this is not an uncommon practice in Britain, it is limited, unorganized, and up to the individual employer. In 1978, less than 20% of all the young people released by their employers for part-time study were women.[32] The extent of in-service or on-the-job training is unknown, but it is generally acknowledged, first, that on-the-job training constitutes the majority of training in Britain and, second, that given the nature of the occupations in which women predominate (clerical, sales) little real chance for improvement and promotion can be expected for women through in-house training. The "proof of the pudding" of training programs is to be found in their effects on employment opportunities. I therefore turn to examine the system of employment services in Britain.

Employment Services

When TSA trainees complete their courses, they are transferred to the Employment Service Agency for assistance in finding a job. Their situation then is similar to any other unemployed person. The creation of the Manpower Services Commission did not change the employment service in Britain; it merely rehoused it. In practice, the employment service continues to be more closely related to unemployment, which is another dimension of labor market policy. Persons who register in employment offices in Britain do so not only to find another job but also to receive unemployment benefits. The legacy of employment offices—that is, a preoccupation with assessing each individual's eligibility for the disgrace of receiving the "dole" rather than an effort to find employment—has been hard to live

[32] Most of these (over 40%) were in miscellaneous services (such as hairdressing). Others were in insurance, banking and finance, and business services; distributive trades; and professional and scientific services. Ibid., p. 58.

down.[33] Not only the negative image but also the function of having to pay unemployment benefits reduce the effectiveness of exchanges in finding jobs. Other factors compound the difficulties. In times of heavy unemployment, the staffs of the exchanges are not increased significantly, and they are simply overworked. More important, since employers are not required to notify the exchanges of their vacancies, the exchanges do not have full information on available jobs. Successful job placement appears to be as much the result of an individual's answering newspaper advertisements or consulting private employment exchanges as from the efforts of the employment service. It is estimated that the public employment exchanges in Britain help fill about 25% of all job vacancies (compared to about 80% in Sweden).[34] As Table 3.2 shows, women are beginning to fare as well as men as beneficiaries of the employment services. However, the excess unemployment apparently is not being well serviced by private initiative either, given that unemployment in Britain has been rising at the same time as unfilled vacancies. We can locate part of the problem of the employment service's inability to close the gap between unemployment and unfilled vacancies in the relationship between the public and private sectors.

To be effective, an employment exchange ideally serves, on the one hand, to employ or re-employ persons according to their occupational abilities and on the other hand, to deploy or re-deploy them according to the labor needs of

[33] Richard M. Titmuss, *Social Policy: An Introduction* (London: Allen and Unwin, 1974), Chapters 1 and 3; Robert Pinker, *Social Theory and Social Policy* (London: Heinemann Educational Books, 1971), Chapters 2 and 4. The Department of Employment tried to change the image of employment exchanges by locating new offices on main streets and brightly painting their exteriors. The cost of such symbolism was curtailed by the Thatcher government.

[34] Santosh Mukherjee, *Making Labour Markets Work: A Comparison of the UK and Swedish Systems* (London: PEP, Broadsheet 532, January 1972), p. 77. The figure is informally accepted as still holding, although no data exist to verify it (personal interview, Department of Employment, May 1982).

TABLE 3.2   Jobs Found Through the Employment Service

Financial Year	Men	Women	Women as % of Total
1975/76	840,374	449,993	34.9
1976/77	973,400	510,700	34.4
1977/78	1,043,020	568,820	35.3
1978/79	1,125,385	680,031	37.7
1979/80	1,161,579	741,985	39.0
1980/81	831,637	702,768	45.8
1981/82	752,010	709,946	48.6

Source: Private communication, Manpower Services Commission, 1982.

industry. The speedier these services, the better for all, including the economy, which is losing productivity from unemployment or inefficient employment. To perform these services, the staffs of employment exchanges must have two sorts of information, one concerning the individuals and the other the economy. Staffs of British employment exchanges interview their clients about their employment desires and abilities. They do not, except on a minimal scale, probe much further by offering aptitude or other psychological tests that would help persons choose from a wider variety of occupations.[35] An Occupational Guidance Service was begun in 1966 as part of the employment service, but its scope is limited. A guidance service could be of great benefit to women workers, especially women returning to the labor market after their children reach school age. In the late 1960s the guidance service was offering advice and counseling to about 600 women returning to work, a meager figure, and overall only about 20% of its clients were women. A number of practical and normative reasons could be suggested for the deficiencies of guidance services in Britain, such as the lack of trained staff, the apprenticeship requirements of trade unions, the practicality of past experience as a determinant of occupation,

[35] Mukherjee, *Making Labour Markets Work*, Chapter 5.

unwillingness to invade privacy, and desire to maintain personal choice. Nevertheless, the task of job steering is futile unless full knowledge is also available about present and future job opportunities. As we have noted, however, employers are not required to notifiy exchanges of all vacancies and labor market and industrial research is not conducted on a major scale. Without such research, proper guidance cannot exist. The public agencies are clearly performing only minimal functions, interfering neither with individuals' occupational proclivities nor with industries' own assessments of labor requirements.

The employment exchanges do nothing different or special for women. In some ways, they do even less for women than for men. The considerably lower use of vocational guidance services by women is one example. Another is that until recently many unemployed married women did not register with employment exchanges. Under the Social Security Act they were allowed the privilege of paying reduced contributions to National Insurance, thereby forfeiting their benefits when unemployed. This, together with the ineffectiveness of exchanges in job-finding, made it useless to register. Those women who did seek assistance and benefit payments through the exchanges also found that separate listings of vacancies were available for men and women. These were based, of course, on employers' preferences and occupational stereotyping. Both of these practices are now unlawful under the Sex Discrimination Act. Whether or not occupational options have thereby opened up for women is another matter.

Job Creation

Given the distaste for interference with job options in the private sector, the other avenue open to the state to absorb the unemployed is to create new jobs in the public sector. Traditionally such employment is temporary because the unemployment it is intended to relieve is considered to be temporary or seasonal. The most common type of public relief work has been in construction, perhaps because such work is finite and seasonal. Ironically, it cannot be conducted in winter when "seasonal" unemployment in the private sector is itself highest. Such public works are often carried on in regions of high unemployment, understandably designed to relieve multiple economic problems. In general, British public job creation has not extended beyond these traditional lines. However, through grants, the government is increasingly encouraging private industries to step up their efforts too, especially during periods and in regions of heavy unemployment. This is part of a newly developing regional policy in Britain.[36] It represents a bolder step on the part of the state to do something about the persisting huge discrepancies in unemployment among regions in Britain. Whether the initiatives by government in grant-giving can be said to represent a leadership role is questionable. Also questionable is the extent to which regional policy is coordinated with national policies for manpower and industrial development. Finally, we must note that women are entirely excluded from public job programs in Britain. The manual nature of traditional public works is one prohibitive factor. Another is the close connection between public works and unemployment and the persisting notion that, since men are the main breadwinners, they must be found work when unemployment threatens. With the increasing youth unemployment in the 1980s, job creation programs in Britain are being further concentrated on the young.

Summary and Assessment

The changes that occurred in the 1970s in British manpower services were first and foremost institutional. The

---

[36] The discrepancies in unemployment and employment opportunities among regions in Britain are acute. In comparing them with Germany, von Beyme and Ionescu note that the German Länder are more actively included in national policy making and (perhaps therefore), the manpower and employment differences among them are small. Klaus von

major consequence of this change was greater volume—in the number of persons assisted and the number of programs and personnel assisting them. In some ways the institutional change was a change in name only, for as we have seen the Training Services Agency and the Employment Services Agency, although housed under the same roof, were not well coordinated.[37] Nevertheless, the changes that did take place were not accompanied by the sorts of qualitative changes that positively affect women's employment problems.

First, in each of the manpower policies we have seen a conception that relates women's employment problems most closely to women themselves—not to the occupational structure, not the economy, not even to women's dual roles. These are taken as the facts to which women must adjust their work aspirations. Some special concessions are made to women, most notably the increase in special training courses for women, including part-time courses and courses for women returning to the labor market after an absence. Insofar as these concessions are singular selective measures and are steering women into the same segregated and hierarchical occupational structure, they are not advancing the employment status of women. The Training Services Agency has also made some effort to adopt an experimental spirit and to understand why, for example, "at least some of the professions have not proved more attractive, or more receptive, to women in the past."[38] Given the sort of investigation the Agency proposes to conduct (consulting institutions on their views and ideas for "remedial action"), it is doubtful that it can go much beyond its present level of solutions.

Beyme and Ghita Ionescu, "The Politics of Employment Policy in Germany and Great Britain," *Government and Opposition*, 12 (Winter 1977): 96-97.

[37] We see this characteristic of British government (interdepartmental fragmentation) in many contexts. In Chapter 5, I attempt to get at its root in another social policy area: day care.

[38] TSA, *Training Opportunities*, p. 19.

Second, it is difficult to find in British manpower policy the "universal framework" that might serve as the guiding force not only for selective measures facilitating women workers but also for some semblance of "full" employment. This latter goal was, after all, the inspiration ushering in the British Employment and Training Act of 1973, which at the time was considered both at home and abroad as the beginning of an "active" employment policy.[39] It did not turn out that way. What went wrong? What in fact guides employment policy in Britain? The answer to these two questions is the same.

By its nature, manpower policy is microeconomic, "concerned with the efficient use of labour at the place of work."[40] This concern, as we have seen, characterizes the British programs. There is another side to manpower policy: "a set of policies operated directly by the national government relating to the utilization of manpower in the national economy and its distribution between various markets—occupational, industrial and geographical."[41] In the terms of my analysis, this function is the equivalent of providing a universal framework within which selective measures can operate purposively. That is, within the orientation based on the economy as a whole one may grasp the fact that labor markets differ and contribute differently to economic goals. British manpower policies do not effectively interrelate the two coordinates, the macro-side of economic objectives and measures with a particular kind of micro approach directed at dual and internal labor markets. The major failings have been of at least three sorts.

First, successive governments have shown a preference for the use of fiscal and monetary measures to stimulate economic growth, that is, macro measures for macro objectives. The potential of labor market policies to contribute

[39] Von Beyme and Ionescu, "The Politics of Employment Policy," p. 91.
[40] Thirlwall, "Government Manpower Policies," p. 165.
[41] Ibid.

to these goals has been underestimated.[42] Second, the fact that labor markets do differ on the basis of a number of factors—not only occupation, industry, and region but also sex, class, and unionization—has not been fully appreciated by those in charge of policy. Third, a micro approach can identify and make use of these facts about labor markets for, on the one hand, labor market policy and, on the other hand, macroeconomic policy. But such a micro approach requires that the state engage in a different role, deeper than the aggregate level and broader than the single-purpose measures that have characterized state intervention thus far.

One example reveals the importance of these many considerations. Britain has done very little research on projecting the future needs of industry. The present level of demand is taken as the basis for occupational training programs. Two factors may be related to this lack of foresight. First, there is very little phasing out of inefficient industries in Britain. The algorithm of rise and fall is not built into the life-cycle of industries. Their need for resources is expected to be constant, or to increase, but not to decrease. In fact, policy has been more successful in attempting to shore up failing industries than in maintaining the pace of rapidly expanding ones. Among other reasons, the strength of the labor unions accounts for the persistence of these practices. A second factor contributing to Britain's lagging industrial research is that British economic planning in general has been less than inspiring. After years of institutional changes and much experimentation, it remains hampered

---

[42] This is slowly changing. For example, Thatcher's Conservative government looked anew at the relationship between housing policy and labor mobility. Because of the low rents in public housing projects and the long waiting lists for new applicants, people are unwilling to move to new areas where labor shortages exist. However, even the relationship between increased labor mobility and economic growth is fraught with any number of intervening considerations. For example, regions with chronic underemployment typically do not have the supporting services needed for an influx of labor.

by "the old instinctive suspicion of positive government, which purports to identify the needs of the community before the community itself has recognized them."[43] The implications of this perspective on the role of the state go beyond planning. We see the same hesitancy with regard to industry and business and individual job-seekers—a deferral of the authority to advise, let alone to direct or redirect.

What all this means for present purposes is that dis/equilibrium in the labor market continues to be measured by the relationship between aggregate unemployment and number of vacancies. The ratio between these variables has been remarkably constant for decades in Britain, and the factors that contribute to the relationship have been largely ignored—for example, the persistent demand for engineers and not secretaries, for workers in Wales and not London. The aggregate relationship between unemployment and vacancies tells us nothing about labor bottlenecks and the gross imbalances that exist among labor markets. And the aggregate measures that have been used to curb unemployment have failed in the long run.[44] While many specific measures could be suggested as stemming from this analysis, such as guiding trainees on the basis of in-depth studies of trends in the labor market, these all rest in the final analysis on how deeply the state is willing to intervene in the private affairs of society. Up to now, the depth of intervention has not been great.

A final word is in order about the implications for women of this conclusion. Women suffer more than men from localized unemployment, aggregate unemployment, and economic stagnation. As the previous chapter demonstrated, the rate of unemployment for women is not as high

[43] Shonfield, *Modern Capitalism*, p. 94.
[44] For an economic analysis of how "imbalances in the labour market exacerbate the conflict between wage (price) stability and 'full' employment . . . [and] . . . also heighten the conflict between 'full' employment, 'full' growth and balance of payments stability," see Thirlwall, "Government Manpower Policies," p. 167, and *passim*.

as for men in Britain, but the rate of change in women's unemployment is much higher than for men. Both women's employment and unemployment are directly related to the cycles of the economy. Women are marginal workers in Britain. That this happens to women workers in Britain is evidence of the lack of selective measures within a universal framework, both designed to maintain as full a level of employment as possible.

LEGISLATION IN BRITAIN

Sex Discrimination Act, 1975

The British Sex Discrimination Act is a landmark piece of legislation not only for Britain but for western Europe as a whole.[45] It mainly specifies the law regarding employment, but it also contains sections on unlawful discrimination in education, as well as in the provision of goods, services, facilities, and housing. It also includes a list of exceptions, such as charities, sports, and elective bodies. The focus of discrimination in the Act is employers or their counterparts in other fields. The Act makes unlawful specific discriminatory practices, such as in advertising, hiring, promotion, dismissal, and granting of benefits. However, while the Act forbids, for example, the refusal to hire a woman because she is a woman, it does not mandate hiring women in general. Positive discrimination (or "affirmative action") is allowed, but achieving a sex ratio is not suggested. Individuals who have proven that they have been discriminated against are financially compensated, but not hired. The burden of proof of discrimination rests with the individual victim. A major weakness of the Act is in its provisions for enforcement and the implications for women that follow. We will look, first, at the meaning of discrim-

[45] It was timed to coincide with Women's International Year, 1975. All of the OECD countries now have some form of legislation for equal employment opportunity. On paper, Britain's is one of the most comprehensive.

ination embodied in the Act and then examine how the Act is being enforced and how continuing discrimination is being dealt with. Finally, I will suggest what long-term contribution to social equality for women we can expect from this Act.

The Sex Discrimination Act distinguishes two kinds of discrimination, direct and indirect, occurring on the grounds of sex per se or against married persons or "victimized" persons.[46] The Act applies to sex discrimination against men, too, except when women are given special treatment in connection with pregnancy or childbirth.

Direct sex discrimination occurs when a woman is treated "less favourably" than a man is or would be treated in similar circumstances. The most common cases occur when a woman is refused a job generally held by a man even though she is qualified and capable of performing it (for example, as a truck driver).

Indirect sex discrimination occurs when the proportion of women who can comply with a requirement is smaller than the proportion of men who can comply with it; when the requirement cannot be shown to be "justifiable"; and when the requirement is to a woman's detriment because she cannot comply with it. For example, an employer may place a particular technical or physical qualification on a job, such as certain weight and height requirements for police or firefighters, when performance of the job does not require the qualifications.

Direct discrimination against a married person occurs when she or he is treated "less favourably" than a single person of the same sex is or would be treated. For example, married women commonly used to be denied positions as flight attendants.

Indirect discrimination against a married person occurs when the proportion of married persons who can comply with a requirement is smaller than the proportion of single persons who can comply with it; when the requirement

---

[46] *Sex Discrimination Act 1975* (London: HMSO, 1975), Part I.

cannot be shown to be "justifiable"; and when it is to a married person's detriment because she or he cannot comply with it. For example, an employer may require periods of in-residence training, which could be offered during regular hours, and which married persons, especially women with children, would be unwilling to take up. Also, an employer might refuse certain promotions to persons with young children, perhaps because greater job commitment and overtime hours are entailed.

"Victimization" occurs when a person is treated "less favourably" because she or he has brought proceedings against an employer or has given evidence or information in connection with the Sex Discrimination or Equal Pay Acts. Victimization can occur when a current employer holds back promotion or a potential employer refuses to hire the individual under question.

The Act gives no specific examples of any of these instances of discrimination, but it does state that the statutes cover the practices of employers in hiring, promotion, transfer, training, and in the allocation of benefits. It also covers trade unions, employers organizations, professional bodies, employment agencies, vocational training bodies, and organizations granting licenses or qualifications. Two exceptions are private households and establishments where the number of persons employed does not exceed five. Other exceptions include work conducted outside Great Britain and in the armed forces. Special provisions are contained for police and prison officers (for example, height requirements are upheld, and restrictions on male governors for women's prisons are removed); for ministers of religion (according to the doctrine of the religion); for midwives (men can now train in a few special colleges); for underground miners (the prohibition against women is upheld, except for inactive mines); and in sports (those sports requiring physical strength, stamina, or a certain physique, putting average women at a disadvantage in competition, can be confined to one sex).

In addition to these special provisions in the jobs listed

above, the Act further elaborates a number of jobs which are an "exception" because "sex," which is in turn elaborated as "being a man," "is a genuine occupational qualification."[47] This includes: (1) a job which requires the "physiology" of a man (excluding physical strength or stamina), such as in dramatic performances; (2) a job which requires a man "to preserve decency or privacy" (no example of a specific job is given); (3) a job which requires that the employee live on the premises and the employer does not or cannot reasonably be expected to provide separate sleeping accommodations and sanitary facilities for women; (4) a job in a men's hospital, prison, or other single-sex establishment, requiring special care, supervision, or attention, so that it is "reasonable" to require a man; (5) a job in which the holder provides individuals with personal services promoting their education or welfare, or similar personal services that can "most effectively" be provided by a man (no specific example is offered); (6) a job which requires a man "'because of restrictions imposed by the laws regulating the employment of women"; (7) a job which "needs to be held by a man because it is likely to involve the performance of duties outside the United Kingdom in a country whose laws or customs are such that the duties could not, or could not effectively be performed by a woman"; (8) a job which is one of two to be held by a married couple.

These exceptions are more important than the bold general premises of unlawful discrimination with which the Act opens for they whittle down the effectiveness of those premises. But the greatest shortcoming is that these instances of genuine occupation qualification require much more clarification than the Act provides. For example, category (5), "personal services that can most effectively be provided by a man," is extremely vague. And category (6), regarding legal restrictions on women's employment, upholds Britain's "protective" laws limiting, for example, the

---

[47] Ibid., pp. 5-6. This discussion keeps as closely as possible to the wording in the original.

number of hours and overtime work that women can engage in.[48] The loopholes are numerous, and the way the Act has been interpreted makes full use of these loopholes, as we will see.

The actual significance of the Sex Discrimination Act for women has been lessened not only because the Act is open to varying interpretations but because of the manner of interpretation and the provisions for enforcement allowed by the Act. When the Act became law, employers and others were informed of its contents and obliged to stop their discriminatory practices henceforth. The Act is not retroactive, but if individuals believe they have been discriminated against in the past, they can file for litigation according to the proper procedure. Not all employers stopped their discriminatory practices when the Act came into effect in 1976. There are various procedures for redress,[49] all of which are to be taken by the individual who has been discriminated against or by a representative (lawyer, trade union official).[50] All complaints must first be made in writing. Those against an employer go to an industrial tribunal, while those in other matters go to county courts, except that complaints concerning education must be made first to the Secretary of State for Education. I focus only on employment.

[48] The extent to which these laws protect or limit is open to much debate. Unions in Britain remain strongly in favor of the laws, especially in such industries as mining. Sweden has rescinded most of its "protective" legislation.

[49] See Patricia Hewitt, *Rights for Women: A Guide to the Sex Discrimination Act, the Equal Pay Act, Paid Maternity Leave, Pension Schemes and Unfair Dismissal* (London: National Council for Civil Liberties, 1975).

[50] By far the majority of individuals represent themselves at both conciliation and Industrial Tribunal hearings. Accordingly, the EOC has prepared a booklet to assist individuals. Equal Opportunities Commission, *How to Prepare Your Own Case for an Industrial Tribunal* (Manchester: EOC, 1979). However, union representation is greater for equal pay than for sex discrimination cases (73% for equal pay compared to 12% for sex discrimination in 1979). About 30% of sex discrimination cases are represented by a solicitor/counsel.

Complaints against an employer must be made within three months of the the alleged discriminatory act. After a complaint is filed with the Secretary of Tribunals, it goes first to a conciliation officer of the Advisory, Conciliation and Arbitration Service. The majority of cases are actually "settled" at this level, or withdrawn. There is very little information available as to how the cases are settled or why they are withdrawn, but there is some indication that women are not the winners. For example, as Table 3.3 shows, several cases commonly are withdrawn with no settlement.[51] Others are settled for token sums (for example, £10 for unfair dismissal, £25 for injury to feelings).[52] Cases that cannot be conciliated are heard and settled by an industrial tribunal.[53] Tribunals are located throughout the country.

TABLE 3.3   Complaints under the Sex Discrimination Act

	1976			1980		
Outcome of Complaint	Men	Women	Total	Men	Women	Total
Conciliation settlements and withdrawals where conciliation attempted:						
Settlements	9	26	35 (14.4%)	13	33	46 (25.4%)
Withdrawals						
private settlement	3	18	21 (8.6%)	4	4	8 (4.4%)
reasons not known	19	49	68 (28.0%)	26	31	57 (31.5%)
Tribunal hearings:						
Application upheld	6	18	24 (9.9%)	5	10	15 (8.3%)
Application dismissed	22	73	95 (39.1%)	14	41	55 (30.4%)

Sources: Equal Opportunities Commission, *The Annual Report of the Equal Opportunities Commission, 1976; Fifth Annual Report, 1980* (London: HMSO, 1976, 1980).

[51] Some of these cases are no doubt based on misunderstanding of the acts. However, the National Council for Civil Liberties claims it has received reports from women who felt they were "bullied" into withdrawing. Jean Coussins, *The Equality Report* (London: National Council for Civil Liberties, 1976), p. 18; see also, Jeanne Gregory, "The Great Conciliation Fraud," *New Statesman* (July 3, 1981), pp. 6-7.

[52] Gregory, ibid.

[53] Industrial tribunals have been operating for decades. Since the Sex

They consist of a lawyer as chairperson, one trade unionist, and one person nominated by management; each member sits for a two-year term. One of the three members should be a woman as a matter of policy, but it is not mandated (and therefore has rarely been observed). Tribunals do not create case law, and their ad hoc rulings vary considerably. Therefore, they have had little consistent impact on women's equality. The burden of proof for discrimination is on the complainant. The employer must rebut the evidence, show that the requirement was justifiable, or show that the alleged discriminatory act is not covered by the appropriate legislation. The tacit assumption is that the employer, the defendant, is innocent until proven guilty.

Table 3.3 indicates that, of those cases heard by an industrial tribunal, few complaints are upheld. The small number of cases brought up for litigation and the still smaller number upheld by tribunals tells us less about discrimination, and its existence and extent, than about the difficulty of identifying and proving it. Furthermore, the decreasing number of complaints since 1976 (under both Acts) ought not be taken as an indication of decreasing discrimination, but rather of the ineffectiveness of litigation. The complicated procedures, the disproportionate number of negative rulings by the tribunals, and the conception of discrimination that emerges from the written statements about some of these cases have been discouraging to new litigants.[54] In addition, if an individual has had a complaint

---

Discrimination and Equal Pay Acts came into effect, their workload has increased, but not their numbers. An industrial tribunal is considered an improvement over a general court or a single judge (common in western Europe), because the members of a tribunal are more specialized in matters of employment. Other cases of discrimination are heard before judges in general courts.

[54] Coussins summarizes a number of written statements of industrial tribunal rulings. She also describes some of the hearings monitored by the National Council for Civil Liberties. In a number of cases, it is difficult to understand the basis for the rulings against the complainants. For example, in "Saunders v. Richmond Borough Council," Saunders, a golfer, was turned down for a job as a golfing professional (she was a top-ranked

before an industrial tribunal, the information is stamped on his/her employment record. Before assessing the fuller impact of this legislation and attempting to explain its form, let us examine the cohort of the Sex Discrimination Act: the Equal Pay Act. These two pieces of legislation complement each other in their consequences for women workers.

Equal Pay Act, 1970, 1976

The Equal Pay Act was passed in Parliament in 1970, with a five-year phase-in period. Thus, it came into effect at the same time as the Sex Discrimination Act. Britain had procrastinated for years in legislating equal pay. Unlike most of the other European nations, Britain did not sign for quite some time (1971) the International Labour Organisation Convention No. 100 on Equal Remuneration (1951).[55] Signing this convention became politically necessary when Britain joined the European Economic Community (whose charter contains an equal pay provision similar to the ILO's), but Britain signed only after its own statute was in operation. The main opposition had always come from the employers' federation, the Confederation of British Industries (CBI), and from private industry. They found sympathetic allies among Conservative politicians.[56] The main issue in contention had always been the meaning of "work of equal value," a broad conception supported by

---

woman player); she had been asked, among other things, whether she would be capable of "controlling men at the tees." Coussins, *The Equality Report,* p. 56.

[55] Britain has still not signed the ILO Convention No. 111 on Discrimination in Respect of Employment and Occupation (1958) because it combines discrimination on grounds of sex and race. Britain has a separate Race Relations Act, 1976.

[56] For the political background, see Graham Wootton, *Pressure Politics in Contemporary Britain* (Lexington, Mass.: D. C. Heath, 1978), pp. 92-100, and the articles by Dipek Nandy, Jeffrey Jowell and Nancy Seear in Ronnie Steinberg Ratner (ed.), *Equal Employment Policy for Women: Strategies for Implementation in the United States, Canada, and Western Europe* (Philadelphia: Temple University Press, 1980).

the main protagonists in this case, the Trades Union Congress (TUC). The CBI insisted that only "same work" could be properly defined and measured and accorded equal pay. After years of negotiations and bickering, a tripartite committee (CBI, TUC, government) finally resolved the terms of the Act. Each woman now has the right to the same terms of contract of employment "on work of the same or a broadly similar nature" or "in a job which, though different from that of a man, has been given an equal value to the man's under job evaluation."[57] The statement is bold; the hitch comes in the exercise of job evaluation schemes.

A woman who feels she is being discriminated against must prove that she is doing the "same work" as a man in order to warrant the same pay.[58] A woman who feels she is doing work of "equivalent value" to a man's, warranting equal pay, must have this proven first through a job evaluation exercise, which is conducted jointly by the union and management.[59] The jobs in question are graded on a point basis according to criteria such as skills, training, manual dexterity. Unfortunately, the points given to the various

[57] This is how it is stated by the Department of Employment in a pamphlet entitled "Equal Pay," p. 3, which is available at local employment offices, job-centers, and unemployment benefit offices. The Equal Pay Act itself says, "where the woman is employed on like work with a man in the same employment" or "where the woman is employed on work rated as equivalent with that of a man in the same employment." *Sex Discrimination Act 1975*, p. 62.

The Equal Pay Act also applies to a man who is being given less favorable treatment than a woman, except in matters related to maternity or other protective legislation. Beside basic pay rates and salaries, the Act covers all contractual agreements in employment, including non-regular work hours and holidays, bonuses and fringe benefits, sick pay, and medical schemes, and membership in employers' pension schemes (but not amount of pension).

[58] During the 5-year phase-in period, some employers got around the new legislation by changing job titles, for example, from shop assistant to trainee manager. Now the complainant must prove that these different jobs constitute "same" work.

[59] Therefore, it is highly unlikely that a woman would be taking part in the evaluation.

criteria are the subject of negotiation between the evaluators. There are a number of ways in which women can be discriminated against in an evaluation exercise.[60] For instance, one perfectly legal factor is length of training, which puts women at an initial disadvantage because until very recently few women have had the same access as men to certain training programs. Other kinds of evaluation can be highly subjective, such as the unequal ratings between manual dexterity as opposed to physical strength. There is widespread dissatisfaction with job evaluation schemes. The fact that there must be a man to whom a woman can compare herself limits the use of these schemes. And the lack of standardized procedures and ratings limits the advantages of job evaluations for many groups of women workers.[61]

A woman who is not satisfied with the results of a job evaluation exercise can take her case to an industrial tribunal according to the same procedure as in other cases of discrimination. Table 3.4 presents the outcome of complaints made under the Equal Pay Act. As with the Sex Discrimination Act, the majority of cases is settled by conciliation, with a high proportion of withdrawals. Of those cases heard before an industrial tribunal, increasingly fewer are being upheld. Also, increasingly fewer cases are being heard. This is not to be taken as an indication that equal pay has been achieved, but rather that the limits of the law have been reached, as I elaborate below.

Appeals of industrial tribunal decisions, regarding both sex discrimination and equal pay complaints, can be made to the Employment Appeal Tribunal. This Tribunal hears only about 10 to 15 cases per year. It appears to be taking a more liberal interpretation of the Equal Pay Act than the Sex Discrimination Act, for about half of the equal pay cases are found in favor of the employee but only about

[60] Hewitt, *Rights for Women*, p. 35.
[61] The Equal Opportunities Commission is attempting to suggest how a more standardized procedure would work. See Equal Opportunities Commission, *Job Evaluation Schemes Without Bias* (Manchester: EOC, 1981).

TABLE 3.4   Complaints under the Equal Pay Act

Outcome of Complaint	Number of Complaints			Percentage of Total		
	1976	1978	1980	1976	1978	1980
Conciliation settlements and withdrawals where conciliation attempted:						
Settlements	106	29	10	6.1	8.5	11.0
Withdrawals						
private settlement	180	49	5⎫			
reasons not known	674	166	50⎭	49.0	62.7	60.4
Other withdrawals						
private settlement	4	0	0⎫			
reasons not known	69	19	⎭	4.2	5.5	0
Tribunal hearings:						
Complaints upheld	213	24	4	12.2	7.0	4.4
Dismissals						
not like or equivalent work	366	22	5⎫			
not same employment	10	0	1⎪			
material difference	78	27	9⎬	28.5	16.3	24.2
other reasons	42	7	7⎭			

Sources: Equal Opportunities Commission, *The Annual Report of the Equal Opportunities Commission, 1976; Third Annual Report, 1978; Fifth Annual Report, 1980* (London: HMSO, 1976, 1978, 1980).

one-quarter of the discrimination cases. Several cases are also regularly sent back to the former or to new industrial tribunals with instructions on or clarifications of points of contention. Some cases are also sent to the European Court of Justice. The decisions of the Employment Appeal Tribunal are important because, unlike those of the industrial tribunals, they set legal precedents and are binding on future deliberations by industrial tribunals.[62]

Figure 3.1 illustrates the difference between women's and men's pay. Legislation has been partly responsible for narrowing the gap. However, incomes policies imposed in 1975 and 1976 also helped, since these benefited low-paid

[62] Further appeals can be made to the Court of Appeals, and then to the House of Lords. None has gone yet to the highest body.

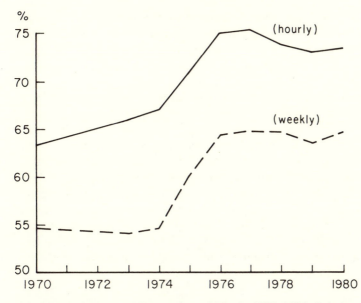

3.1. Women's Pay as a Proportion of Men's, 1970-1980, Britain. Adapted from: Equal Opportunities Commission, *The Fifth Annual Report, 1980* (London: HMSO, 1980).

workers as a whole.[63] It should be noted that after the first spate of complaints, when the Act came fully into effect in 1976, the proportion of women's to men's pay once again declined.

Equality for women in Britain has probably advanced about as far as it can with this legislation. Both the Equal Opportunity Commission, under its chair Baroness Betty Lockwood, as well as the Women's Advisory Committee of the TUC, have proposed a list of amendments to the Acts. These amendments would, among other things, standardize job evaluations; clarify the meaning of "work of equal value"; allow for greater use of "positive action"; and institute class action suits, which EOC and TUC lawyers claim

[63] Nancy Seear, "Implementing Equal Pay and Equal Opportunity Legislation in Great Britain," in Ratner, *Equal Employment Policy*, p. 20.

is completely permissible under the law. These amendments would have but limited impact. The problems that
women workers in Britain face, the problems of occupational stereotyping and segregated labor markets, run much
deeper than the purview of these laws.

In sum, the British legislation is inadequate, a fact that
has also been recognized by the European Economic Commission. The Commission has repeatedly issued directives
to the United Kingdom on provisions in both the Sex Discrimination and Equal Pay Acts. Finally in July 1982, the
European Court of Justice struck down the Equal Pay Act,
charging that Britain had failed to widen its definition of
equal work to conform with the Community's requirement
of "work of equal value." Britain is now obligated to change
its legislation. But after the ruling, the Conservative-led
government "declared that it had no intention of doing
anything about equal pay."[64]

Summary and Assessment

These two pieces of legislation assume that the problem
of inequality in women's employment stems directly from
employers' practices. The mandate that employers stop discriminating has brought some changes for women workers
in Britain. For example, women who apply to work as mechanics are now more likely than previously to be hired if
they are qualified. And women doing exactly the same work
as men are now more likely to receive the same pay. While
some advances have been made because of this legislation,

---

[64] *The Economist,* July 10, 1982, p. 54. The government has since proposed some amendments to the Equal Pay Act. But the Equal Opportunities Commission claims that these proposed amendments do not comply
with EEC requirements. In fact, the EOC warns that "Working women
who have found present equal pay legislation wanting will be in a worse
position if new government proposals to change the law are accepted,"
because they basically further delay and complicate the process of litigation. Equal Opportunities Commission, *News Release* (Manchester: EOC,
March 11, 1983).

we can predict that they will not go much further. The accumulation of instances of individual women who have succeeded after litigation will not change the structural problem in women's employment—dual and internal labor markets. The law may well "reduce prejudice by discouraging the behaviour in which prejudice finds expression."[65] But the law alone is limited as a tool to deal effectively with the forces that produce prejudicial behavior in the first place. At issue is why, for example, so few women apply for jobs in the professions or as mechanics, and why nurses aides are paid at a lower rate than sanitation workers. The legislation examined here does not address these factors. The behavior suggested in these points will continue unaffected, and so too, then, will the force of segmented labor markets.

The British state has taken a prominent position by resorting to legislation specifically designed to facilitate women's quest for social equality. It has put itself in the vanguard and has forced changes that might not have taken place otherwise. The act of state intervention is unquestionably direct; the range of affected areas is wide (despite the long list of exceptions). But if the structure of the problem has not been affected, what can we say about the depth of intervention? Clearly, intervention has been too superficial to affect the structure of the problem. To elaborate, I return to the relationship between a universal framework and selective measures made in the introduction to this chapter.

The Sex Discrimination and Equal Pay Acts can be thought of as special measures directed at some of the special circumstances that create inequality for women in the labor market. But the position that there is a special group with special circumstances lends itself to a peculiarly fragmented perspective. The legislation is not applicable to all women. Those women and those circumstances to which it is applicable must be defined and differentiated from women

---

[65] Home Office, *Equality for Women* (London: HMSO, 1975), p. 4.

workers as a whole, as well as, of course, from workers as
a whole. As we have seen in the case of the Sex Discrimination Act, definition and differentiation have been conducted with a thoroughness that enhances selectivity. In
addition, where clarification is most needed, as in the understanding of certain vague exceptions based on occupational qualifications, it is lacking. The complexity of this
kind of definitional process, together with its selective applicability, makes the generalized concept of discrimination
useless to most of the women who seek to benefit from
legislation on sex discrimination. In addition to the fragmentation that results from the elaboration of specialized
definitions, the enforcement procedure embodied in the
Acts further narrows the impact on discrimination. That
the burden of proof is on the victim of discrimination, and
that so few have been able to prove discrimination satisfactorily for the tribunals, indicates an acute selectivity in
impact. These two Acts do not provide the foundation for
what we know of as "positive discrimination." No group
consistently benefits from litigation. Some women benefit,
but it is impossible to say which ones or under what circumstances. Moreover, the consequences for equality are
unclear. Equality of opportunity has resulted only for those
few who have won after litigation, or whose employers com-
plied with the law in the first place. But equality of outcome
is not advanced in any case. These shortcomings indicate
that a universal framework is lacking, within which selective
measures can function to achieve positive results.

In sum, the act of legislating has given the state the ap-
pearance of playing a greater role in facilitating women's
employment, but the consequences of state intervention
have made that role a token one. Paradoxically, with each
new effort on the part of the state to define and clarify
further the area of applicability of these Acts, the intrusion
of the state becomes greater but the outcome more selective
still. The state is acting, but its intervention lacks depth.
Depth of intervention is evidenced not through the visibility

of the state, but in the effectiveness of the state to alter the rules of the game for the participants.

TRADE UNIONS: AN ALTERNATIVE?

Prior to the development of legislation in Britain, the main means of promoting equality in pay and on the job for women and other low-paid, low-status workers was union activity in collective bargaining. The TUC, Britain's largest blue-collar labor organization, passed a resolution supporting the principle of equal pay for equal work as early as 1888, but for decades little was done to translate the principle into practice.[66] Many unions assumed that formal equality was sufficient and as long as the rule books were followed, actual equality would be achieved.[67] The complacency that so long pervaded union attitudes about women's equality stems from low representation of women in the unions, entrenched sectionalism within the labor movement, and the persistence of wage differentials. I will briefly elaborate these three factors, suggesting that, while they have been mitigated to some extent, they are far from being overcome.

Unions in Britain traditionally have been craft- or trade-based. Only a few crafts or trades include jobs which women traditionally perform, such as textile worker. Thus, by virtue of their occupational segregation alone, women constitute half or more of the membership of only a handful of Britain's many trade unions. (Table 3.5 presents data for selected national unions.) Where women are well-organized, it tends to be in plants or industries where men are also well-organized or in white-collar unions (teachers, public employees). The milieu of the industry or occupation seems to be the most important variable accounting for union activity, regardless, of sex.[68] There are other

---

[66] Seer in Ratner, *Equal Employment Policy*, p. 261.

[67] Valerie Ellis, *The Role of Trade Unions in the Promotion of Equal Pay Opportunities* (Manchester: EOC, 1981), p. 42.

[68] Ibid., pp. 18, 36.

TABLE 3.5 Representation of Women in Selected Trade Unions

Union	Industry	Women Members %	Full-time Officials Who Are Women %	No.	Executive Committee Members Who Are Women %	No.
APEX	Professional, executive, clerical	55	1.9	1	26.7	4
ASTMS	Scientific, technical, managerial	18	7.7	5	4.2	1
ATWU	Textile	45	20.8	5	27.3	6
AUEW (Eng.)	Engineering	14	0.5	1	0	0
BFAWU	Bakers, food	40	3.8	1	22.2	4
CATU	Construction	53	0	0	11.1	2
COHSE	Health service	70	12.5	5	3.6	1
CPSA	Civil, public services	68	14.3	4	30.8	8
CSU	Civil service	38	9.1	1	8.7	2
EETPU	Electrical, telecommunic., plumbing	13	0	0	0	0
FTAT	Furniture, timber	12	0	0	0	0
GMWU	General, municipal workers	33	3.5	10	0	0
IPCS	Professional civil servants	7	21.0	4	12.0	3
IRSF	Inland revenue staff	58	14.3	1	10.7	3

NALGO	National, local government	43	8.9	17	7.6	5
NAS/UWT	Schoolmasters, women teachers	18	0	0	7.9	3
BIFU	Banking, insurance, finance	46	9.7	3	12.5	3
NUDBTW	Textile workers	36	3.8	1	6.7	1
NUFLAT	Footwear, leather	48	4.2	2	6.3	1
NUHKW	Hosiery, knitwear	73	6.5	2	8.0	2
NUPE	Public employees	65	1.7	2	23.1	6
NUT	Teachers	75	7.7	2	14.6	7
NUTGW	Tailors, garment workers	88	15.0	6	33.3	5
SCPS	Civil, public servants	17	15.0	3	15.4	4
SOGAT	Graphics	36	4.3	3	6.3	2
AUEW (TASS)	Electrical	11	5.3	2	3.7	1
TGWU	Transport, general workers	16	0.6	3	0	0
TSSA	Transport salaried staff	22	16.7	10	6.7	2
TWU	Tobacco workers	65	33.3	3	5.3	1
UPW	Postal workers	22	8.3	1	26.3	5
USDAW	Shop, distributive	59	3.0	4	5.9	1

Adapted from: Valerie Ellis, *The Role of Trade Unions in the Promotion of Equal Pay Opportunities* (Manchester: EOC, 1981), p. 61, as drawn from Equal Pay and Opportunities Campaign, *Survey of Unions and the Equal Pay Act*, 1976.

women-specific reasons for the low female representation in unions. People who join unions and are active in union activities also have some sense of job attachment. Job attachment is elusive for women who are transient workers, floating in and out of the labor market in tune with business cycles, and for women who work part-time usually because of family responsibilities. Even when individual women can accommodate their specific drawbacks and join unions, their level of participation is lower than men's, both in terms of attendance at meetings and contribution to union policies and activities. Low participation is connected in part with low job attachment, and in part with conflicting responsibilities, since union meetings tend to be held in the evenings or at other times inconvenient to women with families. It should be added that studies report these same reasons as curtailing men's participation in union activities.[69] We can only assume they are even stronger for women. Finally, male dominance extends to representation in the offices of union hierarchies. Table 3.5 also shows the relationship between women's membership in selected unions and their low representation within the union officialdom. Given, then, women's virtual powerlessness within the unions, it comes as no surprise that unions did not adopt women's causes for decades. In the late 1960s, women's membership within the unions began to increase, as did their militancy in certain isolated strikes. Unions, on the whole, were quick to jump on the bandwagon once the direction of events and the stakes became clear.

In the 1970s, when union leadership finally began to heed the recommendations of their "women's councils," positive action on women's behalf was still slow in coming. One main reason for this continued foot-dragging was the divisions among the various branches of the labor movement. Although many unions are affiliated with the TUC, local

---

[69] John Goldthorpe, David Lockwood, et al., *The Affluent Worker: Industrial Attitudes and Behaviour* (Cambridge: Cambridge University Press, 1968).

unions are completely independent when it comes to taking up TUC policies. The TUC can only suggest what local unions ought to do. On matters such as the status of women, local unions are much more traditional than the TUC. Several unions employing large numbers of women, such as the National Union of Tailor and Garment Workers, have shown little interest in equality issues. Others, such as white-collar unions which organize workers in the public sector and in offices, have shown greater commitment. Interestingly, on political matters local unions tend to be more radical than the TUC.

Some unions have always maintained a "closed shop" principle, barring the entry of women to the trade through certain training requirements. This is now illegal under the Sex Discrimination Act, but it has not necessarily been abolished. Accordingly, when the TUC General Council finally adopted its Women's Conference proposal on equal pay in 1968, no trickle-down effect occurred. Moreover, the TUC General Council was reluctant to push the issue, so as not to " 'rock the boat' . . . in defiance of the government view, consistently maintained since the war, that the principle of equal pay might be good but it was never the right time, economically, to implement it."[70] Since no section in the labor organization felt any sense of urgency about the issue of equal pay for women (except the Women's Council of the TUC), reliance on union initiative in collective bargaining as a means to achieving equality would not have gone much further alone. It required the impetus of legislation and its threatened invasion into the sacrosanct domain of collective bargaining to improve the outcome for women.

Still, the extent to which collective bargaining can advance women's equality is limited. For one, collective bargaining in Britain is a fragmented and complex process. In principle, rates of pay are determined at industry level, but in practice these rates are commonly renegotiated in

[70] Ellis, *The Role of Trade Unions*, p. 47.

an ad hoc fashion at plant and even shop-floor level. Success in this system of bargaining requires some measure of power or support, neither of which women have. For another, among the main consequences of decentralized collective bargaining is the reintroduction of wage differentials among groups of workers. In principle, unions support the justice of equal pay for equal work and eschew discriminatory wage differentials. But they have not taken a unified stand to institutionalize the principle. In practice, each union, at firm, industry or whatever level, attempts to get a better deal for its members. One recent survey asked managers the question, "What would you say are the most difficult problems you have to cope with over pay at this establishment?"[71] Union negotiators were asked which issue "their members felt most strongly about."[72] Of overwhelming importance to both managers and workers was the problem of differentials or comparability of pay of one group in relation to others.[73]

Wage differentials extend not only to different categories of work but also, and more perniciously for women, to different evaluations of broadly similar work. Obviously, women's wages suffer because of persisting wage differentials, for women either are invariably in the lower categories of work or their contribution to broadly similar work is rated lower. The introduction of job evaluation schemes has not helped. As one researcher notes, "job evaluation is essentially a method for resolving problems of differentials

[71] W. W. Daniels, *Wage Determination in Industry* (London: PEP, 1976), p. 38.

[72] Ibid., p. 35.

[73] Ibid. Also high on the list was "basic pay for work by results" or piecework. The concern with comparability of pay is an interesting one, for manual workers tend to compare themselves more with another manual worker than with non-manual (and higher-paid) workers. Furthermore, the sense of relative deprivation vis-à-vis the better-off group is not that high, and not as high in Britain as in Sweden. See articles by W. G. Runciman and Richard Scase, among others, in Dorothy Wedderburn (ed.), *Poverty, Inequality and Class Structure* (Cambridge: Cambridge University Press, 1974).

in an agreed and orderly way rather than of eliminating them."[74] However, success in achieving higher pay through the strengthening of wage differentials is a sign of union power. Those women who are in the more powerful unions are, thereby, better off due to wage differentials. Nevertheless, it is the strength of the union not the differential that enhances the outcome, for men as well as women. Unfortunately, the lack of centralization among unions in Britain makes this outcome unsystematic and unpredictable. Were the labor movement as a whole stronger and more unified in Britain, differentials might be narrowed. Instead, "the relative gap between manual and non-manual workers was wider in 1960 than in 1913-14 and the ranking of occupations by annual average earnings has barely altered in the twentieth century, except for a deterioration in the relative position of the 'lower professions.' "[75]

Both unions and employers would have preferred, of course, to avoid legislation on discrimination in work and pay and to continue to rely on collective bargaining. Since collective bargaining was the established method of workplace arbitration prior to the legislation, the lawmakers attempted to give priority to collective action at the level of local unions and employers. For example, when a discrimination complaint in work or pay is filed, the Advisory, Conciliation and Arbitration Service routinely contacts the local union to encourage its involvement. In addition, there is a separate committee of the ACAS, the Central Abritration Committee (CAC), constituted under the Employment Protection Act, 1975, which handles all grievances involving collective agreements. (It does not deal with complaints from individuals.) Up to now, the CAC has dealt with too few cases involving women as low-paid workers for us to make any judgment as to its effectiveness. It is clear, however, that collective action alone did not do what it could

---

[74] Daniels, *Wage Determination in Industry*, p. 33.

[75] Brian Burkitt and David Bowers, *Trade Unions and the Economy* (London: Macmillan, 1979), p. 31.

have done for women's equality, and there is no reason to expect anything different from such methods now that laws have been instituted. To be sure, unions in general and the TUC in particular are now more supportive of women's equality than they ever were in the past. And they now have women's advisory councils as well as equality clauses in their charters. This apparent change of heart may be more symbolic than real, however. It developed because of certain external factors (legislation, the women's movement, public opinion), none of which has ever been very strong in Britain, and certain internal factors, especially increasing membership of women in the unions. But the change within the union movement has not yet been adequately translated into positive action for women. One indication of tenuous support is the persistence of discriminatory clauses in collective agreements. After receiving several complaints concerning collective agreements, the European Economic Commission decided to bring yet another case against the United Kingdom. Although collective agreements are not subject to legal supervision or enforcement, the matter is being investigated by the TUC and the government.

In sum, the relationship between collective bargaining and legislation for women's equality in Britain is fraught with inconsistencies and ambiguities, reflecting the loose integrity of the country's tripartite system. Just as the state is a distant observer in collective bargaining, so is collective bargaining a weak ingredient in the formulation and implementation of legislation.

CONCLUSION

This chapter has examined two kinds of measures for equal employment opportunity for women in Britain: labor market policies and anti-discrimination and equal pay legislation. At first glance an unexpected contrast appears in the role of the state in shaping these two kinds of measures. Labor market policies reveal the basic liberal paradigm of state/society relations in Britain, with the state taking a secondary role to market forces in directing the allocation of labor resources. Insofar as labor market policies do not exhibit a deep level of micro intervention, they are compatible with general economic policy. As discussed in Chapter 2, the British state favors the use of macroeconomic measures to manipulate in a general way aggregate market factors. The use of these measures is underpinned by a market rationality which assumes that the market is capable of finding its own equilibrium with minimal state assistance. Hence, general economic policies do not effectively form a "universal framework" in that they are ad hoc and weakly integrated. Neither do labor market policies effectively form a set of selective measures to advance the position of women. The various dimensions of labor market policies are based on the conception that women have difficulty in the labor market because of inadequacies in themselves. Training programs thus are oriented to self-improvement for women, so that they can bring themselves up to the level of men in competition for jobs. Structural impediments to women's equality within the labor market have not been touched at all. In sum, women workers in Britain are not significantly better off as a result of labor market policies.

In the area of anti-discrimination and equal pay legislation, the role of the state appears on the surface prominent and deeply interventionist by seeming to obstruct the freedom of employers to hire and fire according to the best wage and price equilibrium they can get. But close examination of the legislation and its enforcement makes it apparent that the state has not interfered too severely with the freedom of employers and their best interests, for only those women who are exactly like men can replace men on the job, and only those women who are exactly as deserving as men receive their due to the same extent as men. This actual low level of intervention on the part of the state is coupled with a conception of the problem in women's employment analogous to the "individual" model. That is, for those women who are capable, employers must only stop discriminating to achieve equality for women in the labor market. The benefits to women of this orientation in state policy have been limited and have already gone as far as they can. Equal access assuming equal qualifications and equal pay for equal work have been achieved, but neither equal qualifications nor equal work have been advanced to any great extent.

Putting together these two areas of measures for women in Britain, we can say that the nexus of equal employment opportunities is weak and fragmented. Even where equality exists as an abstract goal, as in the Sex Discrimination Act, the precariousness of the institutional underpinnings, based on the role of the state, bars the full realization of equality. A fuller comparison of form and consequence of state action in Britain and Sweden awaits the analysis in the following chapter.

CHAPTER 4

SWEDEN: EQUAL EMPLOYMENT OPPORTUNITY

INTRODUCTION

Two frameworks for analyzing labor market policies were introduced in the previous chapter on Britain. The first concerned the conception of the problem in women's employment that informs labor market policies, and three different conceptions were presented: (1) Women themselves are seen as creating their own employment problems because of inadequacies in training, etc.; (2) women's dual roles are held to prevent their full participation in the labor market; (3) the structure of the labor market as a whole is understood as segmented so as to systematically exclude women from full and equal integration. As was suggested in the previous chapter, the individual and role-related conceptions tend to be associated with selective measures for women, which, when used alone, do not contribute to full integration into the labor market. Only a policy framework based on a social structural conception of the problem in women's employment has the potential to improve the situation of women in the labor market. This potential is realized through the greater depth of state intervention that is associated with a social structural conception. We will see in this chapter that labor market policies in Sweden come much closer to the social structural conception than do policies in Britain.

The second framework presented in Chapter 3 concerned the depth of state intervention in fashioning specific labor market policies and shaping the nexus of economic policies within which the labor market functions. In Sweden the state intervenes more readily and more deeply than in

Britain to control both general economic and specific labor market forces with a combination of macro and micro policies. These two frameworks and the relationship between them organize the present chapter on labor market policies in Sweden.

The status of women in Swedish society in the earlier decades of this century was similar to that in Britain and elsewhere. Women were not afforded any special consideration in the economy, in politics, or in law. They were considered, as elsewhere, best suited to be wives and mothers, and so were secluded in their homes—or, in the case of Sweden, on farms—as their husbands' main helpers. The labor force participation rate for women in Sweden was lower than in Britain until the late 1950s. What happened at that time to change the status and situation of women in Sweden was the development of an active labor market policy, whose main features are presented below. We will see that the policy attempts to take a structural perspective on the problem in women's employment, at the same time as it accepts the need for special measures to compensate the accumulation of employment impediments that women have been subjected to over the decades.

The upshot of this analysis concerns the effect of the role of the state on the status of women in society. Traditional conceptions of women's roles are subject to change. One of the main factors precipitating this change is an active state which intervenes deeply in the economy, making optimal use of all available labor for full economic growth. To put this in the terms that were developed above, the principle of full employment for economic growth provides the universal framework within which selective measures optimize labor resources. This sounds like a highly capitalist adventure; it is not entirely so, although the interests of capital are included within a strongly integrated tripartite coalition. State action in Sweden is based on a mistrust of free market forces and of the consequences these forces produce on both labor and the economy. Moreover, state actors in Sweden did not develop an active mistrust of free market forces entirely on their own initiative, but at the behest of a well-organized labor movement. Thus, a second factor facilitating social change in traditional conceptions of women's roles is an active, powerful, and unified labor movement which can place on the public agenda labor's concerns with improving the conditions of low-status, low-paid workers, many of whom happen to be women. Coordination of the interests of capital and labor at the level of the state characterizes the form of state/society relations in Sweden, a form which allowed Sweden to break out of the liberal mode and to develop new approaches to economic and social problems.

In the first section below I present the key ingredients of Sweden's active labor market policy and show how they form a universal framework within which selective measures optimize employment opportunities for women. I then turn to the means through which Sweden has attempted to achieve equality in pay and non-discriminatory employment practices. This involves a detailed discussion of collective bargaining and its significance to Swedish economic management, followed by a discussion of Sweden's recent equality legislation.

Labor Market Policies

Sweden's labor market policy contains three main components: training, employment, and creation of jobs. Unemployment is dealt with at the same time as training. There is only one agent, in fact, one person, and not two offices as in Britain, responsible for the pre-employment and job placement functions. To present the rationale behind the links in labor market policy is to analyze a unique approach to economic management. It rests on the active role of the state in Sweden in redirecting the exigencies of both the labor market and the economy as a whole.

Institutionally, labor market policies and programs are unified through the National Labor Market Board, Arbetsmarknadsstyrelsen (AMS), an autonomous agency not under the direction of the Cabinet. One of the important features of the board is its composition: of its fifteen members, six are union representatives, and three are representatives of the employers' organization. Since the 1950s Parliament has periodically reviewed the operations of the AMS, and has gradually increased its functions and strengthened its capacities. After the first major review of the AMS by a royal commission, Parliament passed a bill in 1966 laying down these general guidelines for labor market policy:

> Labor market policy is . . . an important branch of economic policy. Its aim is to achieve and maintain full, productive and freely chosen employment. This aim cannot be achieved once and for all. Full employment can only be ensured through measures which are constantly adjusted to current requirements.[1]

After a second review, Parliament passed a new bill in 1976 outlining a further development of employment strategy: "The task of employment policy is to give employment opportunities to everybody who wants them."[2] Central to achieving these broad goals is the integration of multiple functions performed at the level of the board's local employment offices.

The Employment Office

When individuals first enter the local employment service office, they can freely browse through the complete listing of job vacancies and contact employers on their own. Since 1976 it has been mandatory for employers to notify employment offices of all vacancies, along with information about the nature of the work required, pay, and promotion possibilities. The employment offices no longer keep statistics on the number of persons they assist. The self-service

[1] "Swedish Labor Market Policy," *Fact Sheets on Sweden* (March 1979).
[2] Ibid.

system and the frequent requests for information by phone make tabulation impossible. It is assumed that all persons looking for a job will consult the employment offices (it is estimated that about 85% do) because of their comprehensive information and other services, and because they are a public monopoly. So as not to overburden the staff, the services offered are "graduated."[3] That is, only when in-depth assistance is required does an individual become an actual client and register with the office. A staff member is then assigned, and forms are filled out. The task of job placement now takes on the quality of "casework," the goal of which is employment or re-employment, not, it must be noted, to provide financial assistance. The employment offices have nothing to do with unemployment benefits, which are dispensed through private insurance funds.[4] To help in vocational guidance, which is an integral part of the services, the staff make heavy use of aptitude tests, which they or coworkers are trained to administer. Furthermore, the staff are knowledgeable about two situations: all immediate and specific vacancies as well as general trends in the labor market. Developments in labor shortages or oversupply are closely monitored at AMS headquarters and are intended as part of the standard arsenal of information for local offices. Computers are also used to help match individuals with job vacancies. The staff/client ratio is high, especially compared to Britain; during the 1960s the ratio was never lower than 1:15; in Britain the analogous ratio approximated 1:119.[5]

Two services offered by the employment offices—job re-

[3] Santosh Mukherjee, *Making Labour Markets Work: A Comparison of UK and Swedish Systems* (London: PEP, Broadsheet 532, January 1972). The following discussion is based on his Chapter 6.

[4] The staff notify the private insurance office, although it is in principle up to the individual to arrange for her or his own benefits. It is necessary to register at an unemployment office in order to receive unemployment benefits. The staff also help arrange for other forms of public financial assistance, if necessary. But this is coincident to the main task of finding a job.

[5] Comparable data are no longer kept.

cruitment and occupational guidance—contain special features to encourage women to enter the labor market and to help them find satisfying, long-term jobs. One means of recruitment is extensive advertising campaigns in the mass media; many contain targeted messages about job opportunities for women and about the services and assistance available at the employment offices. When women seek occupational guidance, they are advised to take jobs that offer opportunities for advancement and security of employment, and if their aptitude tests show potential, they are further advised that many such jobs can be found in fields non-traditional for their sex, particularly engineering and skilled industrial work. The next step in the labor market program is training.

Training Programs

One option available to persons registering at the employment office is to enroll in a training program. This program is open to anyone who is unemployed, threatened with unemployment, returning to the labor market after an absence, or willing to train in fields in which labor shortages exist. The courses are organized and sponsored jointly by the AMS and the National Board of Education. A wide range of courses is offered in almost every occupational category, including some refresher courses for certain professionals. Within the last decade a new type of course has been added to the roster; these are general courses, not vocational, supplementing secondary school certification, preparing individuals for continuing education or reorienting them to the labor market and its requirements.[6] The length of the courses ranges from a few weeks to two years. While enrolled, all trainees receive a stipend which is somewhat higher than they would receive were they to

[6] These are not part of the general adult education courses run by the Department of Education. The AMS courses are enriching, sometimes fulfilling continuing education requirements, but often not. The courses being discussed here are related purposely to future employability.

be unemployed. (It is comparable to the wage in an un-skilled industrial job.) Training is thus an alternative to unemployment, benefiting both the individual and, in the long run, the economy.

In Sweden training serves two broader economic pur-poses: it enables structural change to take place in industry and it counters fluctuation in the business cycle. With re-gard to the first, the rationale of any training program is to enable workers to acquire new skills or to adapt existing skills so as better to meet the changing needs of industry for labor. In Sweden, trends in industrial productivity are a continual component of labor market analysis. With the support of Sweden's largest trade union, the Swedish Trade Union Confederation (LO), the government has developed policy initiatives designed to phase out failing industries and to assist in the expansion of the more productive in-dustries.[7] Of course, the phasing out of failing industries is a rare occurrence (it has actually occurred only in the textile industry), but the lip-service paid to the policy at least means that tabs are kept on the relationship between productivity and future needs for labor. LO support is crucial—it tolerates the unemployment that results from structural changes because, in the short run, unemploy-ment is quickly reabsorbed by the sort of active training program offered by AMS.[8] The long-run benefits for em-ployment and productivity are clear.

Following from this, a second purpose for training has developed and recently has become more important. Training has come to be used as a countercyclical measure,

[7] The British counterpart to LO, the TUC, does not support such a policy. We might note that the previous non-socialist government in Swe-den subsidized some "failing" industries. (The policy of phasing them out is a difficult one to maintain.) However, these were industries in vital primary resources, justifying the measure on non-ideological grounds.

[8] Whenever a plant closes down, there is close cooperation between employers, unions, and local AMS officials on what opportunities to pro-vide each individual worker made redundant. (Personal interview, AMS, May 1982).

designed to absorb excess unemployment during recessionary periods. It is a measure that helps maintain a higher level of aggregate demand than many alternatives, such as unemployment benefits or more costly relief work.[9] During recent periods of heavy unemployment (which began in 1968), the number of trainees has, indeed, increased. Interestingly, when unemployment eased, a decrease in the number of trainees, which might be expected, did not take place. This is probably because the training program has taken on a special quality in its own right. It performs a broad social function, picking up where formal education leaves off in preparing persons for a lifetime of employment. In addition, the training program has been expanded to serve additional groups, such as marginal and handicapped workers, as well as increasing numbers of returnees, mostly women. Each year the National Labor Market Board decides how many training positions will be open and in which fields according to its informed calculation of economic needs.

The training program discussed here is a public sector function. Companies and industries in the private sector conduct their own training programs. The government has encouraged them to adopt the same rationale and to grant the same significance to training that exists in the public programs. For example, during periods of economic difficulty, companies which place employees in training, instead of laying them off or firing them, receive government grants. The amount is not large, but it certainly helps.[10] During the late 1970s, about 5% of the employed labor force participated in company-sponsored training pro-

[9] Britain of course relies on unemployment benefits. One OECD report compared total expenditure on unemployment compensation as a percentage of GDP. The figures for Britain were 0.55 in 1970 and 0.78 in 1979; for Sweden 0.26 in 1970, 0.45 in 1979, *OECD Observer* (May 1982), p. 11.

[10] In 1980 the amount was 24 SwKr per hour per person after the first 40 hours, up to a maximum of 960 hours. One SwKr (Swedish krona) = $0.23 (approximately).

grams, which are of nearly the same broad range as the public ones and are either preparatory to a job or are attended on-the-job. However, in its 1980/81 report, the AMS noted that in-plant training was becoming less extensive than expected. The report added, "The subsidy for persons threatened with redundancy was not a sufficient incentive for firms to choose training rather than lay-offs/short-time work and benefits from unemployment funds. Other forms of in-plant training have likewise been utilized on a small scale."[11]

Nevertheless, adult training, especially in the public sector, is an important component of Sweden's manpower policies, and it received the same support from the nonsocialist as from the Social Democratic government. At least three times as many people attend training courses in Sweden as in Britain, measured in absolute numbers, and Sweden's population is only one-seventh of Britain's. In fact the Swedish training program affects about 1% of the total labor force at any one time, and 3% within the span of a year. In addition, government expenditure on training programs in Sweden is far above that in Britain, again measured in absolute terms, and the continuing increase far outstrips the British.[12] This expenditure reflects many differences between the two countries, not least of which is the centrality of training to labor market policies as a whole.

The special impact of the training program on women is seen in Table 4.1. In the 1960s women constituted only 40% of the new trainees; that figure gradually rose during the 1970s to a high of 55%, but by 1980 it had declined to 49%. The table also shows that the proportion of women in such traditional fields as humanistic, research, and service occupations is declining, and their proportion in such non-traditional fields as agriculture and manufacturing is

[11] National Labour Market Board, *Swedish Employment Policy: Annual Report, 1980/81* (Stockholm: AMS, 1981), p. 17.

[12] Mukherjee, *Making Labour Markets Work*, Chapter 2.

TABLE 4.1   Number of Persons Who Started Labor Market Training, 1970-1980, by Course and Sex

	Total	Women	% Women	Total	Women	% Women
	Technical, Scientific, Sociological, Humanistic and Artistic			Medical and Health Services (included in technical, etc.)		
1970	11,557	7,818	68	6,208	5,978	96
1975	10,006	7,496	75	6,110	5,645	92
1980	23,867	18,768	78	20,140	17,935	89
	Administrative Work			Accounting and Clerical		
1970	55	12	22	7,238	6,020	83
1975	135	33	24	6,282	5,485	87
1980	124	50	40	13,383	11,689	87
	Commercial			Agriculture, Forestry, Fishing		
1970	633	349	55	1,688	129	8
1975	632	351	56	2,201	490	22
1980	1,145	625	54	4,596	1,194	26
	Mining, Quarrying, etc.			Transport, Communications		
1970	100	—	—	1,128	232	21
1975	161	2	1	2,157	377	17
1980	303	51	17	4,875	658	13
	Manufacturing, Machine maintenance, etc.			Services		
1970	20,834	3,886	19	10,398	9,892	95
1975	25,669	6,656	26	8,153	7,475	92
1980	23,824	2,951	12	5,757	4,270	74
	Total (includes work not elsewhere classified)					
1970	79,328	42,107	53			
1975	80,758	44,631	55			
1980	86,445	42,568	49			

Source: National Labour Market Board, *Equality in the Labour Market, Statistics* (Stockholm: AMS, 1980), pp. 12-13.

increasing. However, the trend toward desegregating the occupational structure is not consistent, for the proportion of women in accounting, clerical, and commercial work is also increasing, and the continuing dominance of women in the health services is overwhelming. Of course, public health is also the field in which the greatest number of job vacancies continues to occur (as well as in other traditional women's fields, such as education, and legal, social scientific, and artistic work; see Chapter 2). The AMS acknowledges that these fields are becoming saturated, but it can only advise its trainees to take courses in, for example, technological or manufacturing trades. The training programs are not supposed to be based on client demand, but rather oriented toward opening up bottlenecks, including those based on sex-role stereotyping. However, the AMS has been only marginally successful in performing this function for women. A comparison of Tables 4.1 and 4.2 shows that the distribution of women in training courses closely reflects their basically segregated occupational distribution. All in all, training courses have contributed to an increase in the number of women entering and re-entering the labor market and to some very small changes in occupational choice.[13]

Job Creation

To be effective a training program must be coordinated with other economic measures. One such measure should be designed to ease the burden on training as the main device to absorb unemployment; another should assure that jobs exist after the courses are completed. As for the first,

[13] The best measure of a training program's success would be the number of jobs found by trainees. Unfortunately, such data are not kept. It was acknowledged to me, however, that while women are taking training courses in manufacturing skills (often at the urging of local occupational guidance counselors), they have not been as willing or as able to find jobs in manufacturing. (Personal interview, AMS, May 1982). Traditionalism persists in Sweden, although not on as grand a scale as in Britain.

TABLE 4.2   Occupational Structure of the Labor Force, 1969-1980
            (Annual Average, thousands, Age 16-74)

	Total	Women	% Women	Total	Women	% Women
	Technical, Scientific, Sociological, Human- istic and Artistic			Medical and Health Services (included in technical, etc.)		
1969	707	320	45.3	187	172	92.0
1975	917	443	48.3	263	243	92.4
1980	1,113	585	52.6	336	305	90.8
	Administrative			Accounting and Clerical		
1969	81	10	12.3	413	307	74.3
1975	82	9	11.0	492	386	78.5
1980	98	16	16.3	517	412	79.7
	Commercial			Agriculture, Forestry, Fishing		
1969	360	174	48.3	321	75	23.4
1975	354	170	48.0	272	67	24.6
1980	343	165	48.1	235	57	24.3
	Transport, Communications			Manufacturing, Machine maintenance, etc.		
1969	258	49	19.0	1,239	185	14.9
1975	251	56	22.3	1,218	203	16.6
1980	257	62	24.1	1,099	174	15.8
	Services			Total		
1969	471	372	79.0	3,855	1,494	38.8
1975	541	423	78.2	4,129	1,756	42.5
1980	571	434	76.0	4,232	1,906	45.0

Source: National Labour Market Board, *Equality in the Labour Market, Statistics* (Stockholm: AMS, 1980), pp. 4-5.

Sweden continues to maintain a large program of public relief works that also expands during periods of heavy unemployment. The government has injected the same broad scope into the concept of public works as it has into training. Besides the commonplace construction works, a new category of "archive" work has been added. This is usually general office work in public institutions, but it has also included research or cultural projects. In addition, health and other public services have been expanded under the rubric of relief work. However, whenever an improvement in unemployment takes place, the number of persons in relief work decreases, unlike the number in training. Funding for public sector relief work is the only measure the non-socialist government curtailed, and it did not do so until 1980.

The Swedish government actively uses other methods of creating jobs as well. For example, many of the increases in public sector expenditures have been explicitly aimed at increasing the number of jobs.[14] This measure was favored more by the social democratic than the non-socialist government. Health care and education in particular have grown and have contributed enormously to the expansion of regular, permanent jobs. Also important is what the government has been doing vis-à-vis the private sector. The Swedish government, whatever the party in power, has never been reluctant to give grants or use other inducements to encourage the private sector to follow public policy guidelines. The main method of stimulating the private sector to create additional employment during periods of slump is through a system of investment funds.[15] By law certain companies (incorporated associations, joint stock companies, and savings banks) can gain a tax advantage by allocating up to 40% of their annual pre-tax profits to a special fund, called the Investment Reserve Fund. Each company's taxable profit is then reduced by the amount allocated. The government controls the Fund and releases various amounts

[14] It will be recalled that in Britain the expansion of the public sector in the 1960s was initiated to increase aggregate demand, one indirect consequence of which was to be, it was hoped, an increase in employment. See Chapter 2.

[15] This exists in Britain too, but is much less used and much less institutionalized. The Swedish system is described in detail in "The Swedish System of Investment Funds," *Fact Sheets on Sweden* (June 1980).

back to the private sector for investment to stimulate demand when the labor market is showing signs of slackness.

Another method of creating additional employment is through subsidies to private employers who establish relief jobs. The government covers 75% of the total wage per new person hired for a maximum of six months. At least three-quarters of the persons who enter private sector employment in this way stay on in their jobs after the period of state subsidization is over. Finally, the most recent innovation in the Swedish system of incentives consists of new recruitment grants, subsidies of varying amounts given to companies or industries that increase their number of new jobs. To enable some groups, such as the handicapped, to make the transition to the regular labor market, the government provides grants to employers who hire them (90% of pay for the first year, gradually reduced for successive years). And, as part of Sweden's regional policy, assistance is also given to new industrial establishments in the more remote or less advantaged areas.

The benefit to women of the Swedish conception of relief work is also apparent in the numbers assisted. Table 4.3 indicates that the idea that relief work is for unemployed men doing construction work is fast fading. The latest figures show that over half of the relief work jobs in industry were taken by women. Of course, the proportion of women working in the service sector, and especially in nursing, is also high. Nevertheless, it is noteworthy that these traditional women's jobs have been newly created to accommodate the increasing number of women in the labor market.

Within each of the three components of labor market policy—placement, training, and job creation—something special exists for women. In each program a positive "selectivity" encourages women's full participation in the labor market. However, in each program we can also see a recurrence of one of the main problems in women's employment: occupational segregation. It is incumbent upon us to examine what specifically is being done in Sweden

TABLE 4.3 Persons on Relief Work (Annual Averages)

Type of Work	1972/73			1975/76			1979/80		
	Total	No. of Women	% Women	Total	No. of Women	% Women	Total	No. of Women	% Women
Roads	4,564	87	1.9	2,255	78	3.5	1,098	39	3.5
Water, drainage	2,728	45	1.6	1,392	29	2.0	688	12	1.7
Building	4,545	62	1.4	889	25	2.8	810	22	2.7
Forestry	4,585	163	3.6	3,688	158	4.3	3,282	154	4.7
Nature conservation	1,904	98	5.1	1,069	140	13.1	1,717	86	5.0
Culture projects	797	35	4.4	317	34	10.7	394	19	4.8
Military projects	214	13	6.1	144	4	2.8	114	1	0.9
Tourism, recreation	916	12	1.3	220	9	4.1	328	11	3.3
Industrial	1,865	909	48.7	1,812	932	51.4	673	386	57.3
Services	3,630	1,541	42.5	4,299	2,284	53.1	13,820	7,841	56.7
Nursing	645	537	83.3	760	649	85.4	3,070	2,519	82.0
Totals (includes other projects)	32,644	3,798	11.6	21,280	4,619	21.7	34,282	14,011	40.9

Source: National Labour Market Board, *Equality in the Labour Market, Statistics* (Stockholm: AMS, 1980), pp. 15-16.

with regard to this persisting obstacle to full equality before we can adequately assess the level of conceptualization of the problem in women's employment within Swedish policies.

Desegregating the Occupational Structure

Efforts specifically aimed at desegregating the occupational structure strike at the heart of the problem in women's employment: dual and internal labor markets. This is a structural goal and as such constitutes a universal framework. Special measures for women in the direction of structural change ought to constitute selective measures within the universal framework. As presented below, both of these dimensions, the selective and the universal, exist in the Swedish measures.

Three major labor market measures have been directed at desegregating the occupational structure.[16] The main method in all three has been the provision of special government grants for training and hiring women. One measure is part of Sweden's regional policy, which has stipulated a sex quota in grants to newly developing firms or industries within Sweden's more northern or outlying regions. Unemployment in these regions is higher than elsewhere, and special grants are available to expand or relocate industrial bases outside the large and more prosperous urban centers. Since 1974 these grants have stipulated that companies receiving the grant must hire workers in the proportion of at least 40% of each sex. This is significant in that the jobs are mostly in industry or manufacturing. In addition, it departs from the traditional tendency of having new jobs

[16] Special efforts also are being made in the schools. In 1969 Parliament passed a new bill revising school curricula. All elementary school children now take the same or very similar courses (including obligatory instruction in home economics, child care, and technology) to minimize the influence of sex, social class, or area of residence on choice of field of specialization. However, changes in traditional fields of specialization are barely visible, at either secondary school or university level.

go to unemployed men first. The success of this program has been mixed. The increase in women's labor force participation has been higher in areas receiving regional development support than elsewhere, and, no doubt, more women received jobs than would have otherwise. Women accounted for about 35% of the new recruits, less than the stipulated 40%.[17] The disparity was due, in part, to the granting of exemptions, for example, where persons with special skills were required. This occurred despite the fact that the local labor market board offices received grant applications, tried to keep up with skill needs, and, as much as possible, recruited and trained women to meet the new needs. The program was to have been a five-year experiment, ending in 1979. Because of its limited success, it has been extended, but its future status is uncertain.

Another measure, the "equality grant," was designed to encourage employers to hire and train women and men for positions that are not traditional for their sex. In its first year of operation, 1974, the grant supplemented the wages of 573 persons, but within three years the number went down to 101. Only one man was among the recipients. Recognizing that the scheme was becoming increasingly ineffective because of limitations in the range of occupations it covered, the amount of the stipend, and other restrictive clauses, the AMS pressed for changes—which the government granted. The "equality grant" has now been given renewed strength and, in 1980, supplemented the wages of 883 persons. Still, the government and the National Labor Market Board consider this number to be small, and unless the uptake increases, the grant will be phased out.

A third labor market pilot scheme has been more successful in achieving its purposes. Begun in 1973 in one

[17] Berit Rollen, "Equality between Men and Women in the Labor Market: The Swedish National Labor Market Board," in Ronnie Steinberg Ratner (ed.), *Equal Employment Policy for Women: Strategies for Implementation in the United States, Canada, and Western Europe* (Philadelphia: Temple University Press, 1980), p. 193.

county (Kristianstad, from which the experiment's name is derived) a project was arranged to inform women job-seekers (most of whom were housewives) about training and job opportunities in occupations traditionally held by men. Training courses followed, and certain industries were selected to hire the women.[18] The project spread to six counties within a few years, and 2,000 women found jobs under it. It is still operating, now in fifteen counties. This experiment may have been more successful than others because it did not threaten any male jobs, as did the experiment in regional policy. In addition, the industries participating were already thriving, and grant-assisted expansion was welcome. The grants did not alter anything these industries were doing—they simply added on.

Each of these measures for desegregating the occupational structure was aimed at the demand side of employment—at employers and at the structure of industry and industrial development. These measures complement well, then, the occupational guidance and training components of labor market policy.[19] The conception of the problem in women's employment approaches the social structural level which provides a universal framework within which selective measures have been developed to fully integrate women into the labor market. While granting these policies

[18] Liljeström studied the first experiment, interviewing the women and their husbands, children, workmates, and employers. In the main the women were poorly educated and working class. The new job, and the training and self-improvement gave all of the women great personal satisfaction. However, there were difficulties of adjustment within families, especially on the part of husbands. Rita Liljeström, et al., *Sex Roles in Transition: A Report on a Pilot Program in Sweden* (Stockholm: The Swedish Institute, 1975). Both this experiment and the "equality grant" were devised by an advisory council to the Prime Minister on Equality between Men and Women, which is discussed below.

[19] For further discussions of Sweden's various labor market programs and measures see, Joan M. McCrae, "Swedish Labour Market Policy for Women," *Labour and Society*, 4 (1977), p. 398; *Labor Market Reforms in Sweden: Facts and Employee Views* (Stockholm: The Swedish Institute, 1979); Hilda Scott, *Sweden's "Right to be Human": Sex-Role Equality: The Goal and the Reality* (Armonk, N.Y.: M. E. Sharpe, 1982), Chapter 2.

and measures such theoretical significance, however, we must note the fact that they have not been altogether successful in achieving their goals. In particular, the occupational segregation of women remains a formidable barrier to equality. At this point in the analysis I can only suggest that the reason for this shortcoming is the division of labor within the tripartite system in Sweden. The domain of on-the-job concerns is not that of the state alone, as are education and pre-employment training, for instance. On-the-job concerns have been the official domain of collective agreements between unions and employers since the 1930s (and by tradition since much earlier). In this domain, the agreed norm has been that the state act as a partner in the tripartite system, not as a leader. Its role is to facilitate consensus, not transform relations. We will see this much more clearly when we discuss collective bargaining in wage agreements.

Summary and Assessment

The preceding analysis points out that the Swedish state takes an activating (as opposed to a reactive) role in both the labor market and general industrial policies. The state assumes control for establishing policy and ensures that the means to implement it exist. But the state does not act entirely alone. The private sector is in close concert at every point of state intervention. (Most industries in Sweden are private not public sector enterprises.) State intervention certainly influences the initial course taken by industries, through application of fiscal and monetary incentives that cannot be refused. In addition, the future of industry is strongly influenced by state policy in steering workers according to trends suggested by labor market research and industrial analyses conducted by the AMS. The state justifies its actions in terms of macroeconomic policy; that is, these measures are good for the economy as a whole. It has not applied strong controls to coerce the direction taken by specific industries. Nevertheless, industries follow suit because it tends to be in their best interests to do so. Market-rational factors are not absent from this well-coordinated plan for economic stability. What is novel is the way in which market-rational factors function within the framework of a planned system. An analogous point can be made for the combination of macro and micro factors, in which the macro-level forms the universal framework and the micro-level the selective measures within it.

This combination of factors has particular significance for women. The organizing framework of labor market policy is that freely chosen jobs should exist for all who want them. This policy has positive implications not only for women but also for overall economic growth. The micro-level measures to implement this policy exist in the three components of labor market policy—training, employment, and job creation—as well as in special measures to desegregate the occupational structure.

Swedish labor market policies for women are exemplars of the functioning of Titmuss's conception of "positive discrimination," that is, selective measures within a universal framework. Women's employment and the problems women encounter in employment are not set apart from the norm of employment policy in general, a clear indication that the social structural conception is at work. Women's employment is seen as contributing to national goals, not just to personal goals of self-fulfillment. Since the 1960s the government has actively encouraged women to join the labor market.[20] As we saw in Chapter 2, the demand for women workers stemmed from the robust economic growth Sweden was experiencing at that time.[21] Later, when the econ-

[20] Various government measures have included job creation programs as well as such social and family policies as day care programs. See Chapter 6.

[21] Recall the government's role in stimulating economic growth. In the 1960s part of the new demand for labor was filled by immigrants. Some studies suggest that the government may have turned to women workers to avoid the problems created by vast immigration. Cf. Carolyn Teich Adams and Kathryn Teich Winston, *Mothers at Work: Public Policies in the*

omy slowed down, women's employment remained stable, one indication that women workers in Sweden are not as marginalized within the economy as they are in Britain. We cannot therefore attribute the policy differences simply to the differences in demand for women workers, nor to differences in traditional attitudes about women working. The role of the state in taking the lead to change social attitudes and to assure women's employment stability has been demonstrated here.

This analysis of women and work in Sweden leaves unanswered some nagging questions, the most significant of which concerns the considerable occupational segregation that persists despite occupational guidance and attempts at change. In the next section I will address these questions directly in the context of other facilitative measures for women's employment, specifically measures with regard to pay and discrimination. We will see a peculiar contrast in the role of the Swedish state in these matters compared to those examined above.

Equal Pay and Anti-Discrimination Measures: Tripartism at Work

Labor market policies are concerned mostly with unemployment and employability. They take into account women's special problems, such as sex discrimination and occupational segregation, insofar as these hinder the prospects for full employment of women, especially at entry level. But for a fuller appreciation of what is being done to eliminate employment barriers, we must also look at measures taken on the job, by employers and unions, individually and collectively. In contrast to the active state leadership shown above for labor market and economic policies, when it comes to on-the-job matters the state in

---

United States, Sweden, and China (New York: Longman, 1980). However, immigrants mainly filled service sector and manual jobs, not the professional and clerical jobs that women were entering.

Sweden remains remarkably in the background. Its role is to facilitate the negotiations between unions and employers. This secondary role is most apparent in the implementation of Sweden's recent equality legislation, which gives priority to collective agreements for equal pay. I present first the process of collective bargaining since this is the basis not only of much employment equality for women but also of general economic policy in Sweden.

Collective Bargaining and Equal Pay

Swedish wage policy began in 1938 with an agreement, the Saltsjöbaden Agreement, between the largest trade union organization in Sweden, the LO, and the Swedish Employers' Confederation (SAF). The 1938 agreement

established negotiation procedures including grievance procedure; rules which must be observed in case of dismissals and lay-offs; limitations on strikes, lockouts and similar direct action; and a special procedure applying to conflicts jeopardizing vital interests of the community.[22]

It also established a procedure for future regular bargaining sessions. In one of these, in 1952, the LO and SAF began negotiations on wage policies, eventually including recommendations on working hours and fringe benefits as well. These negotiations were conducted annually for the first few years, then bi-annually. The terms of contract now last for three years. It was only after one of these agreements, reached in 1960, that Sweden ratified the ILO Convention on Equal Pay, even though the convention itself was formulated in 1951. The agreements reached by the LO and SAF are not limited to their affiliates, for "all other categories of private and public employees base their wage demands on [the LO-SAF] recommendation."[23] Since all

[22] M. Donald Hancock, *Sweden: The Politics of Postindustrial Change* (Hinsdale, Ill.: The Dryden Press, 1972), p. 151.
[23] Ibid., p. 152.

unions negotiate with SAF, disseminating the spirit of the LO-SAF framework rests with SAF. Not all unions, for example, the Swedish Foremen's and Supervisors' Union, agree with all of LO's positions and principles. The role of the state in these bargaining sessions is limited to that of observer and mediator, when necessary. When disputes between the LO and SAF require arbitration, or when implementation results in conflict, settlement is reached through the Labor Court and through various laws governing mediation. This has led one scholar to describe the Swedish state's role in labor relations as "relatively passive," adding that "labor market relations in Sweden are virtually free of direct government interference."[24] Since this represents such a clear departure from the active, interventionist state presented above (and in Chapter 7), we must explore it further.

The first point to emphasize is that, although government representatives may appear to sit on the margins of collective bargaining negotiations, they are hardly disinterested observers. Wage agreements are a central factor in the overall functioning of the economy. If wages rise too quickly, a spiraling effect on inflation could result. So how does government let its views be known? As one commentator said about the first Saltsjöbaden meeting: "To prevent legislation was the principal motive."[25] That is, the threat of the use of government authority is "overhanging." This point, too, requires elaboration.

In Sweden the collective agreements between trade unions and employers are part of the machinery of government in two ways. First, the agreements are integrated into overall economic policy. The unions base their requests for wage increases on projections of economic productivity; their requests are responded to within the same framework; and the results are incorporated into policies for, for example, prices, industrial investment, balance of payments. Second,

---

[24] Ibid., pp. 151, 150.
[25] Quoted by Shonfield, *Modern Capitalism*, p. 199.

not only is the outcome of collective bargaining a part of national economic policy but so is the process. So far, representatives of both labor and employers have been as involved as interested bystanders in economic policy making as government representatives are in collective bargaining. For example, government industrial policy could not survive without strong union backing. Swedish trade unions support the policy of phasing out less productive industries in favor of greater investment in the more productive ones. It is a risky policy for labor, for it means layoffs and loss of jobs. Union support is based on the assurance that measures have been developed, some of them with union help, that will pick up the unemployed. These measures include manpower programs as well as policies for assisting labor mobility through moving and rehousing subsidies. We see here how the tripartite system functions—the three partners are mutually interdependent. So, too, is the policy nexus developed through coalition.[26]

Not since 1948 has the government tried to impose an incomes policy in Sweden. Wage policy is the result of collective bargaining, and in this process the visibility of the state is deliberately underplayed in favor of agreement between unions and employers. Unlike the British counterpart, furthermore, wage policy making in Sweden is integral to national economic policy. What does all this mean for equal pay?

Let us examine first the general trend in wage increases over the years. Table 4.4 shows a great deal of fluctuation in the total wage increases of industrial workers. Moreover, industrial white-collar workers, as a group, have fared somewhat worse than all industrial workers. The difference, however, is due not to negotiated increases, but to "wage drift." Wage drift is the increase in wages over and above the negotiated agreement due to productivity increases, overtime or other increased work activity, move-

---

[26] I elaborate the process of consensus-seeking government in Sweden in Chapter 6 in the context of day care policy.

TABLE 4.4   Annual Wage Increases for Adult Industrial
Workers, 1956-1971 (%)

	Negotiated Increase	Fringe Benefits	Wage Drift	Total Increases
1956	4.3	0	3.6	7.9
1957	2.6	0	2.8	5.4
1958	2.6	0	2.0	4.6
1959	2.0	0	2.6	4.6
1960	4.0	2.0	4.2	10.2
1961	3.6	0.7	4.1	8.4
1962	4.8	0.7	3.3	8.8
1963	2.8	1.8	4.1	8.7
1964	2.1	2.3	4.9	9.3
1965	4.2	1.9	5.6	11.7
1966	4.4	0.4	4.1	8.9
1967	3.5	1.4	3.2	8.1
1968	3.2	0.4	3.5	7.1
1969	5.8	0.5	5.2	12.5
1970	3.4	0.7	7.0	11.1
1971	6.8	n.a.	2.2	9.0

Source: Horst Hart and Casten V. Otter, "The Determination of Wage Structures in Manufacturing Industry," in Richard Scase (ed.), *Readings in the Swedish Class Structure* (Oxford: Pergamon Press, 1976), p. 109.

ment of labor from lower to higher paying jobs, as well as idiosyncratic interpretations or applications of the negotiated agreement at the individual union or company level. Wage drift is expected, and it is expected to be higher among blue-collar than white-collar workers. This may explain some of the differences in negotiated agreements. These facts speak to the coordination of wage increases and overall economic activity. Where do occupation-related wage differentials come in? One step earlier.

The LO always asks for greater increases for those industries in which earnings tend to lag behind because of the weak bargaining positions of their individual unions. This accounts for some of the wage drift. Moreover, it is basic LO policy to attempt to narrow pay differentials between various industrial and occupational groups of workers. Its aim "is not to completely equalize wages but rather to establish a pattern of 'rational' differentiation based on differences in 'job requirement.' "[27] Figure 4.1 shows this trend in narrowing the wage gap between higher and lower paid workers.

The heart of the pay issue for women rests on this policy of restructuring the association between occupation and pay, and on LO's commitment and ability to achieve it. LO is the largest, most powerful and, in some ways, the most progressive trade union. Women now constitute over 40% of LO's membership, and their numbers in LO are greater than in any other union. Table 4.5 shows the distribution of women in unions affiliated with LO as well as their representation in union officialdom in 1976. LO's efforts will also affect many of Sweden's women workers who are not

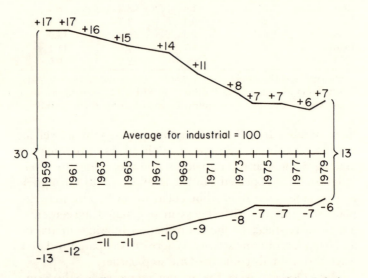

4.1. SAF-LO Collective Agreement Sectors Grouped by Relative Wage Levels, 1959-1979. Figures shown are ranges in percent. Curves show highest and lowest wages as compared to average. Source: Lennart Forsebäck, *Industrial Relations and Employment in Sweden* (Stockholm: The Swedish Institute, 1980), p. 80.

[27] Horst Hart and Casten V. Otter, "The Determinants of Wage Structures in Manufacturing Industry," in Richard Scase (ed.), *Readings in the Swedish Class Structure* (Oxford: Pergamon Press, 1976), p. 101.

unionized.[28] For LO informally represents the lower-paid workers as a group, including those who are not unionized, and women are the majority by far of the low-paid, even controlling for part-time work. To the extent that LO is successful in narrowing wage differentials, we might expect that, for example, nurses aides and sanitation workers together will be paid at a rate more comparable to, say, laboratory technicians.

There is no doubt that the changes in women's pay as a proportion of men's in industry, as shown in Figure 4.2, have resulted from LO's attempts to narrow wage differentials in general. This point should be emphasized; not until very recently has LO addressed collective negotiations specifically to women's issues. Earlier advances in women's equal pay have resulted from a general policy, not a women-specific one. In fact, LO's past concern with women-specific issues has been perfunctory. Only in 1977 did LO begin to negotiate an equality agreement with SAF—and even this was because of the threat of impending legislation. The agreement was very general and basically weak and so was renegotiated in 1982 to give it greater strength.

In the latest round of equality negotiations with SAF, LO coordinated its efforts with another union which organizes many women workers, TCO, the Central Organization of Salaried Employees. TCO represents workers in white-collar jobs. It contains almost as many women as LO, and women now make up about 50% of its membership. Less than rational pay differentials between occupational groups also occur in white-collar jobs, of course. TCO supports the general policy of narrowing wage differentials, saying it "demands a job valuation which will put a premium on the human and social importance of work. Women are above all employed in humanitarian and social sectors."[29] But narrowing of differentials among white-collar workers

[28] By 1980, about 90% of all women workers were in trade unions (about the same proportion as for men); about 75% of all women worked.

[29] TCO, *TCO's View of . . . Family Policy and Equal Opportunities* (Stockholm: Central Organization of Salaried Employees in Sweden, 1978), p. 2.

TABLE 4.5 Representation of Women in Selected Trade Unions (%)

Union (by industry)	Women Members	Congress Delegates	National Executive	Central Negotiating Board	Regional Executives
Garment workers	68.2	45.0	29.0	20.0	33.0
Sheet metal workers	0	0	0	0	0
Building workers	1.7	0.8	0	0	5.3
Electricians	0.2	0	0	0	0
Factory workers	29.0	9.5	9.0	10.0	11.0
Maintenance workers	57.0	16.6	9.5	17.0	24.0
Hairdressers	90.1	58.6	29.0	40.0	65.0
Social insurance, insurance	68.9	37.0	20.0	27.0	39.0
Graphic industry	25.1	5.0	5.8	5.8	13.0
Miners	8.1	3.0	0	0	n.a.
Retail, commercial	70.7	51.0	11.0	47.0	46.0
Hotel, restaurant	79.9	39.0	33.0	0	69.0
Municipal workers	76.8	33.5	45.0	45.0	33.0
Agriculture	17.4	1.8	0	7.6	5.0
Food	39.5	14.0	9.0	9.7	8.0

Metal workers	16.2	1.0	0	0	4.0
Musicians	17.2	n.a.	n.a.	n.a.	n.a.
Painters	0.1	0	0	0	0
Pulp and paper	16.9	4.0	0	0	7.0
Seamen	19.1	5.3	0	0	n.a.
Forest workers	4.8	4.0	0	0	1.6
Chimney sweepers	0	0	0	0	0
State employees	24.8	10.0	6.6	13.0	10.6
Transport workers	11.5	6.8	11.0	13.0	12.5
Wood industry	12.7	1.6	0	2.0	1.4
Total	35.6	15.0	9.0	14.0	13.0

Source: Hilda Scott, *Sweden's "Right to be Human": Sex-Role Equality: The Goal and the Reality* (Armonk, N.Y.: M.E. Sharpe, 1982), p. 177, as drawn from *Kvinnor i facket* [Women in Trade Unions] (Stockholm: LO, 1977).

is only gradually being realized for those in the public sector (a different union) and not the private sector. In addition, a less powerful trade union, but one that represents an important female occupational group, the Swedish Union of Clerical and Technical Employees in Industry (SIF), espouses an alternative policy, based on

> the desirability of an "individual" salary system in the sense that earnings should depend upon the individual's performance and the technical requirements of the job. . . . [T]he range of differentials between different groups of white-collar workers should be allowed to be influenced by the forces of supply and demand . . . in order to "satisfy career aspirations."[30]

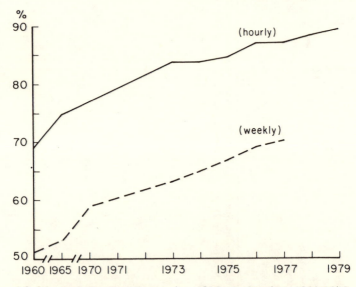

4.2. Women's Pay as a Proportion of Men's, Sweden, 1960-1979. Adapted from Swedish Trade Union Confederation, *This Is How We Work for Equality between Men and Women in Working Life and in the Trade Unions* (Stockholm: LO, 1980), p. 6. "Figures on Men and Women in the Labor Market," *Current Sweden*, No. 260 (November 1980), p. 9.

[30] Hart and Otter, "The Determinants of Wage Structures," p. 100.

This inconsistency among unions may weaken the bargaining positions of LO and TCO.

In sum, union action in Sweden has taken women's pay further than union action and legislation combined in Britain. Union efforts in Sweden to narrow wage differentials have made a significant impact on one of the unequal consequences of occupational segregation. The differences that remain between women's and men's pay reflect the failure of labor market (and educational) programs to achieve further real occupational desegregation through both demand and supply side initiatives.[31]

Legislation for Equality

Before 1980 there was very little special legislation for women in Sweden. A 1939 law, revised in 1945, makes it unlawful for an employer (even in private households) to fire a woman because she had become engaged, had married, or was expecting a child. There also remains some protective legislation for women workers. For example, women are not allowed to work with lead color; exemption is required for a woman to work in an active underground mine; and other safety rules related to pregnancy and motherhood still exist. But protective laws regulating such conditions as women's hours of work have been rescinded because they were considered to be restrictive and not genuinely protective. In 1960, Sweden ratified both ILO conventions relating to women's work (No. 100 on Equal Remuneration and No. 111 on Discrimination in Employment and Occupation). Other than this, legislation has not in the past been the preferred route toward equal working conditions in Sweden. Instead of special legislation, Swedish efforts to deal with sex discrimination in employment have

[31] For further discussions of the role of Swedish trade unions in women's pay and equality issues, see Alice Cook, "Collective Bargaining as a Strategy for Achieving Equal Opportunity and Equal Pay: Sweden and West Germany" in Ratner (ed.), *Equal Employment Policy*; and Hilda Scott, *Sweden's "Right to be Human,"* Chapter 3.

been subsumed under general legislation on job security. The Act on Security of Employment came into effect in 1974.[32] Under its terms an employer cannot dismiss an employee except for "acceptable reasons," which must be stated in writing, and which may be contested.[33] The Act also sets out rules for layoffs, including the order in which employees are to be let go. All dismissals must be immediately reported to the employment service.

Cases of contested unfair dismissal are first taken up by the union, and a settlement may be reached through collective bargaining. The power of this form of arbitration has been enhanced through a new law, the Act on Employee Participation in Decision-Making, effective since 1977 (the "employee" being the shop steward or elected union representative). If a settlement cannot be reached or if the dismissed person is not satisfied with the settlement, the next step would be to have the negotiating process repeated before an industrial tribunal, which would act as arbitrator. If further appeal is requested, the case can go before the Labor Court. Individuals can represent themselves before the Court only if the union refuses to do so. This specialized court is composed of three labor union representatives, two representatives from the employers' organization, and three judges appointed by the government. Since the court sets precedents, a system of rules has developed. The procedure for cases of sex discrimination would be similar to cases of unfair dismissal.

Much like the framework of collective bargaining, this legal framework contained nothing that pertained to the special problems of women workers. Both provided universal frameworks, to be sure, but without selective measures they were becoming stagnant, empty shells. In 1972

[32] Britain also has an Employment Protection Act, passed in 1975. It has no special effect for women beyond the Sex Discrimination Act. It elaborates what does and does not constitute unfair dismissal.

[33] After the written statement, an employee can still hold the job for a period of one to six months, depending on the circumstances, or until a court settlement has been reached.

the Social Democratic Prime Minister established an executive level Advisory Council on Equality Between Men and Women, explicitly to investigate the possibility of special legislation. In its 1975 report the Council took the position that:

> There is always a danger that taking special measures on behalf of one sex will entrench traditional modes of segregated treatment and work against equality between men and women in the longer run. . . . There has long been strong aversion in Sweden to the traditional type of protective legislation for women. Bringing about equality will require very big changes which cut into the whole social fabric. This is not a matter of isolated measures for women. That view has been much too common. The basic requirement instead is a politically all-embracing view of society's social and economic development to underpin reforms that will distribute work more evenly between the two sexes.[34]

Because of an impending election and consequent change in government, the push for legislation remained dormant for several years. Then the Liberal Party in particular began to press for special measures to secure advances in women's employment. Various motives lay behind this position. The Liberal Party wanted to make a symbolic political gesture on behalf of women. The coalition government could not rely on alternative means of influencing labor relations because it did not have the close partnership with organized labor that the Social Democrats had enjoyed. Finally, members of the Advisory Council on Equality, of whatever political persuasion, were unhappy with the apparent stag-

---

[34] Elisabet Sandberg, *Equality is the Goal* (Stockholm: The Swedish Institute, 1975), p. 10. This is a summary of the Council's report. The Council has now become the Equal Opportunity Commission, a permanent executive-level body, with broad advisory and research functions. It is a supporting arm of the Equality Ombudsman's office, which is discussed below.

nation in efforts to achieve equality for women through traditional decentralized methods, and so the Advisory Council more aggressively recommended legislation. Although the Act did not pass the first time it appeared in Parliament, because of Conservative Party opposition, it finally became law in December 1979. The Act on Equality provided what had been missing in Swedish measures for equality: a selective focus on women, but without destroying the strength of the universal framework within which these selective measures operate.

The Act on Equality Between Men and Women at Work

Although there was considerable skepticism about this Act when it was first created, politicians and trade unions alike have rallied to its support. Support did not arise because implementation of the Act has achieved so much more than could have been achieved without it; rather, the enforcement of the Act has strengthened previous tried and true methods of achieving equality for women. This pertains particularly to the process of collective bargaining. Moreover, implementation of the Act is completely within the framework of Sweden's other labor laws, particularly the Litigation in Labor Disputes Act (1974) and the Co-determination at Work Act (1976).

In certain of its main tenets, the Swedish legislation is not significantly different from the British. The Act places the blame for discrimination on employers and sets up a procedure for arbitration of grievances, beginning with attempts at conciliation and ending with the Labor Court. Some features in the Act make it weaker than the British legislation. For example, it covers only employment matters, and where collective agreements exist, these cannot be superseded or altered. Other features, however, make the Swedish Act stronger. For example, the burden of proof rests as much on the employer as on the victim; class action suits are permissible; and an Equality Ombudsman, an office established by the Act, advises claimants and their union representatives if so asked, or represents claimants not covered by a collective agreement. (Thus all claimants are represented, if not by a union, then by the Ombudsman.) If a collective agreement exists, however, the Ombudsman must work within its terms but can make suggestions for improvements. In this sense the Act does not supersede but strengthens collective bargaining. In all cases, the Ombudsman tries to avoid a court proceeding. However, settlements reached "privately" are by no means token—large compensations, similar to what a court might grant, are common.[35]

The Act contains two parts. The first sets out procedure for arbitration of grievances where collective agreements exist; the second part suggests the course of action the Ombudsman should take when there is no collective agreement setting the framework. Under the terms of the second part of the Act, "the employer shall pursue active efforts to promote equality at work."[36] This is basically a nondiscrimination clause, but as elaborated in the Act it includes the "obligation" to pursue affirmative action in hiring and promotion (aiming for a ratio of at least 40% of each sex). If, after an investigation, the Ombudsman finds the employer at fault, the employer "can be ordered to fulfil his obligation under penalty of a fine" or be taken to the labor court.[37]

Thus far, the Ombudsman's job has largely involved dissemination of information to the public at large and to employers and unions. In the first two years after the Act was passed, the Ombudsman's office received over 500

[35] For example, in one case 15,000 Swedish kronor (about $2,500 U.S.) were awarded for "moral injury"; in another case a sum to cover the loss of two years' pay was awarded (personal interview, Jämställdhetsombudsmannen, May 1982).

[36] *Act Concerning Equality Between Women and Men at Work*, Appendix 2 (Stockholm: Ministry of Labour, International Secretariat, July 1980), p. 2.

[37] *The Swedish Act on Equality between Women and Men at Work* (Stockholm: Ministry of Labour, July 1980), p. 2.

complaints, of which about 300 were actual discrimination as defined by the law. These complaints were dealt with either by letter or by negotiations. The Ombudsman took nine cases to the Labor Court (not including cases in which she has assisted union representatives at court). These were all for discrimination, not equal pay grievances. Of the four cases settled within the first two years, all were in favor of the claimant and provided substantial compensations.[38]

In sum, the consequences of this Act on Equality in Sweden cannot be said to herald a significantly stronger role on the part of the state. They do indicate the presence of the state in matters concerning equal opportunity for women workers, but a presence which is similar to the state's traditional role in labor relations. That is, the state closely watches over proceedings with the threat of greater intrusion if matters are not settled properly.

Summary and Assessment

Women in Sweden are in a much better position in the labor market than in most other advanced industrial nations, by almost every measure except occupational segregation.[39] Of their confinement to a limited variety of occupations, we can say that it is at least in higher categories of jobs—for example, nurse rather than factory worker. The measures that have been taken in Sweden to achieve women's relatively high employment status have emanated from both centralized and decentralized institutions. The state has been active in organizing and promoting a general labor market policy involving full employment and economic growth. This has constituted what we might call a universal policy framework for labor as a whole. Within this framework the state has also developed some special

[38] For the Ombudsman's own assessment of her office and its operations, see Inga-Britt Törnell, "The Equality Ombudsman at Work," *Social Change in Sweden*, No. 28 (April 1983).

[39] Organization for Economic Co-operation and Development, *Women and Employment* (Paris: OECD, 1980).

measures to enhance the labor market position of women, measures involving training and incentives to hire women. In this last category in particular, the state has treaded lightly so as not to invade too deeply the traditional prerogative of private employers. At the decentralized level, trade unions, in particular the LO, have adopted a general policy of narrowing wage differentials between low- and high-paid workers as a whole. As a by-product, this policy has advanced the cause of equal pay for women, who constitute the majority of low-paid workers. Not until very recently (with the threat of impending legislation) was collective bargaining aimed specifically toward the benefit of women. However, collective bargaining functions as does any form of pluralism—it is slow and tends to be incremental. Long, drawn-out, piecemeal accommodation does not in the end achieve sweeping change.

Hence, by the late 1970s a certain stagnation point had been reached in the continued advancement of the position of women workers in Sweden. At the behest of the Prime Minister's Council on Equality between Men and Women, an Act on Equality between Men and Women at Work was passed in December 1979. This legislation is limited in its scope and method. On the surface it is not as comprehensive, detailed, or bold as the British legislation. What it does is to reinforce the previous methods that had advanced the position of women workers—equal opportunities in training, hiring, and promotion, and collective bargaining for equal pay. But it takes these measures one step further by placing them within the domain of the state, signifying what was lacking before—a new role of responsibility on the part of the state for specialized, selective matters relating to equality for women workers. Because this Act reinforces a slow process of social change, it is still too soon to assess it fully, except to say that in principle it is promising. In 1982 the Social Democratic Party made a campaign pledge to strengthen the Act and its implementation. The SDP also pledged to renew the state's commitment to child care centers and the various labor market programs for training and employment of women, all of which had faltered under the non-socialist government and all of which are just as important as legislation to equality for women workers.

CONCLUSION

This chapter and the previous one have compared two modes of state intervention by two welfare states in policies to achieve equal employment opportunity for women. In those policies that pertain specifically to the labor market, such as training and placement measures, the contrast between Britain and Sweden is clear and expected. Labor market policies in Britain reveal that the role of the state is secondary to market forces in allocating labor resources, with the consequence that women's position in the labor market has not been significantly advanced by these measures. In contrast, the Swedish labor market policies indicate that the state is taking a strong role in directing the best use of all labor resources in conjunction with a well-developed industrial policy. The consequences for women appear primarily in increased employment rates, rather than a desegregation of the occupational structure.

In another area of policy—measures to reduce sex discrimination and achieve equal pay—an unexpected contrast emerges in the role of the state in Britain and Sweden. The two pieces of British legislation discussed in Chapter 4 seem to indicate a departure from the liberal mode. And in Sweden, the recent and not very challenging legislation to promote equality for women also represents a seeming departure from established, deeply interventionist state action. However, as the analysis has shown, neither apparent departure holds in practice. The British legislation is much weaker in implementation than on paper; its opponents have taken full advantage of its several loopholes and have rendered minimal its impact on women. The Swedish legislation has brought the state into an arena where its presence was needed. State intervention has served to buttress the already strong and successful mode of collective bargaining, making the tripartite partnership as pertinent to equality issues as to economic ones in general.

In sum, these chapters have established that for the achievement of greater equality for women, a concerted effort on the part of the state is required. Matters cannot be left to the goodwill of unions and employers, either individually or collectively. However, state action alone is also insufficient. Strong commitment at the decentralized level, too, is important. In both Britain and Sweden legislation was built on foundations established by collective bargaining. The different results may well be due to the fact that in Britain this foundation was much weaker than in Sweden. Finally, there may also be a lesson to be learned from the differences in the relationship between legislation and collective bargaining in these two countries. In Britain legislation and collective bargaining are rather independent processes, working beside and not necessarily with each other. In Sweden legislation draws on the process of collective bargaining to construct a more unified effort for achieving a common purpose. A fuller statement concerning the role of labor in helping to achieve women's employment equality awaits the analysis in Chapter 7.

CHAPTER 5

BRITAIN: THE ROLE OF
THE STATE IN THE
PROVISION OF DAY CARE

INTRODUCTION

In its approach to social policy Britain tends to follow the principles of a liberal type of welfare state. As depicted in Chapter 1, this means that Britain exhibits a distinct reluctance to intervene in the private affairs of society. A wide range of concerns are considered to be within the domain of public responsibility. However, when the state intervenes in these areas, the depth and mode of its intervention are limited. State action is not intended to alter significantly the terms of the situation that required state intervention: rather, it is intended to alleviate the misfortunes of the situation. The liberal approach is stronger in some areas of social policy than in others.[1] It is particularly strong in the one to be examined here: day care for children.

I chose to look at the provision of day care as a case study of the role of the state because this policy area, more than any of the others relating to women's employment, clearly reveals the tension that can accompany public intervention

---

[1] After World War II the state in Britain readily intervened in health care, but to this day it continues to do little for such victims of misfortune as battered women. There are many reasons, some issue-specific, some not, for differences in level and type of intervention and in general approaches to social problems, within one nation as well as among nations. For example, health care had influential advocates in post-World War II Britain. For a detailed study of differences in policy approaches and outcomes, see Hugh Heclo, *Modern Social Politics in Britain and Sweden: From Relief to Income Maintenance* (New Haven: Yale University Press, 1974).

into the sphere of the private. Child care is closely associated with the traditional role of women; it is a function of the private domain of the family. State provision of day care services interferes with the privacy of child care. A liberal welfare state, which by definition holds to the division between public and private concerns would have difficulty justifying intervention in this issue area. In my analysis, the reluctance of the British state to engage in day care provision, differently and further than it has, is linked to its adherence to liberal principles of state/society relations. This chapter demonstrates the prototype of state intervention in Britain.

The analysis, however, cannot be divorced fully from other constraints on state action in policies relating to women's employment. Both economic determinants and sex discrimination appear in the analysis in this chapter as elements interwoven into the rationale of state policy. That is, both economic constraints and the traditional role of women readily serve as justifications for limited state intervention. They are part of the array of objective criteria supporting an underlying system of action. But, in and of themselves, these empirical justifications are not the basic motivating force. In this analysis, principles of state/society relations form the "deep structure."

The first part of this chapter will review briefly the historical development of day care services in Britain from the early nineteenth century to the present. The short survey of the past demonstrates a familiar adage concerning Britain: "the extraordinary tenacity of older attitudes."[2] The second and main part of the chapter will analyze the mode of state intervention in day care provision. Three dimensions of the mode of intervention are studied: determinants, design, and institutionalization. The first will examine the set of circumstances that justifies the initiation of state intervention and the category of persons for whom

---

[2] Andrew Shonfield, *Modern Capitalism: The Changing Nature of Public and Private Power* (London: Oxford University Press, 1965), p. 88.

the state is intervening. The second dimension, design of intervention, will examine the form of intervention, which in this case is a public program, in terms of the purpose of the program, in both its immediate and long-range connotations, and the quality and quantity of provision. In describing the institutionalization of state intervention, the focus will be on the state institutions which give permanence to the system of day care provision, not only the bureaucracy itself but also the relations among the various agents of day care. Each of these dimensions of state intervention reveals a logic of action that is suggestive of a liberal rationale. The implications of this mode of state intervention for the central problem of this study, social equality for women, will be spelled out within the discussion of each dimension as well as in the conclusion.

The way the state goes about defining the parameters of its intervention and carrying out its goals has consequences, some intended, some not, on social relations. That some consequences are not intended does not make the logic of intervention any less rational. A liberal welfare state does not set out to restructure social relations. It comes as no surprise, then, that social equality is not advanced by the type of day care provision we see in Britain. What gives Britain the right to call itself a welfare state is that state intervention is intended to ameliorate, at least, the misfortunes of those for whom the state has accepted responsibility. My analysis raises questions about the consequences of achieving even this meager purpose. The provision of and the process of delivering this social service is being impaired, not by any lack of good will, nor even simply because it is a limited service for a welfare clientele. At every point of state action, the mode of intervention is reinforcing strong divisions within society: divisions between public and private and between social groups. No doubt this outcome is worse in this issue area than in others because it feeds on already existing strong divisions, based on social classes and the traditional role of women.

HISTORICAL CONTEXT

Before the era of industrialization, the day care of young children, along with other forms of social care, presented no difficulty since, for those women who engaged in some form of labor, either in agriculture or in commerce in the towns, the workplace and the home were part of the same immediate physical setting.[3] If a mother could not, for some reason, be with her small child, another family member was usually present to care for the child. A system of extended household relations also existed among the upper classes, for whom surrogate day care by non-relatives was dominant for centuries. Day care was thus part of the communal structure of pre-industrial society, and it resided within an emotionally diffuse ethos of social relationships.[4]

With industrialization, a process of social change began that loosened the nuclear family from its network of extended relations.[5] Families new to the urban centers were particularly vulnerable to emotional isolation. Social change had different consequences for the child care arrangements of different social classes. Upper-class women and the new strata of middle-class women, who did not work, maintained some form of household help, if not for children then for housework. Poorer women, who were drawn away from work in the home to work in the factory, and who had no relatives or friends to help them, had to leave their children either untended or casually tended by strangers. Eventually, by the twentieth century, one general consequence for child care was similar for all women: the mother became not only the main care-giver but also the emotional bastion of the family. This was particularly evident after

[3] Ross Davies, *Women and Work* (London: Arrow Books, 1975), Chapter 2.

[4] Philippe Ariès, *Centuries of Childhood: A Social History of Family Life* (New York: Vintage Books, 1962), Part Three.

[5] Peter Laslett, *The World We Have Lost: England Before the Industrial Age* (New York: Charles Scribner's Sons, 1965), argues that the extended family of pre-industrial society was a myth, and that industrialization did not transform family relations greatly.

World War I when servants and nannies failed to return to manage households.[6] Most women thus became unable to participate fully in the wider society and were confined instead to what came to be regarded as the "non-productive" sphere of home and family.

The separation of work and home and the development of the modern nuclear family that came with advancing industrialization also separated day care from its traditional, familial setting as a regular feature of everyday living. The first institutionalized day care arrangements for children of working mothers in Britain developed in the early nineteenth century. These were private and profit-making. One form was the "inferior" dame school, run as often as not by uneducated women who crowded as many children as possible into unhealthy quarters and even drugged them.[7] Interestingly, these conditions did not seem to arouse even the voluntary sector, which was actively petitioning for reform in other areas of working life and child abuse. Only later in the nineteenth century and early in the twentieth were a few new-style day nurseries set up, still mostly private and charging high fees.

Dame schools (and, later, day nurseries) contrasted with other "schools" for young children, which were oriented to the educational benefit of young children. Some of these "schools" were specifically for children of working mothers. One example is Robert Owen's nursery school for children of employees in his cotton mill in Scotland. Other schools

---

[6] Gathorne-Hardy's estimates indicate that the institution of the nanny continued in the interwar years, although not as widely as before. The real decline occurred during and after World War II. J. Gathorne-Hardy, *The Rise and Fall of the British Nanny* (London: Hodder and Stoughton, 1972).

[7] Drugging children was a "common practice." Jack Tizard, Peter Moss, Jane Perry, *All Our Children: Pre-school Services in a Changing Society* (London: Temple Smith/New Society, 1976), p. 42. In 1819, a government report, the Hadow Report, estimated that 53,624 children were in 3,102 dame schools, a large enough number although only a minority of the children of working mothers. Most of the others, if tended, were with relatives, friends, or neighbors. Ibid., pp. 50-51.

were attended by children from various backgrounds. For example, "infant schools" were public institutions voluntarily attended by children over the age of three. They were bleak but efficient, with large orderly classes and disciplined instruction in the three R's. Yet another type of nursery setting for young children were kindergartens, based on the child-oriented, developmental techniques of the German educator Fröbel.[8] From their inception in Britain in the 1850s, these enriching educational nursery schools were for middle-class children. They were few in number and mostly private. By the 1870s, however, some of Fröbel's methods were gradually being taken up by some public sector schools, especially in London, where the kindergarten movement began.

These diverse, incipient forms of early education expanded rapidly toward the end of the nineteenth century, followed by an equally rapid decline. Infant schools for 3- to 5-year-olds within elementary schools increased in particular, especially after 1891, when all public sector elementary schooling became free of charge. This also meant that children from both working and middle classes were not attending school. Before the turn of the century, nearly half of Britain's 3- and 4-year-olds were attending some sort of nursery schooling. Within the first decade of the new century, however, and continuing in the years thereafter, nursery schooling declined drastically. The reasons for this are mixed. The number of women workers began to drop in the late nineteenth century, reducing one type of need for preschool care.[9] In addition, compulsory education, enacted in 1870 for all children over the age of 5, may have become burdensome for local governments, es-

[8] Tessa Blackstone, *A Fair Start: The Provision of Pre-school Education* (London: Allen Lane, 1971).

[9] It is difficult to make a direct causal link between the drop in number of working women and decrease in nursery schooling. For one, the time lag is over a decade; for another, working mothers did not necessarily send their children to nursery school.

pecially given the greater financial constraints in providing free schooling.

In sum, two features of day care prior to World War I should be noted. First, the needs of children with working mothers were met meagerly, if at all. Mothers who did work were poor and so, by implication and in practice, were their children's life chances. Second, educational programs for preschool children in general, while enjoying a brief surge of interest, carried no lasting commitment. Most importantly, except for a short period, educationally oriented preschooling was the domain of the middle classes.

World War I, of course, changed the picture temporarily. The need for women to work in the factories brought an increase in all forms of provision by all sectors, but most importantly by the public sector for the first time. Day nurseries in particular expanded. These were simply custodial facilities, pretending to no larger purpose or role than to care for children while their mothers worked in the war effort. Most of the day care facilities were disbanded after the war. The few public programs that continued to operate were brought under the jurisdiction of local authorities by new legislation. In 1918 Parliament passed a Maternity and Child Welfare Act giving the welfare departments of local authorities the power to establish and maintain day nurseries. At the same time a separate Education Act gave the education departments of local authorities the power to establish and maintain nursery schools and classes. The jurisdictional division between these two institutions reflected the differences between two influential professional groups, the medical and educational, in fostering two different kinds of services. This functional and institutional separation between day nurseries and nursery schools was the main inheritance of the post-World War I era. The interwar years saw an increase in interest in early childhood development and child-oriented education. An increase in nursery schools did not result until World War II. From here on the story repeats history. The expansion of provision during World War II paralleled that of World War I, and so did the decline after the war. Very little has changed in the four decades since the war. I turn now to a brief outline of the current form of day care provision in Britain.

CURRENT FORMS OF PROVISION

There are four entirely different types of service in Britain that function in some way as day care: (1) day nurseries, (2) nursery schools, (3) playgroups, and (4) child-minders. All but child-minders are provided by both the public and private sectors. As I describe these services, two points should be kept in mind. First, there is a great deal of variation among the services; each offers something different to working parents. Second, the choice among the services is not wide open, for the services differ greatly in availability and in suitability to the needs of working parents. Tables 5.1A and B summarize the characteristics of each facility.

Day Nurseries

Public.   Public day nurseries, also known as local authority day nurseries, provide all-day care for children who are regarded as being in special need. In this case, special need is usually defined in terms of the child's family's problems (single parent, mother disabled, etc.).[10] Public day nurseries are staffed by qualified nursery nurses, not teachers, and thus offer care, as opposed to purposefully educational attention. Because most of the parents are needy, fees are very low and cover only 8-20% of the running costs. Since waiting lists are very long and places difficult to obtain, very few day nurseries are both willing and able to include "normal" working mothers and children among their clients. The national Department of Health and Social Security

[10] Children with such problems as mental retardation or physical handicap are placed in separate, special public programs, often from the age of two. They are not usually in the public day nurseries or nursery schools and classes being considered here. I do not include these special programs in my study.

(DHSS) leaves a great deal of discretion to local authorities to fashion their own programs, assess the needs of their own areas, and provide day nursery facilities as best they can. Accordingly, there is a great deal of variation in the features and provision of day nurseries among the local authorities.

Private.   Private day nurseries are profit-making and tend to be much more expensive than public day nurseries. Their standards vary so greatly that it is impossible to generalize about them and to make a comparison with other types of facilities.[11] Private day nurseries are supposed to register with their local authority and to follow guidelines similar to those of public day nurseries, but the vigilance of local authorities in matters of registration and inspection varies considerably. There is no firm knowledge even as to how many private day nurseries there are in Britain.[12] If a working parent can find and afford a private day nursery in the area, a place is more easily attainable than in the public counterpart. Some private day nurseries give priority to needy children and families whose fees are paid by the local authority.

There are a few day care nurseries at places of work, exclusive to employees of the company in question. Most offer full-day care, some subsidize parental fees, many do not take children under 2. All are, in principle, subject to the same legislation as other day nurseries.[13]

---

[11] One informal study suggests that, overall, private day nurseries are of lower quality than public ones, noting the lack of inspection and use of poorly trained staff assistants. Barbara Toner, *Double Shift: A Practical Guide for Working Mothers* (London: Arrow Books, 1975).

[12] Most studies estimate that there are more private than public day nurseries. Confusion stems from the fact that statistics for the various private facilities are often combined. There may also be a tendency to confuse private day nurseries located in a private home with child-minders. The distinction between these is up to the local authority.

[13] There are only 90 place-of-work nurseries in Britain (Department of Health and Social Security, *Children's Day Care Facilities as at 31 March 1975*). The labor unions are not eager to expand this type of provision because it limits the freedom of mothers to change jobs. Some hospitals

Voluntary. A few voluntary organizations and charities also run day nurseries, some in conjunction with their residential care programs (for orphans, delinquents, and other needy children). Very little can be said that would distinguish these programs. Public statistics and studies rarely take them into consideration in accounts of day care provision.

Nursery Schools

Public. Public nursery schools are separate (from primary schools), specially equipped facilities, staffed by qualified teachers and assistants and other unqualified staff. They provide educational programs for preschool children. They keep ordinary school hours and holidays, and while some children attend for a full school day, the majority attend either the morning or the afternoon session. They are free (although some charge for lunch, when applicable). All children are, in principle, eligible at the age of 3. However, waiting lists are very long, especially for 3-year-olds. Admission is at the discretion of the headmistress of each school. Public nursery schools are under the jurisdiction of each local authority's education department and ultimately the national Department of Education and Science (DES).

Nursery *classes* are another form of preschool education. They are distinct from nursery *schools* in that they are specially equipped and staffed classes in primary schools. For most purposes, nursery classes are similar to American kindergartens, with approximately 20-30 children, one teacher, and at least one assistant per class. Nursery classes consist mostly of 4-year-olds and what are called "rising-fives," that is, children who are about to be eligible for primary school, compulsory at age 5 in Britain. Finally, some primary schools also have what are called reception classes or first-year classes, in which "rising-fives" are in the majority, waiting for their birthdays. For some reason, reception classes tend to be

---

also provide facilities for employees. One survey is C. Day, *Company Day Nurseries* (London: Institute of Personnel Management, 1975).

less well staffed and equipped than nursery classes, and both reception and nursery classes are less well off than nursery schools. This may be because of numbers—many more children attend reception classes and nursery classes than attend nursery schools.

Private.   Private nursery schools vary a great deal in service, staff, and facilities.[14] They usually keep school hours, are usually headed by a trained teacher, and are usually educationally enriching. All charge fees. All are supposed to register with their local authority, but there is a great deal of variation in registration procedure, including with which department and for what purpose registration takes place. For example, some private nursery schools can apply to be classified as "recognized" (only a small proportion do), if they meet certain requirements similar to those for public nursery schools. They are then subject to inspection.[15] "Unrecognized" nursery schools are not subject to any educational requirements, only safety and hygiene standards. Because there is such diversity among private nursery schools, there is no genuine account of how many there are, let alone how they compare to other facilities. Some local authorities may even classify private nursery schools in their areas as private day nurseries or playgroups.

There are no voluntary nursery schools.

Playgroups

The playgroup movement in Britain has an interesting history, and its achievements have been enormous.[16] Play-

[14] Some are in private homes; others are in separate, more institutionalized settings.

[15] Some private nursery schools used to be eligible for "direct grants" from the government, but this is no longer so. The former Labour government tried to phase out support to all private facilities, including those in health care.

[16] Brenda Crowe, *The Playgroup Movement* (London: Allen and Unwin, 1973).

Table 5.1A Characteristics of Day Care Programs

	Services				Facility		Staff	Staff/Child Ratio (By Law)	Fees
	hours	part/full day	ages accepted	program	type	standards, equipment			
Public Day Nurseries	8:30 to 6:00	both, mostly full, holidays included	0-4, but many do not take infants (0-2)	care	special purpose building	good	qualified nursery nurses & assistants, headed by matron	1:5, more if high proportion of infants under 2	based on means test, fairly low
Private Day Nurseries	"	"	0-4, many take infants	care	private building	not known	head usually qualified but type of qualification varies	"	standard, fairly high
Public Nursery Schools	9-12, 1-3:30, or 9-3:30	both, mostly part; closed holidays	3 and 4	education	special purpose building	good	qualified teachers and assistants, some unqualified staff	qualified staff—1:23 all staff—1:10	free
Private Nursery Schools	"	both; closed holidays	2-5+	education	private	varies	usually headed by qualified teacher	regulation varies	standard, fairly high
Playgroups	2½ hr. sessions	part; usually 3/wk	varies	social play	varies	varies	mostly parents, usually qualified supervisor	regulation varies	very low
Childminders	varies	both	all	home care	minder's home	often poor	no qualifications, no training	1:3-5	vary considerably, fairly low on average

TABLE 5.1B Characteristics of Day Care Programs

| | Principles of Acceptance | | | Jurisdiction | Regulation | Inspection | Clientele |
	Means test	Priority	Waiting list				
Public Day Nurseries	yes, and health visitor interview	special need child or family	long	local authority social service department and DHSS (central)	National Health Service Act 1944 as amended by Sect. 60 of Health Services & Public Health Act 1968	regular	special needs, problems; residents of borough
Private Day Nurseries	no	anyone, priority as above if necessary	varies	"	"	inconsistent	varies

Public Nursery Schools	no	sometimes to 4 year olds	yes, can be long	local authority education department and DES (central)	1944 Education Act	regular	residents of borough
Private Nursery Schools	no	anyone	not known	either local social service or education; DHSS or DES	either 1944 Education Act or Nurseries and Child-minders Regulation Act 1948 and 1968	inconsistent	varies
Play-groups	no	anyone	no	local authority social service department & DHSS	Nurseries and Child-minders Regulation Act 1948 as amended by Sect. 60 of Health Services and Public Health Act 1968	no	tend to be middle class
Child-minders	no	anyone	if registered, sometimes	local authority social service department, & DHSS	"	before registration	varies

groups are in the main voluntary, self-help organizations, most of which are affiliated with the national Pre-school Playgroups Association. (A few playgroups are private and profit-making and a few are run by local authorities.) While voluntary playgroups are not profit-making, all charge a small fee to cover costs. Playgroups are designed to provide children with organized social and play experiences which are not explicitly educational but have educational value. Children attend 1-3 times a week, each session being about 2½ hours long. Most playgroups have a qualified supervisor (usually a trained teacher), but the "staff" consists mainly of parents, that is, mothers, who participate on a rotational basis. A primary purpose of playgroups, especially those associated with the Pre-school Playgroups Association, is to involve mothers and to provide social experiences for mothers as well as for children. Given these features, playgroups tend to be essentially middle-class organizations. Recently, special efforts have been made by other voluntary organizations, some with government grants, to organize playgroups in so-called "priority areas" (poorer districts). Parent participation, however, has been more difficult to achieve and is, therefore, less integral to the programs in these areas. Playgroups are supposed to register with their local authority social service departments, and are subject to health and safety but not to educational requirements.[17]

Playgroups are clearly not in and of themselves a day care service; nevertheless, in the patchwork of programs available to working parents, they have a role. For example, they may be combined with child-minding, perhaps by having the child-minders themselves take the children in their care to playgroups. Use aside, playgroups function in another capacity in the tug-of-war among the various services for official attention and limited assistance grants. There

---

[17] The Department of Education and Science refuses to recognize playgroups as educationally beneficial and to bring them under its wing mainly because of the inconsistent training backgrounds of their heads and "staff."

is a tendency in Britain, to be elaborated and explained below, for the focus on day care as a service for working parents to shift entirely to consideration of day care as a preschool program for children. Insofar as playgroups are one such program, they are being looked at anew by the government. To show its concern for the developmental needs of young children, the government is extending new loans to playgroups, especially those in inner-city areas.[18] One might also suggest that by taking this sort of interest, the government is divesting itself of responsibility to expand other more costly and contentious programs for preschool children, including, of course, day nurseries.[19]

Child-minders

Child-minders are private individuals who care for other people's children in their (the minder's) own home. (This distinguishes child-minders from babysitters and live-in or au pair help, who work in the children's homes.) Child-minders are usually mothers with small children of their own. They care for children of all ages, for a wide range of hours, and for a fee which is usually very little. Child-minders are supposed to register with their local authority social service departments if they are receiving payment to care for more than two children unrelated to them. Upon application their houses are inspected in accordance with minimal health and safety regulations. A good child-minder can provide an excellent type of day care, especially for very small children and for parents who prefer a family setting. However, care by an unknown child-minder can also be a chancy undertaking for parents. No one can be absolutely certain about what is going on in a child-minder's home.

[18] This is being done through an Urban Aid program in the Department of the Environment.

[19] See papers from a conference sponsored by the Department of Health and Social Security and the Department of Education and Science, *Low Cost Provision for the Under-Fives* (June 1976).

It is estimated that nearly half of the nation's child-minders are not registered (despite a penalty of £50), many of them because they cannot meet the registration requirements.[20] From the information being collected by special research groups, it can be surmised that far too many child-minders are providing substandard care for far too many children.[21] Child-minding is the most widely used type of formal day care in Britain, even excluding unregistered child-minders.[22]

At first sight this array of programs might seem as confusing to a social scientist as it must be to parents. There is, however, a rationale to the system of day care in Britain. The following section attempts to explicate this rationale by focusing on the role of the state in providing *public* day nurseries. Day nursery provision is the only public program that genuinely functions as day care. Nursery schools and classes would constitute a day care provision only if they were to accommodate parents who work longer than the regular school hours.[23] However, when parents and interest groups in Britain make demands on the state to expand day care provision, they focus more attention on the Department of Health and Social Security and day nurseries than on the educational system. In the analysis that follows,

[20] Brian Jackson, "Childminding," in Barrie Knight (ed.), *Report of the First National Conference on Childminding* (Cambridge: National Educational Research and Development Trust, 1975).

[21] Brian Jackson, "The Childminders," *New Society*, No. 582, 26 (1973). Another study of forty registered child-minders in London finds that one of the most disturbing problems is the lack of emotional care and warmth. Berry Mayall and Pat Petrie, *Minder, Mother and Child* (London: University of London Institute of Education, 1977).

[22] As far as it can be estimated, it seems that the most widely used system of day care is the informal, non-institutional method of care provided by family and friends. This system is used not always because it is convenient or preferable, but simply because there is no other choice. For example, for those mothers who work at night, fathers are the main source of child care. See the survey by Audrey Hunt, *Families and Their Needs* (London: HMSO, 1973).

[23] Three public nursery schools in London are experimenting with an extended day program. The extra costs are proving to be prohibitive.

public day nursery provision is compared to public nursery school provision to clarify certain distinctions the state makes regarding the purpose of day care. The comparison also demonstrates how the state's approach to each type of provision contributes to the fashioning of a total system of day care.

THE ROLE OF THE STATE

Determinants of Intervention

This section focuses on the circumstances justifying state intervention in the area of child care arrangements. In the case of Britain, we must distinguish two different justifications: one for involvement and one for non-involvement. Historically, the state first provided public day nurseries during a situation of national emergency, and justified its expanded provision on the basis of the country's need for women to work. After both wars public provision returned to its prewar level. Presumably, masses of women were no longer needed in the labor force since men had returned to their old jobs. For whom were those day nurseries which continued to operate intended? And what about those women who continued to work? The answers to these two questions are not interrelated. Different premises underlie the state's provision of day nurseries and its policy position on working mothers.

Bases of Inclusion. During each of the World Wars, national emergencies justified state intervention in the area of child care arrangements. After each war, limited day nursery provision continued. This too was justified on the basis of emergency, only this time emergency situations in the home. Three kinds of emergencies, each signifying a breakdown of some sort, can occur and disturb normal home child care. An individual breakdown, that is, an illness or a personal problem, incapacitates the mother's ability to care for her child. A family breakdown, because of

divorce, desertion, or single motherhood, leaves only one
parent, usually the mother, to care for the child, sometimes
under strained financial circumstances. A market-created
breakdown leaves a family in poverty, usually because the
husband/father earns too little or is only casually employed.
Each of these emergencies constitutes a legitimate condition for placing a child in day nursery care—whether or
not its mother works. On the other hand, only those mothers who work out of financial necessity, because of a family
or market-created breakdown, are accepted as clients of
public day care programs.[24]

The official definition of the state's clientele has been
formulated by the Department of Health and Social Security (DHSS), which is the main government department
responsible for overseeing day nurseries. Periodically, the
DHSS issues "circulars" (memos) to local authorities suggesting guidelines and regulations to be followed in the
delivery of social services. Since 1945 two circulars have
dealt exclusively with government policy on provision of
day nurseries. One of these, issued in 1968 and still op-
erative, delineates the clientele as follows:

> the responsibility of local health authorities should
> continue to be limited to arranging for the day care of
> children who, from a health point of view or because
> of deprived or inadequate backgrounds, have special
> needs that cannot otherwise be met.
>
> The need for day care may arise from one or more
> of a variety of circumstances in which the child or
> family may need help. Priority will normally be given
> to children with only one parent (e.g., the unsupported
> mother living with her child) who has no option but
> to go to work and who cannot arrange for the child to

[24] The only time, other than during wars, when demand for female
labor justified including additional working women among day nursery
clientele was when shortages of teachers and nurses occurred in the late
1950s and early 1960s. In some cases provision was actually expanded to
include this new group.

be looked after satisfactorily. Other children who need day care, some for the whole day, others part-time, will include those:

(a) who need temporary day care on account of the mothers' illness;

(b) whose mothers are unable to look after them adequately because they are incapable of giving young children the care they need;

(c) for whom day care might prevent the breakdown of the mother or the break-up of the family;

(d) whose home conditions (e.g., because of gross overcrowding) constitute a hazard to their health and welfare; and

(e) whose health and welfare are seriously affected by a lack of opportunity for playing with others.[25]

Clearly, public day care is intended for a traditional welfare clientele: children who are already social victims because of their family circumstances, or whose mothers are unable to care for themselves let alone their children. Local authorities vary in the priority they give in accepting children (and families). In general, children who are most "at risk" and in imminent danger of requiring removal from their home and those who are subject to parental abuse ("battering") are taken first. Then, as the circular suggests, priority can be given to the single parent (invariably a mother) who "has no option but to go to work."[26] Being in this position, that is, of having no option but to go to work, places single mothers (as well as those married mothers who are accepted) in the category of a welfare client, eligible for public support.

It is already apparent, and will become more so as I

[25] Ministry of Health, Circular 37/68 (1968).

[26] This is the main clientele. Places are also kept open for such emergencies as when mothers must be temporarily hospitalized. These are considered to be incidental needs. Some of the better-off local authorities, with few priority cases in their areas, do include non-priority children, meaning children of normal working mothers, in their day nurseries. While this does occur, it cannot be considered the norm.

elaborate the British approach to day care, that a late nine-teenth-century paternalistic welfare-ism undergirds the goals and implementation of this social service. We will find some variant of many of the organizing principles of the Poor Laws: "proper limits" to state intervention, deterrence through stigma, strict classification of users, a central in-spectorate.[27] Take, for example, the determination of eli-gibility. If we look closely at how need for the service is assessed, we see that some form of poverty is a constant premise. Moreover, need is less the perception of the pro-spective user than the judgment of a professional authority. Those who become the clients of public day care initially may not even identify themselves as needing the service. Many are already welfare clients who are visited regularly in their homes by social workers or health visitors. Others who are not visited at home still see health visitors at clinics. These professionals identify the conditions of eligibility for day care and refer clients. Of course there are exceptions. A mother who is ill can contact the local social service de-partment for child care assistance. The request is mediated, however, by a social worker or health visitor. Any mother can apply on her own for a place in a day nursery and be interviewed only by the nursery matron. Her acceptance, however, would indicate that she has passed (or failed, de-pending on one's point of view) a means test,[28] bringing her and her children within the sphere of welfare. Many of the clients of day nurseries attend free of charge, indi-cating where they fall on the scale.[29] As it turns out, then, the child who was initially defined as a social victim is, in

[27] Robert Pinker, *Social Theory and Social Policy* (London: Heinemann Educational Books, 1971), Chapter 2.

[28] The exact scale varies by local authority. A very few local authorities do have extra places in their day nurseries and accept non-priority work-ing mothers who pay for the service. Some local authorities also still accept children of nurses and teachers if there is a labor need for them in their areas.

[29] Because so few clients can pay, the income of day nurseries relative to costs is extremely low.

fact, an indirect market victim—the child's family is in the situation of requiring day care at the same time as, and perhaps because, the family is in the condition of poverty.

Why is the conception of the clientele of day care so narrow and confined to poverty-related welfare? The answer will take up the rest of this chapter and more and has several parts. I begin with one formulation: the conception of the proper sphere of state activity. "Proper sphere" has two sorts of referents. First, it refers to an issue area and to who else might be responsible for this issue, if not the state. Second, it refers to what the state ought to do in relation to what can be left to other types of social solutions. There is no longer any question that a modern state must accept the responsibility to do something about poverty. Questions arise, however, about the kind and the level of poverty that states are obligated to do something about. How a state answers these questions indicates how far it is prepared to intervene in the free play of market forces. A second indicator is even more important, however, to our understanding of the path of development of a modern welfare state. If poverty is a minimum responsibility, what related social problems are within the domain of public responsibility? And how are they defined and determined? We can see in the case of day care that the state has not gone beyond the minimum area of responsibility. What creates the need for day care? Poverty or one of its correlates. How far must poverty have advanced? Quite far, such that children are actually "at risk." In other words, first the market determines who is and who is not to become a public responsibility. The state then intervenes but, as we will see below, not to the extent of actually changing (improving) the market-created situation of the persons involved. This is a first indication that the state is acting in a derivative capacity—secondarily to the market, which established the terms of the situation for individuals. The point will be substantiated further as the argument progresses.

A second part of the question about the narrow conception of the clientele of day care begs to be addressed. What about non-welfare, "normal" working mothers? The answer to this question tells us more about why eligibility is so strictly defined and determined—as I show below, it is public policy that mothers who do not have to work should not work, and those who do work anyway should not be assisted.

Bases of Exclusion. The first postwar circular on provision of day care was issued in 1945 by DHSS to explain to local authorities why the majority of wartime day nurseries ought to be closed. It makes clear, at the same time, the state's position on "normal" working mothers. It reads as follows:

> The Ministers concerned accept the view of medical and other authority that, in the interest of the health and development of the child no less than for the benefit of the mother, the proper place for a child under two is at home with his mother. They are also of the opinion that, under normal peacetime conditions, the right policy to pursue would be positively to discourage mothers of children under two from going out to work.[30]

Positive discouragement took the form of not providing child care services or any other assistance to mothers who were not forced to work by unfortunate family circumstances. Although it was not stated as such, the policy also applied to mothers of children aged 2 to 5. The same 1945 circular said that local authorities should provide nursery schools and nursery classes for this age group, but the irregularity of such provision, the lack of state commitment to assure it, and the fact that preschool programs are mostly part-time where they do exist meant that mothers of children aged 2 to 5 were also to be positively discouraged from going out to work. Another circular on day nursery provision was not issued until 1968 and has already been referred to. It did not change substantially the earlier policy

[30] Ministry of Health, Circular 221/45 (1945).

statement, except to drop the notion of "no less than for the benefit of the mother."

This policy on working mothers rests, of course, on a conception of the traditional role of women—mothers ought to be at home raising children. But this is not what the ministers in charge said. They based their position on "the view of medical and other authority." We can surmise that the reference was, in particular, to John Bowlby, the noted British psychologist who was just beginning to conduct research on maternal deprivation. His early work came to the ministers' attention, although the bulk of scientific studies did not begin to accumulate until around 1950 and later. Bowlby's findings about the negative effects on child development of lack of maternal care and affection experienced by children in residential institutions were most disturbing.[31] At the time the incidental relationship between Bowlby's evidence and the situation of children in day nurseries was not recognized.[32] Bowlby's subjects were infants under prolonged institutionalization who had neither mothers nor consistent mother-surrogates to give them care resembling that in a "normal" home. It took many years for social scientists to question systematically the validity of Bowlby's assumptions and conclusions to settings where mother-child separation is temporary, that is, for a certain number of hours each day. Additional research led to a better understanding of the factors that reduced the possibility of deprivation, such as small groups allowing for unhurried warmth in the relationship between child and same-person care-giver. This revived earlier research which had been largely ignored in the 1940s and early 1950s.[33]

[31] His most famous study is *Maternal Care and Mental Health* (Geneva: World Health Organization, 1951).

[32] Peter Boss, "Day Care for the Preschool Child: Policy and Practice in England and Wales," in Pamela Roby (ed.), *Child Care—Who Cares? Foreign and Domestic Infant and Early Childhood Development Policies* (New York: Basic Books, 1973), p. 372.

[33] For example, Anna Freud, and others, wrote on the necessity for gradual transition to new settings and for warmth and constant affection

To this day, however, the full implications of these qualifications have not penetrated the thinking of officials at
DHSS, who continue either to be influenced by Bowlby's
work or to use it to justify limiting day care provision. I
take the latter possibility, that research has been used to
justify policy, as more likely and base the following analysis
on it.[34]

Why does the state limit day care provision so that the
majority of normal mothers who work are excluded? And
why is there no public assistance to normal working mothers in finding or easing the burden of child care?[35] Two
possible answers having to do with Britain's economic situation were the subject of an earlier chapter. First, we might
say that this social service is limited because the nation
simply cannot afford greater expenditure. To be sure, Britain's economy is in a sorry state: its rate of growth is low;
so are its productivity figures. As we have seen, however,
any discussion of public expenditures must include an analysis of priorities: Why are military expenditures so high
relative to social service expenditures?[36] Why are expenditures for some social services higher than for others?[37]
Something special about day care provision underlies its
limited extent. A second, related argument holds that wom-
en's labor is not in great demand. In some ways this is true.
Unemployment is high in Britain; there is little expansion

---

to reduce child anxiety. Cf. Dorothy Burlingham and Anna Freud, *Infants
Without Families* (London: Allen and Unwin, 1944).

[34] My interpretation is based on personal interviews, Department of
Health and Social Security, July 1977 and May 1982. Officials are aware
of other studies but choose to read them selectively.

[35] For example, child care is not tax deductible. In addition, only a few
local authority social service departments maintain a useable, up-to-date
referral service for registered child-minders.

[36] Harold L. Wilensky, *The Welfare State and Equality: Structural and Ideological Roots of Public Expenditures* (Berkeley: University of California Press,
1975).

[37] Arnold J. Heidenheimer, Hugh Heclo, Carolyn Teich Adams, *Comparative Public Policy: The Politics of Social Choice in Europe and America* (New
York: St. Martin's Press, 1975).

in industry. However, the part of the argument that says that women are taking jobs away from men is not true. Women workers are highly segregated in a narrow range of "women's jobs," many of which are in the public sector. The fact that unemployment among women is increasing can tell us more about the public sector, its level of activity, and the role of the state in supporting an active labor force and encouraging its expansion than about the demand for women workers in the economy as a whole. The state in Britain is not active, compared to other welfare states, in promoting full employment. Instead, it allows the market to determine its own level of demand and compensates workers for the consequences.

This conception of the role of the state vis-à-vis the private sector (or society) figures in two other possible answers to our questions about limited and exclusionary day care provision. One is that state action, and inaction in this case, may be reflecting societal ambivalence about the changing role of women. This would be in keeping with a more passive role of the state. However, evidence about such societal ambivalence is subject to much interpretation. For example, in 1968 the government sponsored a study (its only one to date) of issues relating to women's employment.[38] It was a thorough and extensive study, including, among other items, women's attitudes about working and family life. The findings showed that there was, indeed, ambivalence among women about the relative merits of work and family life. But the ambivalence was greater among non-working women than among those who worked. This is not an isolated finding.[39] The "reflective ambivalence" of the state, then, is misplaced. Were working women themselves unsure about their choice, state policy inhibiting their

[38] Audrey Hunt, *A Survey of Women's Employment* (London: HMSO, 1968). The survey was carried out in 1965 on behalf of the Ministry of Labour.

[39] Many other studies find that non-working housewives and mothers are more subject to anxieties and illnesses than their working counterparts. Cf. Margaret Bone, *Pre-school Children and the Need for Day-care* (London: HMSO, 1977), Chapters 7 and 8.

work efforts would be reflective and supportive. As it stands, however, state policy appears to be more selective. It reflects and supports tradition over social change. Is this because many more families are still following traditional role patterns than the newer ones? Evidence on this requires much interpretation too. In 1970 the employment rate of women with preschool aged children in Britain was only about 20% (compared to about 50% in Sweden). The rate of change in the figure for the decade of the 1960s was greater in Britain than in certain other countries, as Table 5.2, below, shows. But this is no longer the case.[40] We might conclude that the direction of social change outpaced the direction of state policy, only to be thwarted in further development by the inertia of social policy. Let us consider more directly a proposition about the role of the state in social change.

Perhaps the state is limiting day care provision and excluding normal working mothers in order to minimize public interference in a matter that is up to families themselves to act upon. Were the state to expand its provision and include among its clientele all working women who wanted the service, it would be engaging in *leading* families toward a particular kind of social change that many families have not yet decided to take up. But what about those families that have chosen to follow non-traditional patterns of work and family life?[41] The state implicitly continues to hold to a policy that "positively discourages" mothers of young children from working by not assisting in their child care needs and by aggravating maternal guilt about leaving children

[40] By 1980 the employment rates of women with preschool age children in Sweden had risen to 75%. In Britain, comparable data are not even available. In its latest report on the subject, the Economic Opportunity Commission still uses the 1970 figure of 20% (and the same source as I do).

[41] Families with two adult wage earners who share household duties are still a minority, but their numbers are increasing and they can be found in all social classes. See Michael Young and Peter Willmott, *The Symmetrical Family* (London: Routledge and Kegan Paul, 1973); Michael Fogarty, Rhona Rapoport, Robert N. Rapoport, *Sex, Career and Family* (London: Allen and Unwin, 1971).

TABLE 5.2 Employment Rates of Mothers of Preschool Children in Seven Countries

| Country | Age range of children | Employment Rate of mothers | | | | Change in rate (%) |
		Rate (%)	Year	Rate (%)	Year	Year
Austria	0-5			26.7	1971	
Britain	0-4	11.5	1961	18.7	1971	+65
Germany	0-5	31.3	1961	31.2	1970	No change
Netherlands	0-3			12.0[a]	1971	
Sweden	0-2	29.0	1967	45.0	1971	+55
Sweden	3-6	38.0	1967	54.0	1971	+42
Switzerland	0-6	7.9	1960	23.2	1970	+201
USA	0-5	20.2	1960	31.4	1971	+56

Source: Jack Tizard, Peter Moss, Jane Perry, *All Our Children: Pre-school Services in a Changing Society* (London: Temple Smith/New Society, 1976), p. 234.

[a] Approximate.

in someone else's care. This is not a laissez-faire stance. It is a position that interferes directly with the free choice of families to engage in alternative life styles. Its consequences are to cause the majority of children with working mothers to be placed with child-minders, a care arrangement about which there is much uncertainty, and to heighten parental anxiety about the care their children are receiving.[42]

Thus, the state justifies its exclusion of many working mothers from limited day care provision on the basis of a preferred conception of traditional sex roles. In so doing, the state is practicing sex discrimination. Moreover, instead of upholding the privacy and integrity of the family, the consequence of state policy interferes with the family's freedom to make choices. State interference is not limited to those who have been excluded from the public domain. As we have seen, the process of determining eligibility for day nursery services also interferes with the privacy and freedom of choice of the selected few. In addition, as we are about to see, the way in which the state provides its services represents an even greater interference in the affairs of society. I elaborate this through an examination of the design of state intervention.

Design of Intervention

The form of intervention that is the subject of analysis here is the public provision of a day care program, specifically, day nursery facilities. I examine how the day nursery is organized in terms of its purpose and the quality and quantity of provision. The state is also involved in some

[42] For example, Hunt, *A Survey of Women's Employment*, found that a substantial proportion of working mothers felt that children suffer when mothers work, p. 189. We do not know what kind of care the children of these mothers were receiving. Other studies show widespread discontent with child-minding. Cf. Bone, *Pre-school Children and the Need*, Chapter 3. Constantina Safilios-Rothschild, "Parents' Need for Child Care," in Roby (ed.), *Child Care—Who Cares?* discusses problems of guilt among working parents, p. 43.

way in the provision of all of the other types of programs
that make up the system of day care in Britain. For example, nursery schools are a public function, and the government gives grants to facilitate playgroups. I will discuss
what is going on in these other programs and what the state
is doing about and for them. The contrast with day nurseries is significant.

Purpose. No firm data exist on the proportion of working
mothers among the users of day nurseries.[43] Still, a mother's work as well as her welfare status are taken into account
in the services day nurseries offer. (The policy recognizes
that some mothers have "no option but to go to work.")
Accordingly, day nurseries are open for long daytime hours
(7:30 a.m. to 6:30 p.m.) and during school holidays and
vacations. For another, the fee is low and based on a sliding
scale according to ability to pay. In this way, day nurseries
allow needy mothers to work. But the purpose of day nurseries is expressed, by those in charge, in terms of the
welfare of the children. Children in day nurseries require
special care because of their (deprived) family situations.
As we will see, the kind of care given to children in day
nurseries is based on their particular class status, as children
from welfare families, and not on their general status as
preschool age children, some of whose mothers happen to
be at work while they are at the day nursery.

The conception of the clientele of day care strongly influences the conception of the purposes of the program.
If day care is for children who are social victims of some

---

[43] Officials at DHSS are under the impression that few of the mothers
who use day nurseries work, and emphasize that day nurseries are for
children in need (personal interview, May 1982). Survey data, however,
contradict this impression and show that mothers with children in day
nurseries do indeed work. Cf. Bone, *Pre-school Children and the Need*; Peter
Moss, "The Current Situation" in Nickie Fonda and Peter Moss (eds.),
Mothers in Employment (Uxbridge: Brunel University Management Programme, 1976), both of whom focus on the type of provision used by
working mothers.

sort, what these children require is the care missing in their
own homes. A good way to ascertain what care means is to
examine the circulars periodically issued by DHSS. Two
circulars in particular, issued in 1965 and 1968, revised the
standards and guidelines to be followed by day nurseries,
updating relevant sections of the Nurseries and Child-minders Regulation Act of 1948. They go into considerable
detail about: the physical setting of the facility (the amount
of space there should be per child; the equipment required,
including fixtures for towels; the allowable improvisations,
such as "wash basins with hot and cold water can be supplemented by portable bowls given an overall provision of
one for each 5 children"); the health of the children (im-
munization records and other information that must be
kept); the feeding of the children (including preferable
items in the diet, such as "a pint of milk a day," as well as
preferable kitchen equipment, such as "a 7 lb. bench model
electric potato peeler").

In contrast to this detail, the amount of space and attention given to requirements in the general care of the children, in relation to their emotional, social, and intellectual
development needs, is small. One page lists suitable toys
and improvised playthings, with the introduction that these
"materials stimulate [children's] curiosity and aid their
emotional, intellectual and physical development." Since
cost must always be considered, it is noted that "the use of
inexpensive domestic articles and junk will meet many of
their play needs." The caretaker's role in all this is briefly
summarized: "She [the caretaker] should have opportunities to talk and listen to the children and encourage them
to form a warm relationship with her and she should be
aware of the undesirability of frequent changes in the people caring for them."[44]

These circulars, and others, reveal that the DHSS has a

[44] Ministry of Health, Circular 5/65 (1965) and Ministry of Health, Circular 37/68 (1968). Parts of these circulars also apply to standards and
guidelines for the other types of facilities under DHSS jurisdiction, that
is, private day nurseries, child-minders, and playgroups.

narrow conception of what care means.[45] The emphasis on physical needs over developmental ones may have something to do with the young ages of the children in day nurseries. Only day nurseries (and child-minders) are authorized to accept children under the age of two. Small children are more subject to infection and their diet requires some attention, so caretakers must be cautious. However, many day nurseries refuse to take children under two, and in those that do, the number of children aged 3 to 5 is far greater.[46] Even so, the program in day nurseries emphasizes the physical care of these older children, not their developmental needs. Other 3- to 5-year-old children, who are not attending day nurseries but are attending other preschool programs such as nursery schools, nursery classes, and even playgroups, are receiving a different service, one that is more developmentally oriented and educationally enriching. The issue to be emphasized is *not* whether children aged 3 to 5 *ought* to be receiving early educational training. What is at issue is the fact that there is a *difference* between what children in day nurseries do and what children in other preschool programs do, and that those in day nurseries are disadvantaged.

Quality.   The main difference between day nurseries and nursery schools is that the services offered by the former are custodial, the latter developmental. Day nurseries are care institutions for welfare children; nursery schools are educational institutions for preschool children in general. The particular vs. the general purpose results in a quali-

----

[45] The latest circular on day nurseries, issued in 1976, similarly described in detail the physical requirements with no mention of program content or guidance on developing children's emotional, social and intellectual needs. Department of Health and Social Security, "Day Nurseries, Design Guidance," LASSL (76) 3 (13 February 1976).

[46] Data on ages of children in day nurseries are close to impossible to obtain. Only one survey seems to have asked about age. It found a greater proportion of 3-5 than 0-3-year-olds in day nurseries. Bone, *Pre-school Children and the Need*, p. 10.

tative difference that disadvantages the children in day nurseries. What underlies this difference and how is it manifest? One can offer a variety of issue-specific reasons. For
example, children are in day nurseries for a long day and
cannot be constantly stimulated, whereas some children
attend nursery schools for a few hours and parents send
them for enriching experiences. These reasons (or excuses)
aside, I suggest that the principal reason for the different
services is the different governmental jurisdictions for the
two institutions: the DHSS and local social service authorities are responsible for day nurseries; the Department of
Education and Science (DES) and local education authorities are responsible for nursery schools. The officials in
each department have their own ideas about what should
go on in their respective institutions. Each department sends
different guidelines to its local office. Each has its own
budget and system of allocation.[47]

One way in which jurisdictional separation leads to differences in quality between the two institutions is in the
different qualifications for staffs and consequent staff behavior. Qualified staff in day nurseries are nursery officers,
formerly known as nursery nurses—and for good reason,
since their specialization is child health. Some day nurseries
may be staffed by registered nurses, whose training is still
considered the equivalent of nursery officers. However, the
majority of staff in day nurseries are unqualified assistants
who may or may not be in training for certification. Nursery
schools are staffed by nursery teachers, and nursery school
assistants are more often than not qualified. Nursery officers and nursery teachers are trained in different institutions and for different lengths of time. The former attend
two-year colleges of further education and technical training. Their courses, run by the National Nursery Exami-

---

[47] It is generally known that the DES tends to be more generous with
supplies and support services to its institutions. Unfortunately, this is a
point that many studies refer to without substantiating. Cf. David C.
Marsh, *The Future of the Welfare State* (London: Penguin Books, 1964), p.
109.

nation Board (NNEB) were once confined to child development and health but now contain more emphasis on social service. Nursery teachers attend a three-year course at a college of education or a one-year postgraduate course with programs in child development, education, and teaching. No formal academic requirement is necessary for the NNEB course; however, prospective teachers must have a minimum of secondary school attainment. The two types of staff also face differences in employment opportunities. Qualified nursery officers and assistants have a wide range of employment possibilities. They can work in day or residential nurseries run by local authority social service departments, in various health services including hospitals, or in nursery schools and in "infant" classes in primary schools. However, when employed by education departments they cannot qualify for teaching certificates because of their training background and their promotional oppportunities in the school system are few. Persons with an NNEB degree can only head day nurseries. Nursery teachers work only in local authority education departments, but they have greater opportunities to progress through the educational system, to teach older children, or to become head teacher. The pay scales for nursery officers are lower than for nursery teachers, especially at the higher levels reached after a few years of experience.[48]

Whether all of this makes any difference to the services provided for young children is debatable, up to a point. A good nursery officer or assistant is probably as capable of offering as high a quality and quantity of intellectual stimulation (and "care") as a nursery school teacher. In the same way, a nursery school teacher is no doubt aware of young children's needs for quiet time, rest, and emotional warmth.[49]

[48] For an elaboration of training and employment differences, see Mia Kellmer Pringle and Sandhya Naidoo, *Early Child Care in Britain* (London: Gordon and Breach, 1975), Chapter 9; also Peter Mottershead, *A Survey of Child Care for Pre-school Children with Working Parents: Costs and Organization* (Manchester: EOC, May 1978).

[49] I wish to emphasize that I am not setting an objective standard against

Nevertheless, studies have found repeatedly that there is a difference between what goes on in day nurseries and nursery schools that is especially important for the 3- to 5-year-old children. It is worthwhile to quote at length the observations of a leading British educationalist, Barbara Tizard, in a 1975 study of preschools:

> observations on staff behaviour were made in 12 different pre-school centres. Four were nurseries rather than schools, and the staff, who were not teachers, disclaimed any educational aim; four were traditional nursery schools, and four were nursery schools which had departed from tradition to the extent of including a special language programme in the school day. In half of the centres most of the children had parents in the manual working classes, whilst in the other half the parents of the children were predominantly from the professional middle-classes. . . .
>
> The results show that significant differences did occur in staff behaviour in the various types of centres. In those nursery schools where a language programme was used the staff spent more time interacting with the children, rather than merely supervising them or putting out play equipment. In the nursery centres which had no avowed educational aim there was least talk addressed to children, the lowest amount of information was given, the fewest suggestions for activities were made, and the least time was spent explaining or showing children how to do things. Further, all types of 'cognitive' staff behaviour, as well as total amount of talk to children, were observed more often in middle-class than working-class centres, whilst in working-class centres the staff spent more time putting out

---

which to measure day nurseries and nursery schools; nor am I suggesting that the one ought to employ teachers and the other care-givers. My analysis focuses on the fact that there are certain differences between the two programs, and the differences affect the services provided, the attitudes of the staff, and thereby, the children involved.

equipment and merely supervising the children. Thus, the greatest 'cognitive' content in staff behaviour was found in the middle-class schools with a language programme, the least in the working-class nurseries not staffed by teachers.[50]

These views are not confined to professional educationalists alone. The London Borough of Camden sent a team of councillors to observe the various facilities for preschool children in that area. The report on day nurseries stated:

We found that for the children under 2½ years of age (a) supervision and cleaning up by staff members accounted for 50% of all staff activity during the time we were observing; (b) Caretaking activities involving some physical contact took up a further 20% of activities. There were practically no instances of affectionate behaviour on the part of staff to children. These children seldom uttered, and adults produced talk carrying informative content only a third of the time.

For the child over 2½, less than half of the time we observed was spent in play activities with adults, although this was the most creative period of the day. . . . Caretaking time for these children took up 30% of the total activities we observed.

There were few differences between the trained and untrained staff in the day nurseries. Trained staff were slightly more affectionate but instances of affection were generally low, the trained staff had far more controlling talk but the untrained staff actually played more with the children. We felt that in at least half the units the toys were not properly accessible to the children. There was also a wide range in the quality of the toys provided.[51]

[50] Barbara Tizard, *Early Childhood Education: A Review and Discussion of Current Research in Britain* (Slough: NFER, 1975), pp. 9-10.

[51] London Borough of Camden, *Report of the Working Party on Provision in Camden for Pre-school Children* (February 1975), p. 21. Camden is a mixed-class borough. It was predominantly working-class until the mid-

In their section on nursery classes, the councillors emphasized the great differences between the teachers and their
assistants, both NNEB-trained and untrained:

> We think that nursery nurses, though trained in caring
> for children, were not sensitized to the educational
> needs of the child as expressed in the purpose of the
> nursery class. . . . The teachers performed small care-
> taking tasks but showed the same amount of play be-
> haviour as did their assistants. They did, however, have
> a higher amount of informative talk. It seems that
> teachers are more sensitive to the need for explaining
> and elaborating things to children rather than just
> chatting, or using language for directing the children's
> activities. The children also talked more when inter-
> acting with the teachers not only in talk directed to the
> teachers but also they talked more amongst each other.
> The teachers showed more affectionate behaviour to-
> wards the children also. . . .
>
> There was less variation in the physical qualities of
> nursery schools. They were better designed to accom-
> modate children in a wide variety of activities. All nurs-
> ery classes had toys accessible to the children.[52]

The Camden Borough report makes much of training
background in conditioning the qualitative differences between day nurseries and nursery schools. Teachers are better sensitized to children's total needs, especially those of
older children; they have a wider range of ideas for interesting and useful activities; and they are better able to organize both their own time (so that even cleaning up is a
learning experience for children) and their classrooms (so
that a higher staff/child ratio is possible and still effective).[53]

1960s, when an influx of middle-class families entered and renovated
houses. Camden is known to be one of the more progressive London
boroughs.

[52] Ibid., pp. 22-23.

[53] Besides the Camden report, a number of other studies note that the
activities of day nursery staff are not simply a function of the fact that

Parents themselves are aware of the qualitative differences between day nurseries and nursery schools. For example, a government-sponsored survey asked parents, both users and potential users of day care, about their preferences and satisfactions.[54] Users of playgroups and nursery schools/ nursery classes were the most satisfied with their arrangements. Users of child-minders were the least satisfied. Nearly one-quarter of day nursery users would have preferred their children to be in nursery schools/classes. These were primarily parents of children aged two and over who, presumably, wanted a better learning environment for their children.

The Tizard report, quoted above, points to additional factors that hamper day nursery staff more than nursery school staff, namely the attitude that is generated by the working environment of day nurseries, including the children's social class and the lack of experimentation in the program (DES and local education authorities are more innovative than DHSS and local social service authorities). This problem will not be solved simply by integrating training and equalizing status, pay, and other conditions of employment.[55] Greater coordination between the two govern-

---

children are in day nurseries for longer periods of time than in nursery schools or classes. In day nurseries the main activity that elicits staff-child interaction is craft work. Craft work also requires a lot of preparation and cleaning up on the part of the staff. Trained teachers are better able to organize a wider variety of activities, and, at the same time, they are more sensitive to the use of both informative and informal talk with children. In general, care-type activities require a higher staff/child ratio than educational-type activities because children in the former are not as busy on their own as in the latter.

[54] Bone, *Pre-school Children and the Need*, p. 15.

[55] These are, nevertheless, worthwhile suggestions, repeatedly made to little avail. Cf. Trades Union Congress, *The Under-Fives* (London: TUC, 1977). Some local authorities, as well as other individual day nurseries, have experimented with the use of teachers in day nurseries. In addition, some local social service and education authorities jointly have established a few so-called "child centres" explicitly to combine the caring and educational functions. These centers tend, however, to place the two staffs side by side, maintaining pay and other differences, rather than fully

ment departments would certainly help. The difficulties and impediments in this process are discussed later in this chapter. The essence of the difference between the two services, and the reason for the inferiority of day nurseries, appears to be based in part on conceptions of the class-related character of day care as opposed to nursery school. Whether or not children in day nurseries are actually from working-class families, they are considered (by authorities, staff, even the public) to be "deprived," because their mothers have had to leave them, either to go to work or to rehabilitate themselves or their home environment. I examine the actual class character of the various facilities one section hence. For now, I examine how the design of state intervention is expressed in quantity of provision.

Quantity. From World War II until about 1970 there was a steady decline in the provision of public day nursery care. Some changes did take place during this time concerning "priority group" placement. For example, when there was a shortage of nurses and teachers in the 1960s, eligibility restrictions were eased, without, however, resulting in a visible increase in the total number of places. A slight increase in the number of places in day nurseries began in the early 1970s (see Table 5.3). But this change was indirect and due to the reorganization of local governments.

In 1965 a government committee, chaired by Frederic Seebohm, was set up to investigate "Local Authority and Allied Personal Social Services." Its report, issued in 1968, recommended major reorganization. One chapter examined social services for children, including a section on services for children under five, with a subsection on the organization of day care. The Seebohm Committee recommended, first, that a new social service department assume responsibility for day nurseries, which had been

---

integrating them. These new efforts are experiencing mixed success, partly because of tensions between the two groups of professionals (personal interview, DHSS, May 1982). See also Peter Mottershead, *A Survey of Child Care.*

under local health authorities, because "the grounds for admitting children to day nurseries are primarily social."[56] Furthermore, it upheld the conclusion of an earlier committee investigating education (the Plowden Committee) that nursery schools and classes for children aged 3 to 5 ought to remain the responsibility of education authorities. The Seebohm Committee recognized, however, that because of nursery schools' hours and holidays these could not "adequately meet the needs of most mothers who have to go out to full-time work and of most motherless families."[57] It recommended, therefore, that the new social service departments "carry responsibility for providing community care facilities when these are required for the periods when 3 to 5 year olds are not attending nursery schools." This amounted to a recommendation to extend day nurseries, part-time at any rate, to children whose mothers have to work full-time (thereby recognizing the category of working mother rather than welfare family). The Seebohm Committee also recommended that local authority social service departments better coordinate their activities with other services used by preschool age children, including those already under its jurisdiction (child-minders, playgroups), as well as those run by education authorities. It specifically recommended greater responsibility in "providing, supporting or supervising play groups for children under 5."

The first of these recommendations, requiring an extension of day nursery provision to children whose mothers work full-time, was not accepted by DHSS. Instead, the broad category of "mothers who have to work" was narrowed to "unsupported or single mothers," a group that was already being given priority. It is highly unlikely, then, that the small increase in number of places in the 1970s included an extension of clientele. However, in deference

[56] Report of the Committee on Local Authority and Allied Personal Social Services (London: HMSO, 1968) (the Seebohm Report), p. 61.

[57] Ibid. Following quotes also on p. 61.

Table 5.3 Day Care Provision in Britain

	Public Day Nurseries		Private Premises[a]		Public Nursery Schools[b]			Public Nursery Classes[c]		Child-minders (Registered)	
						No. of Children		No. of Children			
	No.	No. of Places	No.	No. of Children	No.	Part day	Full day	Part day	Full day	No.	No. of Children
1945	1,300	62,784									
1946	914	43,618			75	—	6,000	—	184,697 (1947)		
1950	884	42,410	326	8,965	416	—	21,079	—	148,428	415	2,638
1955	583	28,024	443	11,679	464	—	23,127	1,000	152,790	777	6,090
1960	477	22,564	601	14,595	454	2,239	21,757	1,703	174,910	1,531	11,881
1965	448	21,396	2,245	55,543	461	7,975	19,927	10,431	197,476	3,393	27,200
1970	453	21,581	10,043	248,883	482	17,779	16,441	28,520	228,292	25,595	84,861
1974	517	24,772	14,843	326,320	548	26,947	15,450	59,660	291,579	30,552	86,954
1980	613	28,400	806[d]	22,000	596	34,377	14,079	150,122	230,342	42,900	107,000
			14,800[e]	500,000							
% population age 0-4 in 1973		0.7		9.0			1.1		9.4		2.5

% children whose
mothers
work
full time[f]
(est. 1974)

| 10.0 | (No playgroups) | 8.0 | 11.0 | 6.0 | 24.0 | 117.0 | 35.0 |

Adapted from: Jack Tizard, Peter Moss, Jane Perry, *All Our Children: Pre-school Services in a Changing Society* (London: Temple Smith/New Society, 1976), appendix tables and p. 88; Department of Health and Social Security, *Day Care Facilities in England at 31 March 1980* (DHSS, 1980); Private communication, DHSS, 1982; Department of Education, *Statistical Bulletin* (DES, February 1982).

[a] Includes private day nurseries, private nursery schools and, after 1960, playgroups. After 1965 constituted mostly by playgroups. 1980 figures separate out playgroups.

[b] Figures are for 1973, not 1974.

[c] Includes other under-fives in primary schools. Figures are for 1973, not 1974.

[d] private/voluntary day nurseries

[e] playgroups

[f] In 1974 there were an estimated 250,000 children whose mothers work full time.

to the Seebohm Committee, the DHSS in 1972 asked local authorities to submit 10-year development plans for provisions for children under five. Furthermore, the DHSS recommended that day nursery places be increased by 2 per 1,000 children in each area, even though it was admitted that this figure might be inadequate even to cover all "priority" children.[58] Although the projections made by local authorities varied tremendously, depending on their current level of provision, many of the plans looked generally favorable to expansion and pointed in the direction of change. This was all very short-lived, however. In 1974-1975 the DHSS cut by 20% the capital expenditure program for local authority social service departments, and the plans for expansion were put on hold. To date they remain shelved. The current policy is one of maintaining what now exists, if possible, although retrenchment in the future is also a possibility.

The second recommendation of the Seebohm Committee, to make better use of other types of already existing child care facilities, was taken up more readily by local authorities. In fact, some local authorities were already doing so. Expediency was beginning to require a new look at the private sector. Note, again, in Table 5.4, the tremendous increase by 1970 in the number of "private premises" (second column) and "registered child-minders" (last column). Let us look at what was happening with child-minders in particular to generate this increase.

The law requires that all child-minders, persons caring for children unrelated to them for at least two hours a day for payment, register with their local authorities.[59] Local

[58] The recommended increase was from the then-current national average level of 6 places per 1,000 children to 8 places per 1,000 children. Tizard, Moss, Perry, *Pre-school Services*, note that it is unclear why this figure for an increase was chosen, p. 88.

[59] Guidelines for registration come from DHSS in its various circulars, and in addenda to the Nurseries and Child-minders Regulation Act of 1948, amended in 1968 (Health Services and Public Health Act, Section 60).

authorities are required to inspect the premises and insure that certain standards are met before issuing registration. Neither of these requirements has ever been fully met anywhere. In addition, the lists of registered child-minders are often notoriously out of date, and, because follow-ups rarely occur, some registered child-minders are caring for more than the legal maximum number of children. Most estimates agree that the number of unregistered child-minders far exceeds the number of registered. In the 1960s some local authorities, for reasons of their own, began the practice of placing children with child-minders. No doubt these were priority children who could not be placed in day nurseries. After the Seebohm report the DHSS began to encourage this use of child-minders, provided that the minder is "carefully selected." Circulars acknowledged that the "best child-minder . . . may be able to offer a more suitable form of care than the large day nursery."[60] A government-sponsored conference on "Low Cost Provision for the Under-Fives" recognized the potential contribution of child-minders, and other previously overlooked resources.[61] Local authorities began more actively to encourage registration of child-minders.[62] Hence the increase in figures. However, the significance of the increase for working mothers is probably negligible. It is doubtful that there has been an increase in the actual number of child-minders, that their quality has improved so as to allay parental concerns, or that normal working parents seeking child care are receiving any greater assistance. A joint DHSS/DES circular issued in 1978 acknowledges that "Parents suffering social and economic disadvantage including many in the ethnic minority groups, tend to a greater extent than others to use child-minders

[60] Ministry of Health, Circular 37/68 (1968).

[61] Besides child-minders, there were papers on playgroups and other voluntary organizations. *Low Cost Provision.*

[62] This was done primarily through poster campaigns in health clinics and social service offices. The penalty for non-registration remained at £50.

to provide day care for their children."[63] What is happening is that more priority children are coming to the attention of local authorities. However, local authorities continue to employ child-minders at their own discretion. Generally, the more hard-pressed local authorities, which are unable to place priority cases in their day nurseries, are more willing to make use of child-minders and to appreciate their services. As of 1980 about 3,400 child-minders were being sponsored by local authorities and caring for about 7,300 children (with various financial arrangements).[64] Better-off local authorities tend to be less approving of child-minders.[65] And yet, despite this change, the waiting lists for day nurseries are not getting any shorter.

The best way to summarize and assess quantity of day care provision would be in relation to need. But the needs of working mothers are not the target of public provision in Britain. As the number of working mothers with young children has increased over the last two decades, the role of the state in providing or in assisting in the provision of day care has not changed. Nor, for that matter, has the slight increase in public provision and greater use of private child care adequately accommodated the kind of need for which the state does accept responsibility, witness the perennially long waiting lists for priority children alone.[66] What

[63] Department of Health and Social Security, Department of Education and Science, "Co-ordination of Services for Children Under Five," Local Authority Social Services Letter LASSL (78)1 (DHSS), Reference No. S47/24/013 (DES), (25 January 1978), p. 3.

[64] Studies are finding that the cost to a local authority of hiring a good child-minder (and paying benefits, as well as wages) is the same as placing a child in a day nursery. Cf. Equal Opportunities Commission, *I Want to Work . . . but what about the kids?* (Manchester: EOC, September, 1978), p. 16.

[65] Community Relations Commission, *Who Minds? A Study of Working Mothers and Childminding in Ethnic Minority Communities* (London: Community Relations Commission, 1975), pp. 14-21 and *passim.*

[66] One parliamentary committee estimated the figure for priority children at 85,000 in 1972, *Sixth Report from the Expenditure Committee: The Employment of Women* (London: HMSO, 1973), p. xvii. A recent survey of facilities in 32 London boroughs found the waiting lists of individual day

we can say about the quantity of day care provision is that it reflects the limited role of the state.

As we have seen throughout this section, the state does not presume to intervene to any great depth in the private family function of child care. Provision in day nurseries does not change directly the home situation that required placement. Provision does offer parents a temporary reprieve from child care, which may allow them, indirectly, to improve the home environment, through employment or medical treatment. Provision also compensates children for the deprivation they suffer at home. But, as has been noted, the kind of services given in day nurseries differs qualitatively from those being offered to other children in other facilities. In many respects, day nurseries can be thought of as an inferior service for a disadvantaged group. Thus intervention does not affect, directly or significantly, the forces that created the disadvantage in the first place. The consequences of this form of intervention, in fact, can be said to aggravate the disadvantages that initially led to state intervention. The elaboration of this point rests on an analysis of the class characteristics of those using the different facilities and the extent to which the state can be said to be reinforcing class divisions by its form of intervention.

Social Class: Cause and Consequence. I have argued that class condition, that is, being in a welfare situation, is the main determinant of eligibility for day nursery services. Moreover, I have suggested that by limiting its services and providing a distinct kind of service to a welfare clientele the state further reinforces the divisions among social classes. Data on the actual class characteristics of children in day nurseries, central as they are to this analysis, are scarce. Local authorities and day nurseries do not, as a rule, keep

---

nurseries to vary from "small" to over 500: Pat Knight, *Survey of London Borough Nurseries* (*mimeo.*, no date). EOC quotes the figure 12,601 priority cases under-five waiting for local authority places in 1976, *I Want to Work*, p. 7.

information on such common indicators of class as family income or parents' occupations. Some scattered surveys do exist, though none is national and none unconditionally substantiates my inferences. But they do lend support to hypotheses about class divisions. I present the findings of the most systematic and most recent survey on day care in Britain, sponsored by the Office of Population and Censuses Surveys in 1974.[67]

First, a word of caution about the survey. Interviewers asked mothers what type of facility their children used, and the mothers' answers were recorded without verification. Differences in definition abound, no doubt based on misperceptions as well as vocabulary.[68] Table 5.4 presents the distribution of type of provision used by father's occupation; Table 5.5 does the same for income. Looking at the figures for day nursery use, which are understandably low, there is virtually no difference between the higher and lower status occupations and the higher and lower income categories.[69] This is most surprising. When I questioned the author of the survey about this, her response was twofold. First, she felt there may have been some irregularity in understanding what day nurseries (as well as the other facilities) actually are. Second, she noted that large numbers of teachers and nurses were among the respondents. Apparently, many local authorities continue to include these two types of non-welfare working mothers among their

[67] The only other national survey was conducted by the Department of Child Health Research Unit, University of Bristol. The report is still being prepared.

[68] This is particularly true of the term "child-minder." This survey made no distinction between taking a child to someone else's home and employing a nanny, au pair, or babysitter in the child's own home. (Responses were open-ended.) The latter practice is, of course, more frequent among the wealthier.

[69] These findings conflict with those of another study which is of much broader scope and greater detail but, unfortunately, is not yet complete. The Research Unit at the University of Bristol is finding that mothers with lower education tend to use day nurseries. In addition, there is a higher use of private facilities by the "well-to-do."

TABLE 5.4 Type of Day Care Used by Children under Five Years, According to Father's Occupation (%)

	All Occupations	Professional	Managerial and Technical	Clerical & Semi-skilled Non-manual	Skilled Manual	Semi- and Unskilled Manual
Playgroup	18	24	21	23	18	13
Nursery/Primary school	9	10	14	5	9	8
Day nursery	2	1	2	2	2	1
Child-minder	3	4	3	2	2	2
Crèche	1	1	1	—	—	—
No day care	68	60	60	68	71	76
Base: Children in social class (= 100%)	2,501[a]	146	415	252	1,121	373

Adapted from: Margaret Bone, *Pre-school Children and the Need for Day-Care* (London: HMSO, 1977), p. 11.
[a] Includes 193 unclassified children.

TABLE 5.5 Type of Day Care Used, According to Joint Parental Income per Week (%)

	All Incomes	£21	–£30	–£40	–£50	–£60	Over £60
Playgroups	18	9	14	16	22	21	26
Nursery/primary school	9	11	7	7	9	13	13
Day nursery	2	4	2	1	1	4	2
Child-minder	3	2	1	1	3	6	4
Crèche	1	1	0	0	1	1	2
No day care	68	74	76	75	65	57	55
Base: Children under 5 years (= 100%)	2,501[a]	161	432	701	490	288	143

Source: Margaret Bone, *Pre-school Children and the Need for Day-Care* (London: HMSO, 1977), p. 11.
[a] Includes 171 children for whom parental income is not known.

priority groups. Another variable may be more revealing. Table 5.6 presents the cost per week of day care provision. Looking down the column for day nursery use, we see that over half of the users attend for free or pay the very lowest fee. Since we know that fees are based on a sliding scale according to ability to pay, we can surmise that some of those in the middle income range and middle non-manual occupations may have been single mothers who need most of their earnings for their own and their children's upkeep. Other surveys confirm that single mothers make up a large proportion of the clientele of day nurseries.[70] One other finding is noteworthy, namely, that playgroups and nursery schools are used more by higher income groups. This finding is consistent in all surveys.[71]

The evidence is skimpy, to say the least, and not altogether reliable. The points that I am making about social divisions based on institutional differences refer to perceptions on the part of nursery staff of the class origin of clientele, and not to the objective economic condition of nursery users. We have seen that staff in the different institutions believe they are dealing with different kinds of clientele and behave accordingly. Parents themselves are aware of the differences between day nurseries and nursery schools. In surveys of preference, both clients and potential users say they would rather have their child attend a nursery school than a day nursery.[72] This is particularly true of parents with 3- and 4-year-old children. We can only conjecture whether this is due to the association of day nurseries with welfare as well as the more obvious worry about the lack of a satisfactory educational program for children in day nurseries.

[70] *Report of the Committee on One-Parent Families* (London: HMSO, 1974) (the Finer Report). In the 68 day nurseries surveyed, an average of 50% of the clients were single mothers.

[71] Besides those already mentioned, Joyce S. Watt, *Pre-School Education and the Family: Relative Responsibilities of Local Authority Departments* (mimeo., 1976).

[72] Bone, *Pre-school Children and the Need*, p. 15.

TABLE 5.6 Cost per Week of Day Care, According to Facility Used (%)

	All Types[a]	Play-group	Nursery School	Day Nursery	Child-minder
Free	16	7	49	33	2
Less than £1.50	56	85	27	20	20
£1.50 but less than £5	11	4	15	26	51
£5 or more	3	0	3	16	20
Not known	13	3	7	4	8
Base: Children using day care provision (= 100%)	790[b]	459	148	49	65

Source: Margaret Bone, *Pre-school Children and the Need for Day-Care* (London: HMSO, 1977), p. 12.
[a] Includes crèches, some of which are provided by mother's employer.
[b] Includes 83 children at primary school.

I return to the concept of class and social division in the conclusion of this chapter. The next section carries the theme of differentiation into another setting—within the structure of government itself. The focus moves beyond the individual institutions to the wider system of responsibility for day care.

Institutionalization

The concept of institutionalization has two dimensions: process and structure. I analyze these two dimensions of the institutionalization of day care as follows. A study of the decision-making process within government allows us to focus on the first dimension. The analysis shows that it is difficult to say who decides on day care, for while all other branches of government absolve themselves of responsibility and defer to the DHSS, the DHSS itself defers to traditional conceptions, local authorities, and financial constraints. Policy making thus emerges as an incremental process, fraught both by casual interest and piecemeal information. The structural conterpart of incrementalism is fragmentation. Evidence of this attribute of the day care system at the level of government is drawn from an examination of unsuccessful joint efforts by the DHSS and the DES to integrate and inspire day care programs. In addition, fragmentation can be seen in the relations among the various actors involved in deciding on or implementing day care policy.

Here we will continue to develop the theme that was first suggested in the previous two sections on state intervention. We have seen that day care is organized on the principle of differentiation between mutually exclusive categories— between the eligible and the ineligible, and between one kind of service in day nurseries and another in nursery schools. Such differentiation also separates one branch of government from another. In this case, the closed and autonomous spheres of government delimit lines of responsibility at the same time as they limit the ability to act.

Throughout this section I attempt to locate a potential source of change for day care policy. The search within government proves fruitless, and the conclusion of this chapter explains why.

BRANCHES OF GOVERNMENT

The DHSS is the main branch of government responsible for formulating day care policy and overseeing its implementation. However, other branches of government could and have concerned themselves with matters related to day care policy. Before turning to the DHSS itself, I will review the involvement of these other branches of government.

Parliament is the most important "other branch." Its major contributions to women's employment have been the Sex Discrimination and Equal Pay Acts (discussed in Chapter 4). Neither of these acts mentions day care, nor has Parliament as a whole ever considered day care or other provisions for preschool children.[73] Some parliamentary subcommittees have considered matters related to women's employment and noted in passing the problem of day care. For example, the 1972 Expenditure Committee issued a report on the employment of women that was largely concerned with educational and training problems. It did, however, contain sections on facilities for children, both preschool and school age, and on "lone" mothers. The committee noted the inadequacy of existing facilities, and recommended

the rapid expansion of day nurseries and nursery school provision with flexible hours adjusted to the require-

---

[73] Services for preschool children are not statutory (except for health-related matters). That is, local authorities do what they can, under advisement from central government departments. However, local authority social service departments are under statutory obligation to do something about children who legally become "public wards," for example, orphans and battered children, once they are removed from their homes. Thus, Parliament itself can only recommend, not legislate, on preschool provision, unless, of course, its legislates to make certain preschool services mandatory.

ments of working mothers, and in particular, we support the establishment of nursery centres under the
supervision of the Department of Education and Science.[74]

No legislation followed this report. Both the DHSS and
DES were advised of the recommendations.

Short of legislation, Parliament indicates its concern on
issues which are topical or neglected by establishing special
investigatory committees called royal commissions. These
are composed of interest group representatives, experts in
the field, and politicians. No royal commission has ever
been set up to investigate women's employment or related
matters.[75] Nevertheless, two recent royal commissions on
other subjects found it necessary to mention local authority
provisions for preschool children. The Plowden Committee
on Education, reporting in 1967, did not suggest any change
in day care, but did suggest an extension of part-time nursery school.[76] It agreed with the DHSS position on the pro-
priety of young children remaining home with their own
mothers. A second royal commission, the Seebohm Committee on Local Authority and Allied Personal Social Services, agreed with the Plowden Committee on nursery schools.
But, as we have seen, the Seebohm Committee suggested
an extension of day nurseries to better meet the needs of
priority groups as well as to take into account the vast numbers of mothers entering the labor force. The recognition
that mothers with young children work was a major step.
However, the Seebohm Committee did not supplement its
perceptiveness by suggesting any restructuring of day care,
probably because it conceptualized "need" within the same

[74] *Sixth Report . . . Employment of Women*, p. xviii.

[75] The background materials for the Sex Discrimination and Equal Pay
Acts were gathered by a parliamentary committee and handled at the
ministerial level. For the politics behind this legislation, see Graham Wootton, *Pressure Politics in Contemporary Britain* (Lexington, Mass.: D. C. Heath,
1978), pp. 92-100.

[76] *Children and Their Primary Schools* (London: HMSO, 1967) (the Plowden Report).

basic paradigm as DHSS, that is, as stemming from economic necessity.

Parliament took both of these royal commission reports seriously, and both resulted in major changes.[77] The most important consequence of the Plowden Report for our purposes was the extention of part-time nursery schools and the reaffirmation of day care as unsuitable for very young children. As for the Seebohm Report, day nurseries were brought under the newly reorganized local authority social service departments, but they were not expanded systematically to include working mothers. Only some individual local authorities, those which were already providing well for their priority cases, took it upon themselves to follow the Seebohm Committee's suggestions—with DHSS approval but without its guidance.

In addition to Parliament and the royal commissions, the concern with day care on the part of two other branches of government requires mention. One is the Department of Employment, which is responsible for such matters relating to women's employment as training, job placement, sex discrimination, equal pay, and benefits. But the Department of Employment is not responsible for day care, nor has it exhibited any concern with day care. Another branch of government, one which has expressed interest in day care, is the Office of Population and Censuses Surveys (OPCS). This is a research arm of government. It undertook two major surveys that have been referred to in this chapter (one on women's employment, another on preschool provision). It is not up to OPCS to do anything with its reports other than publish them, and nothing more has been done. Some of the findings have been referred to by various committees and in departmental reports, but selectively.

What emerges from this overview of the involvement of other branches of government in contributing to day care

---

[77] Not all royal commission reports are debated in Parliament; some become pro forma only.

policy is a generalized unwillingness to accept any great depth of responsibility, if any concern even exists. The centrality of the DHSS appears sacrosanct. Two other branches of government that have contributed to day care policy and might rival DHSS's centrality are the DES and the local authorities. The important points about these other branches are best made in relation to the DHSS. I turn now to an examination of the key agency in day care policy to see to what extent it actually "decides" on day care.

THE DEPARTMENT OF HEALTH AND SOCIAL SECURITY

Every central government department is headed by a cabinet minister, who is also a Member of Parliament. In principle, the minister is responsible for policy development. Potentially, the minister is also the main source of policy innovation, since s/he represents fresh blood and outsiders' views; but, of course, there is no assurance that renewed authority at the top invigorates the policy process below. One study of the cabinet ministers' conceptions of their roles found a fairly even division between those who saw themselves as policy initiators or as policy selectors.[78] Which function a minister performs is entirely up to her/him—there is no constitutional division of labor within government that specifies the process of policy making. The DHSS has been headed for years by ministers who prefer to perform neither of these roles, in an active sense, with regard to day care policy. They have all preferred to allow departmental policy to be carried on as it is.

If not ministers, who else might take an active role in formulating day care policy? Civil servants, perhaps. The role of civil servants varies considerably by department and issue area. Understandably, the stronger the role of a minister in policy making, the weaker, but more supportive,

[78] Bruce W. Heady, "A Typology of Ministers: Implications for Minister-Civil Servant Relationships in Britain," in Mattei Dogan (ed.), *The Mandarins of Western Europe: The Political Role of Top Civil Servants* (New York: John Wiley and Sons, 1975). Heady's is a finer typology than the more common weak-strong dichotomy.

the role of civil servants. There are two categories of civil servants. Top personnel are known as "generalists," versed in matters of administration flexibly applied to any branch of government and any department within it. On a lower tier are civil servants who are less mobile. Their educational background is somewhat more specialized, and they become more specialized in the matters of one department.[79] In the DHSS, responsibility for day care has been placed in the hands of this second group. The persons who have headed the Division of Child Welfare have been specialists in social work or social services. This fact may have contributed to the dominant conception of day care within DHSS, and it may be contributing to the continuing commitment to that conception. It does not, however, explain the lack of innovation in day care policy. We can only say that civil servants, as well as ministers, have been responsible for the passive reaffirmation of past policy. We cannot add that the conceptualization of a problem offered by a single profession is limiting the ability of civil servants to re-think the problem.

The situation within DHSS is the same as the situation elsewhere in government—no actor or agent is willing to accept greater responsibility to do much more to change day care policy. Everyone else defers to DHSS. Does the DHSS fully accept all responsibility for day care? The answer is no. It, too, engages in this game of deferment—it yields to local authorities (and, of course, to the current economic situation). In interviews, civil servants (in both DHSS and DES) stressed the fact that central government can only "suggest" to local authorities. Grants may be provided to encourage local authorites to follow suit, but action is up to them. This nominal local independence is true for both expansion and experiment. Indeed, officials at DHSS concede that most of the recent innovations (for example,

---

[79] The Fulton Committee, which investigated the civil service and reported in 1968, criticized both specialists and generalists, as well as the dichotomy between them. While reforms are being made in some departments, they are slow and disparate.

in neighborhood and combined child centers) were initiated by individual local authorities. Let us now turn to the local authorities' side of the picture to see what is hindering them from taking greater initiative in day care policy—besides deferment to DHSS.

LOCAL AUTHORITIES

Local authorities have the potential to be innovators in social policy. In principle, they are remarkably free agents. They are allowed to assess their own needs, sometimes in their own terms, and they can provide their statutory services accordingly. As a result of this sort of formal autonomy, variations in actual provision among local authorities are great. Area of residence can be the major determinant of the type of service that is available to individuals.

In practice, however, local authorities are far from being free agents. The crucial power of the purse belongs to central government. Financial arrangements are usually divided at approximately 60% + central government and 30% + local authority. Many local authorities are consistently (and traditionally) hard-pressed to fulfill their statutory obligations. Central government tends to prescribe aims and standards and to suggest changes without providing or assuring the resources to meet them. Local authorities are expected to perform juggling acts within set budget allotments.[80] Local differences in these skills also increase the gross inequality in provision by area of residence. Local authorities are also subject to the variations among central government departments in both subtle and obvious ways. Different central government departments not only have established different relationships with their local authority partners but also differ among themselves in their generosity with allotments. The Ministry of Education, for instance, is noted for its frankness and close cooperation with local authorities and its ample provision

[80] The Seebohm Report, p. 196.

of supplies and educational materials.[81] This has meant, among other things, that changes and expansion in nursery school provision have been quite responsive to public expressions of need and demand, more so than have social service provisions. For example, the growth of the play-group movement spurred an expansion in part-time nursery classes for preschool children.[82] We can see that those factors that are conducive to experimentation and innovation by local authorities are ad hoc. In the past decade or so, the central government has provided some carrots, but no sticks. There have been special grants (for example, under the Urban Aid Programme), but local authorities have had to take the initiative to apply. The same is true of the current attempts at coordination among services for preschool children as recommended by the Seebohm Committee. Some special funding, limited of course, is available for experimental programs, but no doubt it is the same local authorities as always who are taking advantage of the new opportunities. Indeed, they may now be using these funds to do what they were previously doing within existing financial constraints. Other, less experimental authorities can easily shy away from change by invoking the doctrine that they require specific statutory authority for their actions. Unsystematic central guidance and idiosyncratic local characteristics lead to fragmented implementation of incrementally developed policies.

What is going on here? We cannot discover a single actor or agent who decides on day care, let alone suggest who could possibly contribute to change in day care policy. How-

---

[81] Marsh, *The Future of the Welfare State*, p. 109. The different "cultural milieux" of the two departments can only be suggested. For a "cultural" study of British government, see Hugh Heclo and Aaron Wildavsky, *The Private Government of Public Money: Community and Policy Inside British Politics* (Berkeley: University of California Press, 1974).

[82] This was the avowed aim of the early organizers of the playgroup movement. The DES refuses to recognize playgroups as educational because their instructors are not always trained teachers. It therefore also refuses to bring playgroups under its jurisdiction.

ever, we now have a sense that there is something outside of single actors or agents and consistent among them that is constraining them. Let us turn our attention, then, to the relationship among the entities to see if we can locate the key to this apparent reluctance to change. The most important relationship in which coordination has been attempted and which allows a glimpse of the latent problem, namely the persistence of traditional "domains," is that between DHSS and DES.

DHSS/DES

Since approximately 1976 DHSS and DES have attempted to forge some form of coordination of their many services for children under five. Representatives from these two departments, as well as outside advisers and representatives from other departments and organizations, meet every few months for consultations. As a result of the meetings, a first joint DHSS/DES letter was issued to local authorities in 1976; a second, in 1978, advised them of the new spirit of cooperation at central level and suggested how it might be put to practical use. The first of these letters was characterized by a mild and noncommital tone, a tendency to put the onus of implementation on local authorities, and a diffidence in the suggestions for coordination. (For example, if space is available in a school a room should be rented out to a playgroup; if everyone agrees, a few selected children can be taken from a day nursery to a nursery school, accompanied at all times by a day nursery staff member.[83]) Many of the suggestions were already being tried out by local authorities at their own initiative. Some of the local attempts at coordination had already been assessed by a government committee as less than satisfac-

[83] Department of Health and Social Security, Department of Education and Science, "Co-ordination of Local Authority Services for Children Under 5," Local Authority Social Services Letter LASSL (76)5 (DHSS), Reference No. S 21/47/05 (DES) (9 March 1976).

tory.[84] Others, such as the combined child centers, were experiencing difficulties (in integrating staff) requiring greater central guidance, which has yet to be forthcoming.[85]

The grand attempt at coordination at the central government level is an example not of leadership but of central sanctioning of courses of action already being taken by local authorities and individual institutions. Together DHSS and DES have managed to maintain the distinctions between them while displacing the burden of implementing coordination onto local authorities. One of the main impediments to the greater coordination of central government has been the tradition of the legitimate domain of each department. Up to now, DHSS alone has been responsible for the "care" and welfare of children under 5, DES for the educational enrichment of children over 3. The problem of the overlap of jurisdiction for children aged 3 to 5 has been handled according to the kind of institution the children attend. Moreover, DHSS has always stood to lose from any integration of provisions for preschool children, and DES has stood to gain. Day nurseries were (and still are) roundly criticized for limiting their services and not providing the same enriching programs that other institutions, such as nursery schools, are providing for the youngsters under their supervision.[86] In contrast, educational programs for preschool children are not criticized for providing insufficient attention to "care" factors—except by DHSS officials. In the face of this criticism, DHSS

[84] The Seebohm Commitee concluded "[we are not convinced] that any of these means of securing co-ordinated action work satisfactorily. Although the success achieved obviously varies in different areas, overall the impression is of very limited success despite the expenditure of much time and energy," p. 28. These attempts at coordination within individual local authorities were, of course, totally ad hoc.

[85] The problem of integrating staff at the child centers, referred to above (footnote 55), is a central government responsibility since it involves such matters as pay, training, and promotion.

[86] This criticism comes from such groups as the TUC and several well-known educational research institutes, as well as from individuals within government.

representatives stressed more firmly the need for more background in social work for those working with priority case children and their families, sensing that coordination with DES would mean that the "care" and the social work specializations of day nurseries would be diluted. DES, however, could expand its educational views into new fields and for a new type of "clientele."

The outcome of this struggle for domains is apparent in the second joint circular issued in 1978. There is one reference to the fact that staff in day nurseries working with children who have multiple problems should hold or be encouraged to obtain a certificate of qualification in social work. In contrast, references abound on the need to enhance the educational content of programs for preschool children. For example, "Many children receiving day care do not attend such [nursery] schools and classes and the Departments hope that all authorities will examine the possibilities of improving the educational content of the various forms of day care available in their areas." And, "increasingly, authorities are also recognizing the educational needs of children who attend day nurseries and in some areas teachers are visiting nurseries to work with their staff."[87] Statements such as these reflect the changes in attitude that are beginning to seep into central government, changes that were already present among the actual providers of day care at the local level.

In sum, the institutionalization of day care in Britain is characterized by a fragmentation among the government authorities involved and a division of responsibility reflecting the persistence of fiefdomship. No single branch of government is consistently willing to assume leadership for much needed change in the provision of day care. Each branch defers in this role to another. However, when threatened by an invasion of its domain, the central agency in the whole operation, DHSS, tends to tighten its rein. This has taken the form of a strict interpretation of such

[87] DHSS, DES, "Co-ordination of Services" (1978), p. 3.

standards as who attends day nurseries and what provisions are required for the maintenance of day nurseries, as well as an insistence about the social work qualification for the providers of the service. For a time, strict rules and definitions put firm closure on the issue of day care as a whole, minimizing the need to make substantive considerations about change.

One can now see signs of an impending breakdown in the system of day care provision in Britain, due in large part to its organizational and provisional inadequacies. Innovative local authorities, fed up with the lack of leadership from the top, are improvising on their own. While their efforts are much to be admired, the consequences of ad hoc organizational arrangements and selective innovation will not help the problem of piecemeal provision for working mothers as a whole.[88] Only those clients lucky enough to live in certain districts will benefit. In addition, the DES has now entered, by government mandate, the field of day care provision. Its influence is being felt by the gradual erosion of the care versus education division that has plagued the British system for so long. Thus far the two functions, where they coexist at all, tend to sit side by side rather than being properly integrated. Still, this is the common path of change in a liberal system. Incrementalism rids the system of one particular problem; at the same time, unfortunately, it gives rise to the unfortunate consequences of single-targeted change.

CONCLUSION

Among the many meanings of the term welfare state, there is "a central core of agreement" that it implies "a state commitment of some degree which modifies the play of market forces" in the attempt to achieve a greater measure

---

[88] Martin Bradley, *Co-ordination of Services for Children Under Five* (DHSS, DES, 1981). The great variety of forms of coordination can be both praised for its innovativeness and criticized for its contribution to bafflement.

of economic and social equality.[89] This chapter has examined one instance of state intervention, day care provision, which neutralizes market forces in particular cases rather than generally redirecting these forces, and which compensates for inequality rather than seeking greater equality. I have briefly reviewed the parameters of state intervention in day care provision, emphasizing the consequences of intervention. The form of intervention that we see in British day care provision reinforces two kinds of social divisions—those pertaining to economic class and those pertaining to women as a class. The dynamics which in interaction produce this outcome have to do with the class basis of the provision of care, the exclusion of normal working mothers, and the institutionalization of intervention.

Why does the state in Britain provide day care in the first place? State intervention is justified by the existence of an emergency situation, if not war, then some form of family breakdown or other irregularity requiring the mother to be absent from her normal child-rearing duties.[90] What is the purpose of state intervention in relation to this breakdown? By providing for child care in a public institution, the state is allowing parents to improve or set aright their family situation. But this outcome is not assured; the form of intervention, day care provision, is only indirectly related to the needs of a family in distress. However, insofar as day care enables parents to work or gives a sick mother the rest needed for a return to health, then the provision can be said to directly facilitate the (re-)establishment of family normalcy. That is, if the need to care for their children is preventing parents from improving the family situation,

---

[89] Dorothy Wedderburn, "Facts and Theories of the Welfare State," *The Socialist Register* (1965), pp. 127-28.

[90] This is called a "residual" conception of welfare. Breakdown and rehabilitation are thought of as temporary; so too, therefore, is the need for state intervention. Harold L. Wilensky and Charles N. Lebeaux, *Industrial Society and Social Welfare* (New York: The Free Press, 1965). John M. Romanyshyn, *Social Welfare: Charity to Justice* (New York: Random House, 1971).

then the provision of child care directly facilitates improvement. The purpose of intervention must also include a conception of what the children need while they are away from their mothers. By examining the program and staff of day nurseries, we saw that care is thought of as custodial. The program does no less for the child than would be done in a normal home, nor does it do more. It does not improve the child's situation, except indirectly by removing the child from possible neglect or maltreatment. The fact that the purpose of day nurseries is not improvement is significant primarily because it contrasts with the purpose of programs for preschool children in other institutions, in particular in public nursery schools and nursery classes. The differences in the programs disadvantage children in day nurseries.

In both of these dimensions of state intervention, justification and purpose, the factor of class appears to be significant. Personal or family breakdowns can occur in any family. However, the need to seek public assistance when breakdown occurs is more likely among poor families with fewer resources. This suggests that public assistance is not the preferred or normal means of help. The conception of the need for day care as being related to poverty is expressed in the strict criteria of eligibility for day nursery provision, as well as in official statements and guidelines concerning day nurseries and the attitudes and behavior of staff. In this way the existence of social classes and class-specific needs may be said to determine state intervention. The program provided in day nurseries is based on this conception of the clientele as recipients of welfare. Once the state has accepted and defined its area of responsibility, it adopts a paternalistic approach to its clientele, fully absorbing all considerations into standardized bureaucratic rules, thereby reducing the exercise of discretion in individual cases. There is no inherent reason why welfare children should not be taught to read in the same way and at the same time as middle-class children of the same age in nursery schools. That children in day nurseries are thereby disadvantaged and their class status thereby maintained may well be simply an anomaly of the institutionalization of day care in Britain. We have no evidence that it is anything more. But the fact remains that a reinforcement of social divisions based on class *is* a consequence of the mode of state intervention in the provision of day care programs for preschool children.

When we look at the way in which intervention is institutionalized, we see another mechanism by means of which social divisions are maintained. This one has nothing to do with whether or not the state itself has a class basis. It refers more generally to the institutional mechanism of differentiation based on division of responsibility. Responsibility for day care is not readily or fully accepted by any department or level of government. Deferment is based on many factors, including traditional jurisdictions as well as concern with having to confront what is wrong with day care and doing something about it. Nevertheless, the branch of government to which most of the responsibility falls, the Department of Health and Social Security, has an institutional interest in maintaining the status quo in day care, particularly the care and welfare component. For broadening the scope of day care means sharing power and resources with the Department of Education and Science. To distinguish "us" from "them" becomes imperative for the bureaucracy. The resulting fragmentation permeates the logic of intervention in day care. Nevertheless, circumstances are forcing DHSS to relax its strict definition of the situation. The consequence thus far is even greater central deferment to local authorities, with the attendant greater lack of consistency in quality and quantity of day care provision for current and would-be users.

The implications of this analysis for women go beyond the immediate facts that day care provision is limited and that the negative attitude toward working mothers is not conducive to freedom of choice. We saw in Chapter 2 that working women in Britain function as an economic class—they are a "reserve" of labor, fluctuating in and out of the labor market according to the business cycle, and working in low-status, low-paying jobs. Their marginality in the economy places them in the lower strata of the class structure. This chapter suggests that working women are placed in the position of a marginal social class. Public day care provision excludes the interests of non-welfare working mothers. By implication the state deems it to be in the public interest not to provide universal day care. The interests of working mothers are thus fragmented from the norm, subordinated to it, and particularized.

The kind of intervention that we see in British day care provision is characteristic of a liberal welfare state. A commitment to welfare determines that the state intervenes; a commitment to liberalism determines how and to what extent it intervenes. This particular combination of welfare-ism and liberalism is peculiar to Britain. It is not the case in Sweden. The next chapter demonstrates that in Sweden welfare-ism is combined with a form of corporatism, with significantly different consequences for working women and social equality. How any combination of approaches to social problems comes to be the dominant mode in any one country is the essence of the contemporary debate concerning the theory of the state. This debate as it pertains to Britain and Sweden will occupy the last chapter.

CHAPTER 6

SWEDEN: THE ROLE OF THE STATE IN THE PROVISION OF DAY CARE

INTRODUCTION

The development of day care policy in Sweden has to be seen in light of the previous chapters on changes in attitudes toward working women in Sweden and in policies for them. Women's labor force participation increased dramatically in the 1960s largely due to government policies in the fields of economic management and labor market programs. Because of women's increased labor force participation and the continuing demand for women workers, and in full recognition of the desirability of social equality for women, other facilitative social policies, such as day care programs, also developed. Thus, day care was both a catalyst for the further employment of women and a supporting measure serving the needs of women who work.

Day care policy and programs in Sweden are presented here in counterpoint to the policies and programs in Britain. Issues of care vs. education, clientele, class, and delivery of services are discussed within the framework of the role of the state. Many of the problems posed by these issues in Britain have also existed in the past in Sweden. But because the state in Sweden has taken a different role, one which has been evolving for some time and which took shape in the 1960s, these problems by and large have been overcome. A different policy process has produced a different policy outcome. The form of policy making that has developed in Sweden is a corporatist version of social democracy. I first elaborate what is meant by corporatism and corporatist social democracy in particular, and then go on

to show how state intervention in the social function of
child care has become an important addition to the bundle
of policies facilitating the ability of women to work.

CORPORATIST SOCIAL DEMOCRACY

The concept of corporatism has become an increasingly
refined analytical tool for studying the role of the state in
advanced capitalist societies.[1] In broad terms, corporatism
may be defined as "a system of interest and/or attitude
representation, a particular modal or ideal-typical institutional arrangement for linking the associationally organized interests of civil society with the decisional structures
of the state."[2] The groups so linked to the state represent
a particular hierarchy of social power, a particular *blocco
storico*, in Gramsci's terms, around whose shared interests
social control and social rewards are organized.[3] Moreover,
once so linked to the state, these groups cease to be strictly
speaking voluntary, since access to effective decision making in society is mediated by them. And, lastly, this form
of interest association is non-competitive, insofar as these
groups are incorporated more or less permanently into
parastatal decision-making bodies. Within these broad
characteristics, two types of corporatist systems may be dis-
tinguished: state corporatism and societal corporatism.

In a state corporatist system, the state coalesces and sanc-

---

[1] The concept of corporatism was first used to describe fascist Italy. In
some contexts it still has a connotation of authoritarianism. Usually the
locus of power is with the state, as in Latin America, but sometimes organized private interests, either labor or business, are in control. The
various meanings of corporatism stem from the variety of national settings
to which the concept has been applied. For a list of the uses of corporatism,
see Philippe C. Schmitter, "Still the Century of Corporatism?" *The Review
of Politics*, 26 (1974), pp. 87-88.

[2] Ibid., p. 86.

[3] This discussion is based on ibid.; Ruth Berins Collier and David Collier,
"Inducements versus Constraints: Disaggregating 'Corporatism,' " *American Political Science Review*, 73 (December 1979); and J. T. Winkler, "Corporatism," *Archives Européenes de Sociologie*, 17 (1976).

tions the groups that are then incorporated under state auspices into the dominant mechanisms of social decision making. In its extreme, fascist, variant, the state may create these groups in the first place. In any case, the state directly constrains the organization and functioning of the incorporated groups. In a societal corporatist system, interest groups occupy powerful social positions in their own right, without state intervention. The state accepts, as a working basis of governance, such dominant social coalitions as may have emerged within society. The state seeks the expertise and the support of the groups that represent these coalitions, and co-opts them into the decision-making mechanisms by means of inducements. Under the societal type of corporatism, mutual adjustment rather than hierarchy governs state-group relations.

These, of course, are ideal types. For purposes of analysis, however, Sweden may be said to approximate a specific form of societal corporatism, the social democratic variant.[4] Corporatism emerged in Sweden in the 1930s, when the Social Democrats first came to power. They were dependent on the active support of a number of interest groups, in particular labor. But labor and employers' groups had already worked out their own institutionalized form of collaboration. The state simply incorporated this form of collaboration into the governing process, and the fundamental compromise that labor and employers had managed to reach became the very foundation of Swedish socioeconomic policy from that time on. Building on this basis, but never departing from it, Swedish societal corporatism developed

[4] Swedish scholars themselves are unhappy with having the term "corporatism" applied to their cooperative form of governance. For, even with the adjective "societal" as a prefix, the term carries too strong a connotation of state dominance. Walter Korpi, for one, prefers the term "social bargaining." See his book, *The Working Class in Welfare Capitalism: Work, Unions and Politics in Sweden* (London: Routledge and Kegan Paul, 1978). It is my argument, however, that the somewhat stronger role of the state under a Social Democratic government provided the necessary extra impetus that led to the development of such strong policies for women as, for example, day care.

into a broad-based system of interest group representation, drawing in particular on functionally specific expert groups who can translate the fundamental compromise into working policy for each new set of social problems to which the state addresses itself. The active participation of these groups has become indispensable to the formulation of sound and acceptable policy, and the policies in turn are more likely to be implemented successfully because these groups can mobilize support on their behalf.[5] Thus, group participation has become not only a tradition in Sweden but even a necessity.

In the 1960s, changes developed in the Swedish form of societal corporatism, because of the expanding role of the state. What became distinctive about the societal corporatist form in Sweden was that the state under a Social Democratic government began to take a somewhat stronger role than is suggested by the pure societal corporatist model.[6] Within the governing coalition, the state acted increasingly in a directive rather than simply a supportive role.[7] In a supportive role, a state initiates actions within a prescribed and broadly accepted framework. A directive role still places heavy reliance on inducements to achieve compliance, and state intervention is governed by the tenets of social democracy, but the compliance inducements may be so strong as to verge on constraints.

I will argue that the form of corporatist social democracy that we find in Sweden, including the recent shifts in the role of the state, is largely responsible for the remarkable achievements that have made Sweden a "model" welfare state.[8] This chapter examines Sweden's social achievements

[5] Olaf Ruin, "Participatory Democracy and Corporativism: The Case of Sweden," *Scandinavian Political Studies*, 12 (1974), 174.

[6] Collier and Collier suggest that it is useful to treat the distinction between state and societal corporatism not as a dichotomy but as a continuum. "Inducements versus Constraints," p. 279.

[7] Winkler, "Corporatism," pp. 103-109.

[8] With the change in government in 1976 the role of the state changed slowly to a more liberal mode of intervention in some issue areas. However,

in one issue area, policies and programs for child care, where the consequences of the shift in the role of the state are particularly evident. The advancement of social equality for women and children is fully accepted by both socialist and non-socialist governments in Sweden, and the state has acted positively to assure implementation of clearly articulated and egalitarian goals into excellent and successful programs.

At the same time, there are also tensions and problems in the Swedish system of child care. A gap exists between goals and accomplishments, and quality sometimes is compromised by necessity. I analyze this gap not simply to show *that* it exists, which would scarcely be surprising. It is, in any case, a much smaller gap than exists in Britain. I analyze it rather from the point of view of showing *why the particular forms of shortcomings* exist, rather than some other forms. The explanation for this too lies in the nature of the Swedish state, as we shall see, specifically in that the form of interest aggregation assured by Swedish societal corporatism systematically excludes certain kinds of interests. I conclude by arguing that whatever "welfare backlash" may exist in Sweden is due less to a reaction against welfare and its cost[9] than it is due to the patterning of authority relations incorporated into the Swedish state via the prevailing form of corporatist social democracy.

In this chapter, I will follow the same format as the previous chapter on day care in Britain, except that for Sweden the analysis of each of the dimensions of the role of the state is divided into two parts: purpose and practice.

HISTORICAL CONTEXT

In the last few decades the issue of day care and its formulation on the public policy agenda in Sweden has

the development of the day care policies under consideration here took place under a Social Democratic government in the 1960s and early 1970s. I discuss below how the non-socialist government affected day care policy.

[9] Harold L. Wilensky, *The "New Corporatism," Centralization and the Wel-*

undergone a transformation that reflects a profound change in social attitudes toward the family. In earlier years day care was essentially a welfare issue in Sweden as elsewhere. The first Swedish "crèche" was set up in 1854 in Stockholm to care for children of poor working mothers. These early "day nurseries" were poorly equipped and strictly custodial.[10] The way in which the state, as well as the private sector, thought about day care and provided it was similar to Britain. The clients of day care facilities were "wards" of society, children whose families were in financial need or who for some other reason were left uncared for. Day nurseries provided a measure of relief for parents by at least allowing them to work, even though full-day institutional care was not thought to be in the best interests of the child. Nursery schools, on the other hand, were an entirely different matter. The few of these that existed were private and provided part-day educational enrichment for children whose families were better placed in society.

In 1935 a government Population Commission upheld this dualism of institutions and purposes. It questioned the value of supporting the institutional care of the youngest infants, although it recognized, reluctantly, the necessity for day nurseries to meet needs other than those of the children.[11] However, the Commission did suggest that the pedagogically motivated half-day preschool system deserved financial support from the state. Children from about the age of 3, the Commission contended, "needed some complement to their home environment, regardless of the nature of that environment."[12]

These suggestions remained just that until the 1940s. In 1941 another Population Commission reviewed the question of day care and preschools. It decided that while there

---

fare State (Beverly Hills: Sage Publications, 1976), argues the cost case.

[10] Ragnar Berfenstam and Inger William Olsson, *Early Child Care in Sweden* (London: Gordon and Breach, 1973), p. 81; Kenneth Jaffe, "The Politics of Child Care," *Social Change in Sweden*, No. 11 (March 1979).

[11] Bodil Rosengren, *Pre-school in Sweden* (Stockholm: The Swedish Institute, 1973), p. 11.

[12] Ibid.

was a difference between the two, both institutions deserved to be supported by state grants. The change of heart with regard to day nurseries can be directly related to the outbreak of World War II and the ensuing need for women workers.[13] To enable women to meet the labor force and production needs of the nation, publicly provided day care facilities became more readily available. The Commission's proposals for the facilities, particularly the concern with staff training, program activities, and integrated health and social services, were far-sighted, and the financial system to assist implementation was very supportive. But this boom in day care was short-lived. When, in 1950, a Committee for Semi-Open Child Care made thorough and far-sighted proposals concerning the many questions surrounding day care and preschools, its proposals were shelved. The 1950s were a period of mild recession in Sweden, in both the economy and social change. Because women by and large had returned to their traditional roles in the home, the quantity of day care returned to its prewar levels. While there was not a retreat to traditional philosophies regarding day care (even though Bowlby's work on maternal deprivation was as misunderstood in Sweden as elsewhere), there was renewed criticism of the effect of an institutional environment on children and of the quality of child care facilities. Once again, public centers were being used primarily by the needy, and, as always, the majority of children with working mothers were being cared for privately. With little support and little justification for expansion, the number of places in day nurseries increased by only 2,000 between 1950 and 1965. However, an upsurge of interest in part-time, pedagogically motivated nursery schools led to a doubling in their numbers between 1950 and 1960.

The story of modern day care in Sweden begins in the 1960s. At that time an upsurge in female employment took place in response to the new wave of industrial develop-

---

[13] Although Sweden was not in the war, men were conscripted to military service as a precaution against possible invasion. Women workers were required as a temporary replacement.

ment. The lack of day care facilities and the inadequacy of their institutional features were becoming all too obvious. A number of concerned groups, including industry, the unions, and the press, began to advocate reform measures. As is the custom in Sweden, a number of government commissions were set up throughout the decade to investigate aspects of the problem. A change in public policy toward day care was beginning to take shape. Finally, to consolidate the findings within the framework of a comprehensive government approach, a Royal Commission on Child Centers was appointed in 1968. The Commission's report, issued in 1972, proposed a revamping of the entire system of public day care, based on new conceptions of needs and purposes. These included: (1) recognition that, while all children need some form of preschool, the need for day care itself is directly related to the needs of normal working parents; (2) recognition of the harm done in the past because of the institutional separation of care and education; (3) a public commitment to meet the preschool needs of children and parents, quantitatively and qualitatively. The Commission's recommendations were formulated into a Preschool Act which was passed by Parliament in December 1973. As the municipalities began to act on their new mandates, additional legislation (a Child Care Act) to assist their efforts was passed in 1975 and 1976. A brief outline of the present system of day care in Sweden follows.

Current Forms of Provision

There are two basic types of public day care programs in Sweden: preschool groups and family day homes. Preschools are either full-day or part-time. In some publications one still finds the first being referred to as day nurseries and the second as nursery schools, even though the Commission insisted on use of the new terms to dispel connotations of the old. My terminology follows the Commission's wishes.

Full-time Preschool

The new full-time preschool groups differ from the former day nurseries in a number of important ways. One concerns the clientele, another the purpose and program of day care. Full-time preschool groups are no longer intended primarily for the needy. Special need is still a first priority for admission, and this includes children with special requirements arising from physical, mental, social, and linguistic handicaps. However, some of these children may attend part-time. Full-time preschool groups are now also explicitly intended for children of working parents or student parents. Fees for attendance are based on a sliding scale of parents' income and the number of children in the family (reflecting the recognition that there is a mix in parental ability to pay).[14] Another difference between day nurseries and full-time preschools is, as the new name suggests, that all preschools are now educational and not custodial. Children attending full-time (five or more hours per day) have such extra activities as outdoor play, rest periods, and meals, which part-time attenders do not necessarily have. But the program of play and social and educational learning is roughly the same in all preschool groups, and staff training for all preschools, whether full- or part-time, is the same, as is their salary scale. Full-time preschools accept children from the age of 7 months, or when maternity leave is over, until the age of 7 years, when compulsory schooling begins.

Part-time Preschool

In principle, the only differences between full-time and part-time preschool are the number of hours attended and

[14] The average income in Stockholm in 1976 was 41,000 SwKr per year. Parents who earn more than 5,000 SwKr per month pay the maximum amount of 20 SwKr per day per child (private communication, Social Welfare Board of Stockholm, November 1977). The average fee is still 400-500 SwKr per month, but the range is now greater: 0-1,500 SwKr

the ages of children in attendance. Priority for part-time preschool is given first to all 6-year-old children, who now have the "right" to attend preschool free of charge for one year prior to compulsory education. These children attend for three hours a day, five days a week.[15] When the new law requiring preschool was passed, some local authorities had to build new facilities in a hurry. These local authorities were therefore unable to offer part-time preschool to younger groups for some time. However, most preschools are open to younger children and to priority groups who for some reason do not attend full-time preschool.

Where possible, full-time and part-time preschools are to be housed in the same building. Just how much interaction takes place between the two groups is up to the individual center, and depends on the facilities and number of children. The Commission on Child Centers recommended as much integration as possible of full-time and part-time programs to assure comparability and to enable the development of "sibling groups."[16] Aside from pedagogics, the main intention of integration is that every community have a comprehensive child center which sees not only to each child's preschool needs but also to health and other needs. Since 1972 each child is registered with a local center at birth, and thereby "enrolled" for the services and activities provided by the center. Mothers bring their children to the centers for regular check-ups, consultations, and other services or activities. The center is to meet all the child's needs as these arise.

---

per month (personal interview, Swedish Association of Local Authorities, May 1982). The fee for a second child decreases immensely—parents can pay nearly the maximum fee for a first child and close to the minimum for a second.

[15] Rural children who have to travel long distances usually attend for fewer days and longer sessions.

[16] Rather than keep all same-aged children together, various mixes of ages are attempted, depending on the center. Where children under 2 are involved, however, a higher staff/child ratio is required. All new facilities have combined age groups.

Family Day Homes

A remarkable feature of Swedish day care is the change in the status of persons who provide child care in their own homes. In other countries such persons are called child-minders or babysitters; in Sweden they are now called day mothers. They are women who often have children of their own at home. They have always provided the majority of day care in Sweden. Consequently, when government commissions began again to investigate the day care situation in the 1960s, one of the first areas reviewed was this primary form of private child-minding. A family commission reporting in 1965 felt that child-minding in a home was making a valuable contribution to day care provision in two ways. First, in terms of sheer quantity, it was filling the gap between the need for day care and the lack of facilities. Second, it provided an alternative form of day care especially for children who for some reason, usually health, were not suitable for day care centers, or whose parents did not want them in centers, perhaps because they were still infants. The Commission realized that to assure the continuing contribution of quality child-minding toward meeting the need for day care, reorganization and assistance were necessary. After reviewing the problems of child-minding from the point of view of the providers and the parents, the commission decided that the best way to utilize the system was to place it under public auspices. In a memorandum entitled *The Expansion of Public Childminding Services* the commission suggested that child-minders be employed by the local authority with all the benefits this implies, such as holiday pay and pensions, and all the requirements, such as inspection of premises and training (a ninety-hour three-week course in child care).[17] The incorporation of

---

[17] The course is voluntarily attended by about 30% of day mothers. As everywhere, because personnel is limited, inspection, monitoring, and assistance to day mothers is irregular. But the homes are visited at least once a year (personal interviews, Social Welfare Board of Stockholm, September 1977; Swedish Association of Local Authorities, May 1982).

family day homes into the local authority began in 1966. The local authority refers parents to available homes, collects the fee (the same scale applies as in preschool) and pays the day mother (at the same rate as aides in preschool, plus benefits for food for the children and use of the home). The 1968 Commission on Child Centers reaffirmed the role of family day homes in an integrated system of day care, especially for certain children such as infants or children more prone to infection. But because of the inherent weaknesses of this form of care, compared to the more developmentally enriching program in public centers, the commission wanted to limit the expansion of family day homes and to encourage local authorities to put their major efforts into preschools.[18]

After-School Centers

One of the more outstanding features of the Swedish day care system is the recognition of a continuing need for child care once a child with full-time working parents begins school. After-school centers provide care and activities for such children aged 7 to 12. These centers are housed either within the preschools, on school premises, or within other activity centers. The same scale of fees applies as in preschools. Some school children who cannot be accommodated in after-school centers are given places in family day homes for after-school care.

Experimental Programs

In addition to these programs, the government is supporting a number of experiments in selected areas, either to compensate for gaps or to complement existing programs. For example, certain centers are testing the exten-

[18] There is a bias against family day homes on the part of research staff and others connected with the various commissions of inquiry, based primarily on the inferior quality of family day homes compared to child centers. However, many parents and local authorities prefer a traditional home setting.

sion of provision to evening hours for parents engaged in shift-work. Thus far, experiments are favoring the use of personnel attached to the center who babysit in the child's home during these hours. (The same personnel provide care for sick children at home while their parents work.) Another experimental program is called the open pre-school. It provides activities for mothers or day mothers together with children.

There are some cooperative or private forms of child care in Sweden. Information about these is not widely available, but they include cases such as the following: a group of students at Uppsala University developed a three-family system of child care. One "day mother" is hired to care for the children of the three families and the meeting place for the group is rotated each week among the three homes. Such experiments are assisted by special government grants.

There are a few private day care/preschool facilities in Sweden run by churches or charities.[19] In 1968 these constituted only 2% of total provision. They have not expanded and so by now are insignificant. There are no regulations pertaining to private facilities, but local authorities must include them in their plans for future provision. There are also private child-minders, but no company-run day nurseries.

The change that has taken place in the last decade and a half in the Swedish approach to day care is remarkable. How it came about, how it has been put into practice, and what it signifies is the subject of the following analysis.

THE ROLE OF THE STATE

Determinants of Intervention

The specific state intervention which is investigated here is the expansion and change in day care in Sweden that began in the 1960s. As we saw in earlier chapters, "demand"

---

[19] Many receive state grants, except church programs which have special tax benefits.

for labor led to an increase in women's labor force participation in the 1960s and framed government policies for
working women. Expansion in day care occurred at the
same time as the increase in number of working mothers,
as Tables 6.1 and 6.2 show. Throughout the 1950s, the
number of places in public day nurseries remained constant
at about 10,000. From 1965 to 1970, the number of places
in just this one type of public facility more than doubled.
During this period the number of places in other types of
public facilities also increased substantially (over three times
in family day homes, and not quite one and one-half times
in nursery schools). Concurrent with this was an increase
in the number of women at work. Between 1965 and 1970
the total increase in the number of working women was
about 5½%, but the increase for women with young children was 12%, and this rate continued throughout the 1970s.
Thus, we can see a clear relationship between the increase
in day care and the increase in working women, especially
women with young children.

This relationship was mediated, however, by another factor. The government did not respond directly to the increase in the number of working women by immediately
expanding day care provision. It first set up a commission
of inquiry. In the early 1960s, government committees of
one sort or another began redefining the issue of day care
and suggesting changes in its organization. A Family Commission in 1962 first suggested a new system of state financing for a new type of integrated "child center." Another Family Commission in 1965 examined the system of
child-minding and recommended that it be integrated into
the system of public services. Throughout the 1960s Parliament passed bills, acting on each commission's recommendations. As provision began to expand and organization became more integrated, another committee was
convened in 1968: the Royal Commission on Child Centers. This Commission can be thought of as a continuation
of earlier inquiries on child care, since it culminated the
work of earlier commissions and saw through to fruition

Table 6.1 Provision of Day Care in Sweden

| | Number of Children: | | | | | |
	Full-time preschools	Part-time preschools	Family day homes	After-school centers	Private paid child care	Other child care (relatives)
1950	9,700	18,700	—	2,400		
1960	10,300	38,400	4,000	2,400		
1965	11,900	52,100	8,000	3,000		
1970	33,000	86,000	32,000	6,500		
1975	73,700	123,500	67,300	23,000		
1980	132,600	119,500	81,100[a] 34,500[b]	49,700	97,000	44,000

% of children aged 0-6 with gainfully employed or student parents (full- and part-time):

	Full-time preschools	Part-time preschools	Family day homes	After-school centers	Private paid child care	Other child care (relatives)
1965 (base: 254,000)	4.7	20.5	3.1			
1970 (base: 386,000)	8.5	22.3	8.3			
1975 (base: 440,000)	16.8	28.1	15.3			
1980 (base: 517,000)	25.6	23.1	17.0	—	18.8	8.5

Adapted from: "Child Care Programs in Sweden," *Fact Sheets on Sweden* (December 1981); Göran Sidebäck and Lars Sundbom, *Local Politics and Social Planning: Some Cross Community Differences in Day Care Programs in Sweden* (Stockholm: Swedish Institute for Social Research, January 1982), p. 35.

[a] Ages 0-6.
[b] Ages 7-12.

TABLE 6.2   Labor Force Participation Rates

	1963	1965	1970	1975	1980
All women	54.5	53.8	59.3	67.9	75.1
Single women	69.6	67.2	65.9	70.8	74.4
Married women	47.0	47.2	56.1	66.2	75.6
Women with children under 7 years	38.0	36.8	49.7	60.5	75.3

Source: National Labour Market Board, *Equality in the Labour Market, Statistics* (Stockholm: AMS, 1980), p. 8.

the total change in the Swedish system of day care. The work and reports of this commission give us clear evidence of changes in the role of the state in day care provision.

The Royal Commission on Child Centers carried on within the conceptual framework formulated by earlier commissions, but added greater substance to that framework. The Commission's task was simplified by the clear set of directives issued by the Ministry of Family Affairs, which established the Commission. These directives clarified, at the outset, the multiplicity of concerns involved in the issue of day care, stating:

> The responsibility for the upbringing, supervision and care of children rests chiefly with the home. The community has, however, to a great extent undertaken a responsibility in this field, among other ways through the provision of child centres by local authorities. Changes in the family structure and living conditions have brought a greatly increased demand for public measures to assist parents with the care of their children. In increasing numbers of families both parents go out to work. For unmarried and divorced parents organized child care is a condition for their ability to support the family by paid work. Child Centres also fulfill an important educational function in teaching children group activities under pedagogic guidance.[20]

[20] Rosengren, *Pre-school in Sweden*, p. 17. This is the official report of the Royal Commission on Child Centers.

Implicit in this statement is the duality that has plagued attempts everywhere to resolve the problem in child care provision: the needs of parents on the one hand, especially working parents and/or single parents, and the needs of children on the other, both with regard to, and regardless of, their family situation. This duality is often seen as a conflict, stemming from the fact that young children need to be with their parents. Through its deliberations the Commission developed a conception of the clientele of child care that attempted to recognize differing needs within a common framework.

The first step was to establish the fact that the pressing need for child centers arose primarily because of the increasing number of working mothers. In gathering and presenting the relevant data, the Commission was very matter of fact; no moral judgments accompanied the data on working mothers. The Commission simply assumed that working parents provide one area of need/demand for child care, indeed the major one. The Commission recognized that negative or negligent public policy, that is, a lack of child care facilities, does not prevent mothers from working, but it does harm the children involved. Furthermore, in recognition of the equality of the right to work, they began to use the terminology of "working parents," or "gainfully employed or student parents." The Commission did not elaborate these points further (nor, for instance, speak to the integration of family, child care, and labor market policies, which a later Family Commission did). However, the premise was clearly accepted throughout the report that the majority of preschool children are in child centers because both parents work.

But working parents are not the only clientele of child centers. The second task for the Commission was to elaborate other needs for child care and in so doing to clarify selective vs. universal dimensions of the clientele of child centers. For this purpose, the commission shifted its focus of the clientele from the family to the child. First, it was agreed that children with special learning or social needs require preschool programs. Second, the problem of the general need of all children for enriching preschool experiences was confronted. This is especially important in view of the fact that the focus on the "need" for child centers in terms of family situation otherwise creates a selectivity and corresponding inequality of access to the services. The Commission dealt with this issue by formulating a general preschool plan, which contains two main features. The first is the integration of all preschool programs and a similarity in the programs offered to all children, regardless of their reasons for attending or of the length of time they attend. The second feature is an expansion of preschools, gradually, to accommodate all those who wish to attend. Compulsory schooling begins quite late in Sweden, at age 7. The plan mandated that all 6-year-old children be given a place in part-time preschools, and that if more places became available, and certainly as provision expands, younger children should be given places too. Attendance at part-time preschools is voluntary and free of charge.

Thus, selectivity was not meant to be a factor in the Swedish system of preschool provision. But then neither was universality. Not all children attend preschools (although it was hoped that all 6-year-olds would attend part-time). Far fewer children attend full-time than part-time. The Commission intended to make the question of universal vs. selective services a moot point—as moot as the division between care and education, day nurseries and nursery schools, and so on. The idea was to establish a "child center" that every child would attend, for various reasons and for various lengths of time. The services offered at the centers were to range from health check-ups to open playgroups, and were to include parents as well as children. But the concept of universality vs. selectivity inevitably emerged in another context, when the Commission was forced to consider the practical question of quantity.

There are not sufficient full-time places in child centers to accommodate fully all working parents, either in 1970 or in 1980. (I turn to the data in a later section.) Which working parents are given priority? Despite its attempt to rise above the issue of priority (and, therefore, selectivity), the Commission had to deal with differences in need for day care. One difference concerns the number of hours parents work, another parental income. Each has implications for the universal-egalitarian goals of the Commission.

A place in a full-time preschool is open first to children whose "social situation" (which includes the family's economic situation) places them in special need; then to children with a sibling in the center. Of those children who do not fit these priority categories, only those with *full-time* working or student parents are accepted.[21] Thus, mothers who work or study part-time, the majority of mothers with preschool age children, generally cannot be accommodated in the preschool. Only a few can fit their work schedules with the three-hour sessions of the part-time programs. Many of the children in part-time preschool have part-time working mothers, but most must combine preschool with family day homes or other babysitting arrangements.[22] Since part-time preschool is not intended to accommodate working parents, additional problems, such as school holidays, are up to parents to handle.

Full-time working parents also have different "needs" for public day care, stemming from their economic situation. The wealthy can afford to hire private babysitters; the poor have had to rely on relatives, perhaps with parents themselves alternating work schedules. In confronting these differences in financial need among social groups, the Commission tried to focus on the long run, and hoped that each child center, from the beginning, would resemble the type of center that would eventually exist when supply and demand coincided. The Commission therefore recom-

[21] Some local authorities may choose to interpret working or student parents as a special "social situation," depending upon the family's income.

[22] Placement in a part-time preschool is based on the child's age, not on whether or not the mother is working part-time.

mended that each local authority accept for each center a clientele from mixed backgrounds, social and income groups, as reflective as possible of the wider area of residence. Accepting a mixed clientele really means accepting the middle classes, which is difficult to do when there is a shortage of places and when a greater "need" exists among working-class families. In recognition of this, the Commission added that: "During a long period of construction, particular weight will have to be given to priority on social grounds in the allocation of preschool places. Case-finding activities by the authority responsible play a major role in this context."[23] In fact, this is exactly what did happen. Case-finding found enough welfare-based need to fill the limited number of day care places during a period of construction that became much longer than anticipated. The traditional conception of social need as being an objective welfare condition was thereby reactivated in practice, displacing the more universal social category of working parents.

Let us examine, as best we can, how the reality of quantitative constraints and corresponding selectivity has affected implementation of the goal of universality. I focus on full-time preschool care, since this is where the greatest tension exists between need and quantity. Information on the socioeconomic background of children in full-time preschools is not generally kept. The impressions and general knowledge of the authorities will have to suffice to make the points here. In the full-time preschool, first priority is given to single parents, then to parents who are financially pressed, then to other groups as determined by officials of the local authority or child center. It was estimated that in Stockholm about 30% of the children in full-time preschool have single parents.[24] There is much less certainty about the occupational or income characteristics of parents.[25] In

[23] Rosengren, *Pre-school in Sweden*, p. 33.

[24] Private communication and interview, Social Welfare Board of Stockholm, 1977.

[25] I was told by one authority that all professions are represented among parents in Stockholm's child centers. However, another acknowledged the

general, we have to assume what is tacitly acknowledged in Stockholm—that given the limited places and high number of priority cases, many higher income or middle-class working parents cannot be accommodated in urban full-time preschools. And yet, the larger urban centers in Sweden are doing much better than the more rural areas in meeting the need/demand for day care. It is estimated that the municipality of Stockholm currently meets 86% of its need for day care through preschool and family day home provision and that the suburban municipalities around Stockholm meet about 70% of their need.[26] This figure decreases gradually across Sweden's 252 communes to a low of 22% for the more rural areas.

Before we can say anything, then, about the extent to which provision discriminates among families with different needs, we must distinguish among different communes. A recent study of local variations in provision of day care services found that the commune's economic structure accounted for more of the variation in provision than any other factor.[27] The more rural areas also have the lowest level of women's employment, but as noted above they barely meet the meager need for day care that does exist. I return to the issue of local differences and the role of the state in handling these differences later in the chapter.

In sum, the timing of state intervention in the area of day care provision was determined, in the first instance, by an increase in women's labor force participation and, second, by the recommendation of government commissions of inquiry and, third, by specific social needs. Three general kinds of social need were to have determined the timing,

---

tacitly well-known fact that middle and higher income parents have great difficulty receiving a place in a child center.

[26] "Need" is defined as working or student parents. The relevant data appear in *Barnomsorgen i Siffror 1981* (Stockholm: Socialstyrelsen, 1981), pp. 49-54.

[27] Göran Sidebäck and Lars Sundbom, *Local Politics and Social Planning: Some Cross Community Differences in Day Care Programs in Sweden* (Swedish Institute for Social Research, January 1982).

organization, and extent of state intervention: the needs of all working parents, the needs of children with educational, physical, or social handicaps, and the needs of all preschool children for some enriching experiences outside the home. In the abstract, market forces were not to have entered the picture at all. The category of working parents was to be conceptualized in terms of the principle of equality in the right to work. In practice, however, the general social category of working parents has been narrowed to the point where market factors are instrumental in determining eligibility and access. The first intrusion of the market occurs because of the expense of the program, which necessitates a selection process differentiating among clientele. This has meant, on the one hand, that there are different criteria of access to full- and part-time programs: family situation for the former, and child's age for the latter. On the other hand, access to full-time programs has been narrowed further. Aside from social need for day care because of single parenthood, financial need has determined eligibility (except for the municipality of Stockholm and its environs), introducing once again the force of market factors. A broader explanation for the erosion of principles and goals in program implementation must await the analyses in the following sections.

Design of Intervention

To meet the three areas of need for day care as formulated by the Royal Commission, the state established preschools with programs and features that could accommodate all the needs at the same time. The key concept guiding this multifaceted achievement was integration. Each center was to offer a holistic system of services, together with special features for special needs. The idea is similar to one we encountered in an earlier chapter: a universal framework within which selective measures can "discriminate positively with the minimum risk of stigma, in favour of those whose needs are greatest."[28] I look first at the special features provided for working parents, and then at how special needs are integrated into a unified system of services.

MULTIPLE NEEDS AND MULTIPLE PURPOSES

The conception of the purpose of preschools, as expressed by the 1968 and other commissions of inquiry, is to offer enriching experiences for children while they are there. The general needs of children, and, in particular, the special needs of children who attend full-time, are to be met within a developmental program of social learning, pedagogically similar for all, but with necessary variations and additions for those attending full-time. Preschool, for whatever length of time, is explicitly thought of as a supplement to the family, not a substitute.

However, special needs, bordering on substitution, arise because of the long working hours of most full-time working parents. Most centers are open from approximately 6:30 a.m. to 7:00 p.m. on weekdays, and some are open on Saturday mornings. The commission felt that child care needs outside of these hours (because of odd hours of work, especially evening or weekend shift work), required not only a great deal of consideration but also a great deal of experimentation. It recommended that certain state-subsidized pilot projects be launched, some of which are still continuing in a few municipalities. One, for instance, involves having child care personnel babysit in the child's own home in the evenings. The commission also suggested that the whole set of issues involving working hours and family life were of such importance that a special commission ought to be set up to investigate the matter. In 1974 a Family Commission was appointed which has considered a variety of special considerations that would ease the situation of working parents and their children, such as the

---

[28] Richard M. Titmuss, *Commitment to Welfare* (London: Allen and Unwin, 1968), p. 135.

possibility of flexible and/or shortened hours for working parents.[29]

Other worries of working parents include the care of sick children. The Royal Commission recommended that child centers be involved in this matter. Parents whose children are ill can now choose whether to take time off work in accordance with a new sickness benefit plan, or have their child cared for at home by a child-minder who is attached to the preschool.[30] These special services for parents are complemented by the universal framework of pedagogics for their children, as we will see.

INTEGRATION OF SERVICES

The distinction between care and education for young children existed in Sweden in the past and was associated, as elsewhere, with the division between day nurseries and nursery schools, and between full-time and part-time programs for young children. One institutional feature, unique to Sweden, enabled the displacement of these divisions in

[29] Some members of the Family Commission wanted to recommend that working parents with small children have the right to a shortened workday with compensation for time lost. Opposition from other members was too strong, however. In particular, the representative of the LO argued that working parents would be unduly discriminated against by employers. The representative from SAF agreed. As it now stands, a shortened workday is possible under the parental insurance scheme. Of the total nine months parental leave, the last three months can be divided in various ways with regular compensation until the child is 8 years old (personal interview, Family Commission, September 1977). The Family Commission's final report, *Day Care for Small Children*, was issued in 1979.

[30] Of course, the choice only exists for those parents whose children are in child centers with additional personnel. Often, a local authority social worker (or a child-minder) comes to the child's home. The sickness benefit can be taken by either parent with the same compensation as the parent would receive for her or his own illness (usually 90% of pay). It allows for 12 days off per year per family with one child under 10; 15 days for a family with two children; and 18 days for a family with three children. The parental insurance scheme also entitles every parent to take a leave of absence (one day per month) to participate in the day care center program.

the plans for new integrated services. The education department has never been involved in preschool programs except in a consultative capacity and in teacher training. The Royal Commission on Child Centers decided to emphasize this already existing division between preschool and formal schooling, and to make all preschool programs part of family and social policy.[31] There is no attempt to teach preschool children to read or write.[32] There is general agreement among all concerned that children can wait to learn these skills until they are in school. Nor is there any desire to lower the compulsory school age, which at age 7 is rather high compared to other countries. Accordingly, the Commission adopted a philosophy of learning that stressed child development, applicable to all preschool programs. Guided by the theories of Erikson and Piaget, the pedagogic objectives emphasize that the preschool ought to provide the

conditions in which the child can develop and stabilize a conception of itself as an individual . . . [to] develop its communicative ability in interplay with its environment . . . [to] understand fundamental concepts, and understand a certain interplay between concepts and simple system relationships. The child is to acquire not primarily knowledge, but a method of learning; it is to acquire a capacity to utilize concepts in the solution of problems.[33]

The term "dialogue pedagogics" is used to describe the methodology of interrelationships in a preschool—"a mutual giving and taking of feelings, experiences and knowledge." Since the Commission's final report, these abstract pedagogic aims have been systematized into a "working plan for the preschool." It was drawn up by the National

[31] Siv Thorsell, "Pre-School in Sweden," *Current Sweden*, No. 55 (March 1977), pp. 3-4.

[32] However, pre-reading skills are taught, and one sees words and books in the "classroom."

[33] Rosengren, *Pre-school in Sweden*, pp. 22-23.

Board of Health and Welfare in collaboration with the National Board of Education, and consists of a four-volume "programme" with practical suggestions on implementing "planned free activity." Although advisory only, it is the official common work program for all preschools.

This pedagogical and jurisdictional unity of preschool programs has broken down the former divisions between day nurseries and nursery schools, and between full-day and part-time programs. In addition, however, it was necessary to eliminate two other features associated with this division: separate institutions and differently trained personnel. With regard to the first, the Commission recommended that wherever possible all preschool programs be offered within a single center. As mentioned, child centers are intended eventually to meet all the needs—health and social—of children in an area, keeping track of each child's development and changing needs from birth. This has not been possible everywhere. Great problems arise in rural areas, where the population is widely scattered. Moreover, not all parents have wanted to make use of the services offered, making it necessary for local authorities to "find out why."[34] Although all preschool programs are housed within the same building, an internal physical separation still occurs between full- and part-time programs. In some centers, the organization of the two programs requires separate space and separate facilities, although all the children may meet in common outdoor play areas or on other occasions, depending on the center. Whether this separation in program facilities makes any difference for the children has not been investigated.[35] As long as teacher's attitudes and services offered are not affected, the children ought not be affected either.[36] The current trend in Sweden, however, is toward sibling group arrangements (including chil-

[34] This then takes on the character of social casework. Ibid., pp. 26-27.

[35] This separation is justified as better for the children since they associate with the same set of playmates at all times.

[36] Recall from Chapter 4 that British studies show the attitudes of nursery staff seem to affect the kind of program children receive.

dren up to age 12) and an emphasis on group interaction rather than teacher-child centeredness. The essence of the Commission's meaning of integration was service and pedagogics designed to overcome the discrimination entailed by the division between care and education. This aspect of its plans has apparently been successful.

Consolidation of staff training and salaries for child center personnel was fairly easy to achieve, but problems linger on. All preschool programs (full- and part-time) are now headed by preschool teachers, comparably trained and paid. The only status differences in child centers are between teachers and aides. Aides are not trained for as long a period and receive a much lower rate of pay than teachers. The staff/child ratio for both full- and part-time programs is the same, and is based on children's ages. The main problem arises with the differences in status and pay between preschool teachers and compulsory level school teachers. Sweden maintains a scale of pay that increases by level taught, making university professors the highest paid teachers. Moreover, preschool teachers are paid by the more financially hard-pressed local authorities, and compulsory school teachers by the more generous central government. The salary differential has been narrowed somewhat in the last decade. The primary reason for this was the effort to attract men to the preschool.[37] Many of the urban child centers have a least one male teacher. Their low representation reflects continuing sex-role stereotyping, as well as pay differentials and fewer promotional opportunities in the preschool.

The greatest remaining difference between full- and part-time programs, and potentially the most problematic, concerns the payment of fees for the services. Part-time preschooling is free of charge. Parents pay for full-time preschooling (and for the after-school program).[38] There is

---

[37] Special concessions are made for male applicants to teacher training programs as well.

[38] A discrepancy arises in that parents of 6-year-old children who attend full-time pay, whereas part-time attenders do not.

much talk of making all the services free, but given the current financial situation in Sweden, pessimism prevails.

It is clear that the Royal Commission devised a high quality, egalitarian day care system, integrating the needs of working parents and their children into the mainstream of a public program. State intervention in the area of preschool provision was to be as legitimate an activity as public provision of compulsory schooling. The Commission made a strong case for preschools in terms of the needs of all children, and attempted to express the longer hours provided for some children as a dual function of the programs, that is, serving working parents as well as children. The Commission fully recognized the needs of working parents and accepted responsibility on behalf of the public sector to assist working parents. As we look now at the expansion of preschools, we see that while all working parents are included in principle, only full-time working parents are served in practice. We also see a second feature of state intervention, namely, growth in public sector control of day care.

EXPANSION OF PROVISION

The Commission submitted its report in 1972, and various acts of Parliament followed, legislating expansion in preschool facilities. It was made mandatory that by 1975 local authorities have sufficient part-time places for all 6-year-olds. Expansion in full-time places was not made mandatory. All expansion was to be achieved through special financial arrangements between the central government and the local authorities; these are discussed in the next section. However, the Commission did set specific goals for expansion of full-time preschools commensurate with its conception of the purpose of the programs. It hoped that by the mid-1980s all of the need for places, measured in terms of the number of children of gainfully employed parents, would be met. The plan for reaching this goal called for ever-greater increases per year in the number of new places. Table 6.3 compares the Commission's goal for increases

TABLE 6.3   Goals for and Growth in Full-time Preschool Places

	Goals for New Places (Increase per year)	Actual Increase per year (estimate)	Actual Number of Places (estimate)
1976	16,000	1,500	77,500
1977	18,000	14,600	101,600
1978	20,000	11,200	112,800
1979	22,000	11,500	124,300
1980	24,000	8,300	132,600

Adapted from: Bodil Rosengren, "More Time for the Children," *Current Sweden*, No. 131 (October 1976), p. 15; "Child Care Programs in Sweden," *Fact Sheets on Sweden* (December 1981).

with the estimated actual increases in full-time places.[39] It can be seen that the actual increase falls short of the hoped-for increase. Had the plans materialized, by 1980 there should have been 100,000 new full-time preschool places, meeting about 55% of the need, with another 25% of the need being met by family day homes.

Nevertheless, as Table 6.4 shows, full-time preschool and family day homes together meet about 65% of the need for day care. Compared to the extent to which the need for day care is being met in Britain, the figures for Sweden are laudable. But compared to what the state in Sweden has defined the problem to be and what it wants to achieve, the results are wanting. The greatest area of need is among part-time working mothers. They are not accommodated in full-time preschools, nor in part-time preschools if their children are under 4 years of age. Yet they constitute 60% of working mothers with preschool age children, a figure often quoted in policy contexts. At least one-third of the need for day care comes from part-time working or student

[39] These estimates are derived from the plans submitted by local authorities to the central government. We can speculate that the real increase is even less than the planned estimates, given persisting financial difficulties and reluctance to expand on the part of local authorities in some areas. Rita Liljeström, "Integration of Family Policy and Labor Market Policy in Sweden," *Social Change in Sweden*, No. 9 (December 1978) p. 7.

TABLE 6.4 Meeting the Need for Day Care[a]

	No. of children needing full-time places[b]	No. of children in full-time preschool	% of need accommodated	No. of children in Family Day Homes	% of need accommodated	% of children not accommodated
1976	241,000	77,500	32	61,200	25	43
1977	248,000	87,500	35	62,100	25	40
1978	254,500	96,300	38	63,700	25	37
1979	261,300	104,000	40	65,400	25	35
1980	—	111,400	—	66,400	—	—

Source: Bodil Rosengren, "More Time for the Children," *Current Sweden*, No. 131 (October 1976), p. 15.

[a] Estimated figures.

[b] Children with full-time working of student parents.

mothers.[40] The Royal Commission had implicitly suggested the coordination of day care policy with labor market policy. The latter was seen "to give employment opportunities to everybody who wants them."[41] The former was intended to assure freedom of choice in decisions about work, including part-time vs. full-time employment for mothers of young children. In the event, constraints in expansion have hampered the goal of policy coordination.

These plans for expansion reveal a final characteristic of the design of state intervention in day care provision: a greater reliance on public institutions over private homes. Both the 1968 Royal Commission and the 1974 Family Commission suggested that the expansion of family day homes be limited in favor of preschools. During the transition and construction period, the increase in the number of family day homes was not to exceed the increase in full-time preschool places. Eventually, reliance on family day homes was to taper off, so that the number of places would be less than one-quarter of the total provision. The reasons for decreasing use of family day homes were based on their inferior quality compared to preschools and the difficulty of supervision.[42] Later studies justified the preference for preschools on the grounds of finances too; contrary to popular belief, studies found that family day homes were not cheaper to subsidize than preschools.[43] This was especially so when children over 3 were involved and additional costs for toys and food were included.[44] Studies also found that,

---

[40] Part-time means less than five hours per day or less than five days per week. Calculated from data in *Statistiska Meddelanden, S 1980: 20* (Stockholm: Statistiska Centralbyrån, 1980), pp. 82-87.

[41] "Swedish Labor Market Policy," *Fact Sheets on Sweden* (March 1979).

[42] Inferior quality is based on lack of formal training of day mothers, lack of pedagogical activities in family day homes, and the frequent changes of day mothers that many children undergo. See Anita Söderlund and Elin Michelse, "Day Nurseries and Family Day Care in Sweden," (*mimeo.*, February 1977).

[43] These studies were conducted by the 1974 Family Commission, which favored an emphasis on child centers.

[44] Family day homes are cheaper for children under 3 because the

again contrary to popular belief, there was not a lower incidence of illness among children in family day homes. The value in keeping family day homes was for children under 3 who were not ready for group learning or whose parents preferred a non-institutional environment.

However, local authorities continue to find that family day homes are cheaper in the short run than constructing new preschools because they require no new capital outlays. In addition, family day homes provide a traditionally valued alternative to preschools, especially for younger children; and they are necessary to fill the gap between provision and need. Those who cannot be accommodated in preschools are usually assisted by the local social welfare agency in finding a place in a (local authority) family day home. Table 6.5 indicates that family day care is popular and, accordingly, it remains an integral part of the day care system. In fact, the figure of 25% of family day homes in total provision has recently been revised upward to about 30%, to reflect local needs and desires. However, as Table 6.5 also indicates, the preference for preschool care (indicated as "day nursery" in older sources) is far greater, although its popularity has tapered off.

In sum, we see that the state has taken the upper hand in formulating and organizing quality day care programs in Sweden. It has not been fully successful in realizing the intentions of its interventions, however. Most significantly, the pressures of expansion have created a tighter set of criteria for eligibility than intended. While all those children in full-time preschools (and many in part-time preschools) have working parents, only a limited percentage of working parents are being offered child care assistance in their efforts or desire to work. In the next section I will analyze the nature of the resistance to expansion in terms of the institutionalization of decision making about and implementation of day care.

---

caretaker/child ratio is lower than is required in preschools (1:4 compared to 1:2 or 3).

TABLE 6.5   Child Care Use and Preference

Kind of Care	% at present in care		Mother's preferred kind of care	
	1972[a]	1980	1972[a]	1980
Day Nursery	9	31.4	48	44.5
Family Day Home	20	23.5	24	24.9
Domestic Help	14	⎫	13	⎫
Relatives	11	44.6 ⎬ private	5	29.4 ⎬ private
Relative in child's own home	13	⎪	6	⎪
Other	33	⎭	4	1.2 ⎭ not asked

Adapted from: *Förskolan Del 2* (Stockholm: SOU, 1972), p. 27; *Statistiska Meddelanden*, S 1980: 20 (Stockholm: Statistiska Centralbyrån, 1980), pp. 100-102.

[a] Halmstad region, 1972

The Form of Institutionalization

The formulation and provision of day care services in Sweden involves both the central government and local authorities. The central government is the primary agency of goal setting, and the local authorities of implementation. At the level of the central government, the Royal Commission, as we have seen, analyzes problems and recommends policy responses. Based on its reports, Parliament enacts legislation and directs local authorities to implement the provision of care. Monitoring of the implementation phase is performed by the National Board of Health and Welfare, which oversees the planning and programming of local Social Welfare Boards.

The success of day care provision in Sweden is largely due to the fact that the central government accepts a strong leadership role in every phase of policy development and program implementation. The inadequacies in day care provision are largely due to the fact that local authorities, not the state, implement national goals according to local needs and abilities. Moreover, local authorities are often reluctant to implement the quantitative and qualitative goals formulated by the central government. As we shall see, financing is not the problem, since the central government has come to assume much of the direct cost. The problem goes deeper. Local authorities in Sweden are overwhelmingly rural and reflect values and interests of a more traditional character, especially when it comes to the social and economic roles of women. These values and interests are not reflected in, and to some extent are incompatible with, the consensus reached by the dominant social coalition at the national level. A fundamental disjuncture exists, therefore, between the social bases of policy formulation, on the one hand, and policy implementation, on the other, and this disjuncture largely accounts for the remaining gaps between goals and outcomes in day care.

In the attempt to narrow this gap, the central government is responding to one problem but contributing to another. The response of the central government to the shortcomings in day care provision has been to take on an ever-increasing role for itself. This in considerable measure has resulted in even greater quantitative and qualitative accomplishments than were achieved before. However, the assumption of additional authority by the central government, acting through the parastatal network of dominant interests, has had the consequence of removing the policy-nexus of day care still further from the ultimate users of the service: working parents. Parents, who were more readily able to influence local authorities, are unable to participate *qua* parents at the level of the central government because the pattern of interest aggregation represented in the governing coalition includes no such category of organized interest. And since this coalition is organized principally on the basis of social relations of production in the economy, it is difficult to envision the future incorporation of working parents in it.

Below, I briefly elaborate and document these arguments.[45] I first describe the constitution and functioning of

---

[45] Evidence for this section is derived largely from personal interviews

the Royal Commission that was concerned with day care. I then discuss the tension that exists between the central government and the local authorities in this domain of policy and what the central government has attempted to do about it. In the conclusion, I return to the emergent consequences of this response by the central government and to the more general and growing problem of "user-participation" in policy making for social services in Sweden.

THE ROYAL COMMISSION AND SOCIETAL CORPORATISM

The issue of day care and the inadequacy of provision in the face of increasing demand were first brought to public notice through a variety of concerned groups: labor, employers', and women's groups; representatives of children's groups; and the mass media. In Sweden, grass roots agitation is usually directed toward a single, general outcome—that government do something.[46] And in Sweden that something is usually, first, to appoint a royal commission. Thereafter, the formation of public policy is largely beyond the reach of the public at large. It becomes the work of an elite network, albeit a well-informed and representative elite.

The institution of the royal commission is well-established in Sweden, dating back for centuries. Almost every issue is now dealt with first by such an inquiry.[47] In fact, by the time a commission reaches Parliament, the only role left for Paliament is to vote on particulars, since a working compromise on the broad principles and basic contours of

---

in Stockholm with: (1) members of the Royal Commission on Child Centers, including its chairman; (2) officials at the Ministry of Social Affairs, National Board of Health and Welfare, and Association of Local Authorities; (3) members of concerned interest groups and users of the service.

[46] Sten Johansson, "Liberal Democratic Theory and Political Processes" in Richard Scase (ed.), *Readings in the Swedish Class Structure* (Oxford: Pergamon Press, 1976).

[47] About 75 new commissions of inquiry are appointed each year.

policy will have already been reached.[48] A royal commission thereby limits the range of policy choices of Parliament. It is allowed to do so for two reasons. The first is the thoroughness of a commission's investigations. The second concerns a commission's membership.[49] We have seen the first factor at work in the Royal Commission on Child Centers. With regard to the second, the members of a commission represent constituencies that are deemed to count, both because of their position in the network of leading social groups and by virtue of expertise. The majority of members on most commissions are civil servants, both top-level experts in the particular field of inquiry as well as more junior-level research staff. The other members are appointed by the minister in charge with an eye to representation. Some are Members of Parliament, while others are members of interest groups, which invariably include labor and employers' groups.

Thus, the core membership of any royal commission reflects the tripartite coalition of labor, employers, and the state bureaucracy. Tripartism permeates policy making in Sweden, even in a field such as day care. There are several reasons for this. One is that day care in Sweden is an integral part of labor market policy, which in turn is the very essence of Swedish economic management. In addition, tripartism institutionalizes what might be called the hegemonic social consensus. Labor, employers, and the state bureaucracy have to find a basis for agreement before anything can be done, and once they do agree, the social and institutional basis for public policy exists. The Royal Commission on Child Centers also included representatives from

[48] In the case under consideration here, one can simply compare the similarity between the report of the Royal Commission on Child Centers and the subsequent Child Care Acts of 1975 and 1976. For accounts of the more general pattern of policy making, see H. Meijer, "Bureaucracy and Policy Formation in Sweden," *Scandinavian Political Studies*, 4 (1969); and M. Donald Hancock, *Sweden: The Politics of Postindustrial Change* (Hinsdale, Ill.: Dryden Press, 1972).

[49] Meijer, "Bureaucracy and Policy Formation."

other groups, as do royal commissions in general. These are chosen because they represent a more particular interest concerned with the issue under consideration, such as representatives of women's groups who were members of the Royal Commission on Child Centers, or by virtue of their expertise, such as the child ombudsman and the educators who also sat on that same commission. But the fundamental consensus on which any would-be policy has to be based is that reached by the tripartite coalition.

Once appointed, a royal commission receives no further direction from Parliament. The commission as a whole meets regularly and extensively to discuss the work of its research staff. Occasionally during its deliberations, but always after its report is complete, each commission reports to a number of groups and individuals who have a particular concern or expertise on the issue under consideration. Only after this consultative process is the report submitted to Parliament. Major differences on issues will have been resolved by now, and a compromise will have been reached. Each commission report contains specific proposals for legislation, which Parliament then takes up.

In sum, it is because day care is included within the wider framework of labor market policy, which in turn occupies such pride of place in Swedish economic management, and because of the political support and the expertise which a royal commission reflects and its report embodies, that day care policy in Sweden is as ambitious, holistic, and successful as it is. We can note that the Royal Commission on Child Centers was appointed by and worked under a Social Democratic government. In principle, this ought not to have affected the composition or work of the Commission, since membership on a commission is supposed to be broadly representative and since civil servants are non-political appointees. As I elaborate below, however, the leadership role of the state, including the Royal Commission, was strongly influenced by the fact that the state was at the time in the hands of a Social Democratic government.

LOCAL AUTHORITY/CENTRAL GOVERNMENT RELATIONS

The Royal Commission on Child Centers set the goal of fully meeting the need for preschool places within ten years, that is, by the mid-1980s. This goal placed a heavy financial burden on the local authorities which actually implement the programs, and required a revised system of governmental responsibilities. In an earlier period, from the 1960s to the mid-1970s, central government subsidies for child care programs accounted for only 35% of the costs of building and operating preschools. The system was a combination of grants and loans; different amounts were given for initial construction and for eventual maintenance. Local authorities paid 50% of the costs, and parents' fees covered the remainder. The Royal Commission on Child Centers helped devise a new system of grants to assist local authorities expand their program in accordance with the new goals.

The new system was based on a considerable increase in the central government's contribution. It went into effect with an Act of Parliament in 1976. The change in the structure of finance is shown in Table 6.6. As of January 1977, the initial grant for constructing new centers was raised to cover over half of the cost of building and operating full-time places in preschools. Moreover, the central government's contribution took the form of direct grants. As shown in Table 6.6, the proportion of costs accounted for by local authorities has decreased considerably as the central government attempted to assume the increased burden of providing expanded services.

The change in the mode of central government funding, from loans to grants, represented a significant change in the relationship between the central government and local authorities. Previously, the burden of responsibility for providing child care programs was clearly on local authorities. Central government grants supplemented by loans were used as an incentive for local governments to expand their provision, and an operating grant assured continued

TABLE 6.6 Paying the Costs for Full-time Preschool

	Central Government				Local Authorities ·			Parents	
	Amount per place per year (SwKr)				Amount per place per year (SwKr)	%		Amount per place per year (SwKr)	%
	Grant	Loan	%						
1970	2,800	2,500	35		7,500	50		2,250	15
1975	7,500	2,500	50		7,800	39		2,250	11
1977	14,000	—	55+		7,780	30+		2,560	10

Source: Private communications from the National Board of Health and Welfare, and from the Social Welfare Board of Stockholm (September 1977).

central government support. The incentive system acknowledged the fact that expansion of child care provision was not a statutory local task. Local authorities were obligated to provide facilities to the extent that they deemed necessary and possible. The new parliamentary acts passed in the mid-1970s made certain kinds of expansion mandatory, and removed all references to "as far as possible." At the same time, the role of the central government was transformed from that of a catalyst to that of a major provider. Instead of a limited contribution, the substantive and financial burden of child care began to rest squarely on the central government.

In addition, the central government increasingly began to exercise stronger control over the direction of expansion of child care provision. Grants reflected both the quantitative and qualitative goals set by the state. For example, since 1966 the central government has not funded the construction of new centers providing only part-time preschooling. New legislation stipulates that in joint centers at least two-thirds of the places must be for full-time supervision, or according to need. Similarly, to limit the reliance on family day homes, new regulations at first required that these homes may constitute no more than 25% of total provision. But because of resistance from the local authorities, this stipulation was revised upward to about 30%. However, the central government contribution to the costs of maintaining family day homes has remained at 35%, not 50 + % as for preschools. Still, many local authorities prefer family day homes on philosophical grounds and argue that they are also cheaper to operate—though it has been shown that they are in fact as expensive as child centers, if not more so, when all costs are reckoned. Thus, the preference boils down to normative grounds.

When the Royal Commission completed its work, the central government agency that took over responsibility for child care was the National Board of Health and Welfare, which is the research arm of the Ministry of Health and Social Affairs. Besides conducting research and development projects and gathering information, it guides the local authorities in a supervisory capacity. Every year each local authority is to assess its current and future needs for pre-school places within the framework for expansion suggested by the Commission and enacted by Parliament. These are rolling-type five-year plans, and must include all the data relevant to the goals (for example, the proportion of full-time places, part-time places, and family day homes, changes in need/demand, etc.). The plans are submitted to the National Board of Health and Welfare, which keeps track of the changing relationship between supply and demand at the national level, and revises goals for expansion. Representatives from local authorites and the central government meet periodically to discuss these plans and changes.

Within the context of national goals and plans, the local Social Welfare Boards exercise some measure of discretion in the administration of tasks. But most of the matters they "decide" were already remarked on in some way either by the Royal Commission on Child Centers or in the handbook "A Programme for Preschools" issued by the National Board of Health and Welfare.[50] These guidelines were meant to be suggestive only, but they convey the central government's desire for uniformity on the one hand and, on the other, for earnest efforts to realize the standards of excellence and achievement proposed in the national reports. Local authorities also have some measure of discretion as to the involvement of other local resources, such as private or voluntary case agencies. They can use part of the central government grants to support such alternative arrangements, as long as the use of the funds is approved by the central government. They can also decide whether to try out certain experiments, such as open preschools. Local authorities with special problems, for example, a greater number of immigrants, are given special grants, but since these are not earmarked, local authorities can decide for themselves how to use the extra funds.

[50] *Arbetsplan För Förskolan* (Stockholm: Socialstyrelsen, 1975).

Thus, the role of the central government, which began by providing incentives to local authorities, became increasingly directive. This extension of the role of the state took place under a Social Democratic government. When a non-socialist government was first elected in 1976, it was obligated to carry out legislation and plans enacted by its predecessor. After several years in office and a worsening economic situation, the non-socialists began to cut back the ambitious goals for expansion in child care that had been devised in a different era. As part of an agenda for a more limited role for the state, the financial arrangements between central and local government for expansion in child care were gradually revised. Rather than the 60% of costs suggested in the mid-1970s, the state decreased its contribution to 40%. The change reflected both economic and political reality. The state's financial contribution was index-regulated to the average salary of public employees. Toward the end of the 1970s, the costs of child care, including both wages and building, increased so much that the state's proportion to total costs decreased. The non-socialist government attempted to institutionalize this change with a 40% across-the-board contribution to all local child care costs. In another general economic measure, the central government limited local expansion overall to 1% per year. Those local authorities which exceeded the limit had their funds cut.[51]

Accordingly, expansion in child care slowed down by 1980. The retrenchment reflected a changed political as well as economic situation. Non-socialists simply did not support child care as much as socialists, neither the electorate nor the elected, at neither local nor national level. The slow-down in expansion in the late 1970s could have been expected, then, on purely ideological grounds. However, even when the socialists are in power, a political and ideological division exists between central and local gov-

[51] Personal interview, Swedish Association of Local Authorities, May 1982.

ernments which can lead to manifest tensions. Consistently more non-socialist than socialist officials are elected at local than national level in Sweden, and non-socialists hold the majority on various local boards. The progressive goals for day care which have been discussed here were at times at variance with the normative preferences of local authorities. Local authorities that do not conform to centrally determined goals and plans cannot be compelled to comply, for although grants are contingent in principle, in practice they cannot be withheld. As a result, considerable variation in the provision of day care developed and still exists in Sweden, with the more rural, traditional local authorities being unwilling to provide fully the care specified by the central government, and large urban local authorities being unable to do so.

In sum, centralization in the provision of day care increased because of the gap between centrally determined goals on the one hand, and local ability and willingness to implement these goals on the other. It was inevitable that some disjuncture would have emerged, and to some extent it was anticipated by the central government when it provided for increased financial assistance to local authorities. Before this assistance could begin to close the difference between objectives and accomplishments, however, a new non-socialist national government and a worsening economic situation retracted expansion in day care. Nevertheless, greater centralization could not have overcome, and indeed, would have exacerbated, the normative constraints on the expansion of services posed by local authorities. Each local authority retains the constitutional prerogative to define its own particular situation and needs, and each local authority is responsive to its own particular clientele and their interests and values. Except for the largest urban center of Stockholm, local politicians are more traditional than the national elite. In 1982, the Social Democratic Party campaigned on a platform which included expansion of day care. Their election heralds a return to greater centralization in policy development and program implementation, measures which are necessary for day care expansion, but which at the same time risk widening the fissures that exist within the Swedish welfare state between the leaders and the led.[52]

Conclusion

This chapter has shown that the need for day care in Sweden is conceptualized in universal terms. Day care services are intended to assist working parents and provide social learning experiences for preschool children, irrespective of socioeconomic status. There is full acceptance of the idea of working mothers, and day care policy itself is embedded within the broader framework of labor market policy. Moreover, all component services in the provision of day care are institutionally integrated and deliver the same standard of care. The result is a quantity and quality of care that far exceeds that available to working parents and their children in Britain. I attribute both the vision upon which day care provision rests, as well as its accomplishments, to the form of societal corporatism that prevails in Sweden (except during the temporary reign of a nonsocialist government). The corporatist mode of governance, which has evolved since the Social Democrats first came to power, has institutionalized under the auspices of the state the broad social compromises reached by labor and employers. Moreover, this social and political basis for public policy has been operationalized in successive policy areas by drawing upon such expertise as exists within the coalition of state bureaucracy, labor, and employers, as well as among other concerned interest groups in society at large. The specific institutional mechanism through which these social coalitions formulate the policy that Parliament

[52] While these fissures exist, nevertheless polls consistently show that Swedes do not want a cutback in the welfare state and its services, and are willing to pay small user charges for the services. See Hans Zetterberg, "Maturing of the Swedish Welfare State," *Public Opinion* (October/November 1979).

then acts upon is the Royal Commission—on Child Centers, in the case of day care.

At the same time, I have shown that two sorts of problems remain in the Swedish provision of day care. First, in some residential areas, particularly where the need for day care greatly exceeds the number of places available, priorities for placement have had to be introduced. The result has been to exclude de facto many middle-class working parents from the benefits of the service. This is a source of tension because those so excluded of course complain about the disjuncture between the ideal and the actuality for them. A second problem is more serious, because no "easy" solution exists, and it, no less than the successes of the policy, results from the corporatist mode of government. This problem results directly from policy decisions on the part of local authorities in the non-urban and more traditional areas of the country. A normative disjuncture exists between the interests and values represented at the level of the more traditional local authorities, where the national hegemonic consensus does not hold and indeed in some measure is seen as being inimical to the prevailing normative conceptions of women and family. An institutional disjuncture exists in the sense that the central government, which designs policy, is set against local authorities, which implement policy. The obvious solution was thought to be greater centralization, but this was forestalled by a non-socialist government. The return to further centralization now threatens not only the delicate relationship between two levels of government, it also removes still further from the ultimate users of the service, from working parents, any say over the making of policy, because centralization absorbs policy making into the parastatal elite network of legitimized interests.

CHAPTER 7

WOMEN, WORKERS, AND STATE/SOCIETY RELATIONS

INTRODUCTION

This study has asked the question: Why are the policy responses to women workers so different in Britain and Sweden? The policies that have been examined concern the provision of facilitative services prior to employment, such as training programs; during employment, such as day care for children; and policies to advance the equal position of women in the labor market, such as legislation or other measures to overcome sex discrimination in job placement, promotion, and pay. Within each of these policy areas, a systematic pattern has emerged in both Britain and Sweden.

In general, the British are more traditional in their conception of the role of women. For example, there is less effort or concern about breaking down occupational segregation on the basis of sex. Though a Sex Discrimination Act exists, women are expected to take the initiative themselves to seek to enter male-dominated fields of employment. There is little incentive or support for them to do so, either in terms of prior experience in the educational system or in proving discriminatory practices to industrial tribunals. In addition, the traditional conception still prevails that women are mothers first and foremost. This is seen in the conditions for eligibility for day care services in Britain. Only those mothers who have to work for financial reasons or because they are welfare clients can receive a place for their children in public day nurseries. In addition, the implementation of the British programs also shows evidence of a peculiar role for the state, peculiar in the sense that Britain was, at one time at least, said to be a welfare state in which, by definition, the state supposedly intervened readily to modify the play of market forces and to reverse their inegalitarian consequences. Yet in each of the policy areas that have been examined here the state has intervened hesitantly, and intervention has not altered significantly the impact of market forces on the social and economic status of women.

Swedish policies indicate a prevailing conception of women as potential or actual workers. Swedish policies are explicitly designed to overcome the traditional barriers that have prevented women from participating in the labor market, barriers such as young children, sex discrimination, and economic recessions. For example, in programs that prepare women for the labor market, there are courses especially designed for women re-entering after an absence of some years. There is extensive aptitude testing to assure a comfortable fit in a future occupation, as well as extensive analysis of labor market trends to assure secure, well-paying, and productive employment. These policies anticipate that once individuals enter the labor market they will remain there. This expectation is further advanced by the countercyclical measures that increase funding for public works projects, including research and hospital work in which women are heavily employed. In the area of day care, Swedish programs provide services that begin when a mother's maternity leave is over (7 months) and continue until the child enters school (7 years). Even then, after-school facilities provide activities until the hours when full-time working parents return home from work. Those parents who cannot be immediately accommodated by child centers are assisted in finding a place in family day homes, many of which are under local government supervision. In sum, the state shows no hesitancy to intervene so as to facilitate women's employment. (The only exception concerns those special areas that are the exclusive prerogative of collective bargaining, namely, on-the-job matters. Yet, even here, the state is not absent; it nudges and if necessary threatens legislation to achieve desired outcomes.) The state has met little resistance from management and labor. Both unions and employers not only have agreed with state policies for women, but also have participated in the development of those policies. We saw too, however, that in each of the policy areas that have been examined, further progress for Swedish women workers may be reaching certain limits.

To account for these contrasting patterns in policy responses to working women in Britain and Sweden, I focused on three major areas of possible explanation: economic determinants, sex discrimination and other women-specific factors, and the role of the state. Concerning the first two, I have shown that in each of the policy areas economic determinants and women-specific factors are more significant in explaining policy responses in Britain than in Sweden. British policies in the area of labor market demand for women workers take market demand as a given. For example, the state accepts that more women are employed as secretaries, and structures public training programs accordingly. There is no attempt in Britain to shape or alter any given structure of labor market demand. Furthermore, women-specific factors such as the traditional view of women as mothers first are of central importance in the determination of eligibility for day care programs and in estimating the overall need for day care. In contrast, the Swedish state has taken a more active role in reversing market forces that, for example, place women in the lower paying categories of occupations, and in attenuating the impact of business cycles on women's employment. Labor market policies as well as the provision of day care also seek to overcome sex discrimination as a determinant of the economic status of women.

We begin to see from these differences that, while each of the three areas of explanation plays a part, the role of the state is critical, for it *mediates* the effects of the other two factors in addition to having an independent impact of its own. To demonstrate in greater detail this dual significance of the role of the state—as both independent and intervening variable—I looked more extensively at a single area of policy: day care for children of working parents. And I developed two ideal-typical forms of state-intervention: the liberal-welfare and the societal-corporatist. These forms of state intervention, approximating the actual cases of Britain and Sweden, respectively, may now be seen to characterize British and Swedish policies toward working women more generally.

The basic contrast that I drew was between the liberal-welfare orientation of the state in Britain and its societal-corporatist orientation in Sweden. In Britain, the interests of women workers are placed within a framework of market-determined priorities. This means that the timing and the nature of the state's response to the concerns of women workers are based on the immediate "needs" of the economy for women workers and less on the needs and abilities of women workers themselves. The relationship between the market and women workers has been mediated only weakly by the state. The strongest instance of state mediation in Britain, the Sex Discrimination Act, has resulted in very little improvement in the conditions of employment for women workers because the basic system of allocation and rewards, as determined by the market, has not been affected. The weakest instance of state intervention to facilitate women's opportunities to work, namely the provision of day care facilities, demonstrates an outright capitulation to traditional conceptions of the role of women and to market-determined criteria of the need for welfare.

The key to the changes that have occurred in Swedish policies for working women is the close association between concern for women, the labor market, and economic productivity. Unlike the British situation, where women's concerns are specific only to women themselves, in Sweden they are placed within the mainstream of economic policy. Productivity and growth constantly form clear, visible goals and constitute explicit and direct objectives of economic policy. Whatever needs to be done to achieve these ends is done (including changing traditional attitudes about the role of women in the workplace and in society). However, the state in Sweden has never acted alone, either in developing or in implementing policies. Never has there been unilateral enforcement of economic or social measures. The state always acts as part of the tripartite system. The critical body of support for state policies and goals initially comes from the labor movement. The close association between the labor movement and the Social Democratic Party and the longevity in office of the latter has certainly been helpful in providing a strong basis of support for policies. The concerns of women workers have found expression through their adoption by the labor movement and the Social Democratic Party. They are also adopted by management as a result of political pressure and collective bargaining. This provides the foundations for the societal corporatist policy nexus. These policies for women are effective because they are placed within the framework of labor productivity and economic growth.

In sum, the role of the state in Britain allows the "free play" of such societal factors as economic determinants and sex discrimination to shape the economic status of women, whereas the state in Sweden has adopted a role of strongly mediating if not actually controlling the impact of these societal factors. The task that remains is to show that these forms of state intervention are not unique to the particular issue area of working women—to show, in other words, that the role of the state as an independent and intervening variable in the domain we have examined here is not itself a function of "state/women" relations but represents a more general modality of "state/society" relations in Britain and Sweden.

It is my thesis that the differential role of the state vis-à-vis *women workers* in Britain and Sweden reflects the differential status of *labor* more generally. Two differences are critical for present purposes. First, labor itself is far more fragmented in Britain than it is in Sweden. Second, in Britain labor is an inferior partner in the governing coalition comprising labor-capital-state; in Sweden labor is fully integrated as an equal partner in the tripartite system. This in turn has two major consequences, one for economic policy concerning labor in general, the other for policy concerning women workers in particular. British macroeconomic policy subordinates the interests of labor to neo-liberal strictures that stress the needs of external financial stability over domestic welfare. Labor is compensated for its sacrifice by means of micro-level interventions by the state in sectors like health and housing. But these interventions are inadequate to bridge the pre-existing antipathy between labor and the state that is reinforced by the general pattern of macroeconomic planning. In Sweden, the interests of labor are the very essence of a form of economic management that presumes external stability to be a function of domestic welfare. Far greater trust and perceived interdependence therefore exists between labor, capital, and the state. And women workers in Sweden increasingly are becoming less of a particular group than part of a more universal category called simply workers, which in turn are more fully integrated and equally represented in the governing coalition. In contrast, in Britain working women are a particularistic claimant in an internally fragmented constituency, which itself plays an inferior part in relation to capital and the state.

In sum, the argument that I will establish in this concluding chapter is that the key to understanding the differences in the role of the state toward women workers in Britain and Sweden is the respective status of labor and its relation with the state.

I proceed as follows. In separate sections on Britain and Sweden, I first trace the development of the labor and social democratic movements, the initial working relationship that developed between them, and the understanding each had about the meaning and goals of socialism. Next, I examine how the strength and integrity of the labor/state relationship were tested by certain critical developments earlier in this century, primarily the economic dislocation caused by the Depression and the changes produced by the world wars. I turn finally to the contemporary scene. Here I examine the relationship between labor and the state from the vantage point of macroeconomic planning in Britain and Sweden, as well as incomes policy in Britain and labor market policy in Sweden. In a concluding section, I discuss the implications of the relationship between labor and the state for women workers.

LABOR AND THE STATE IN BRITAIN

A fundamental cleavage exists between labor and the state in Britain which both shapes policy proposals that affect labor and conditions the ultimate failure of these policies to achieve even their minimal objectives. This cleavage remains no matter which party is in power. In the 1920s and 1930s, the Labour Party and organized labor were temporarily united by their visions of socialism. But, since the late 1940s, whenever the Labour Party has been in office, it has consistently adopted a highly particularistic interpretation of the "national interest" that has not differed in essence from the Conservatives. The change in Labour's doctrine occurred after World War II. During the war and for a few years thereafter, the governing Labour Party was still firmly committed to the primacy of full employment and the need to control market forces. But this position was constrained by certain national and international factors.[1] As a result of wartime losses, Britain was utterly dependent upon American aid, first the loan of 1945 and later Marshall Plan assistance. This the United States was willing and even anxious to provide, but on the condition that Britain return quickly to more orthodox liberal economic arrangements, including full convertibility of sterling and the abolition of imperial trade preferences.

[1] Stephen Blank, "Britain: The Politics of Foreign Economic Policy, the Domestic Economy, and the Problem of Pluralistic Stagnation," *International Organization*, 31 (Autumn 1977).

United States demands met with the approval and support of the City of London, with the Bank of England and commercial banks themselves being eager to resume sterling's international role. But an international role for sterling in turn implied a high priority for domestic price stability, which could only come at the expense of social expenditures and the level of wages. Thus, external financial constraints, together with the internal orthodox financial constituencies they encouraged, subordinated Britain's commitment to full employment and social policies. This was the compromise Labour was obliged to accept: domestic social measures that directly affected the international role of sterling and the balance of payments would be constrained by orthodox financial policy; in return, social sectors whose direct international ramifications were minor, such as health and housing, could be socialized. In sum, the Labour Party, no less than the Conservative Party, has clung to certain central tenets of economic liberalism as the primary framework of economic policy.[2]

Although labor leaders, at times, have followed suit in the application of this policy framework, rarely have rank and file union members succumbed in heart, despite legislative coercion. From the point of view of workers, their "fair share" has still not been realized. Accordingly, limited trust was placed in the centralized hands of the labor movement. Even this is being withdrawn of late in favor of renewed "shop-floor" activism.

The liberal tenets of the welfare state in Britain mean that the market determines economic conditions, including the position of and rewards for labor; thereafter, the state may ameliorate these conditions, as the situation requires. However, as we have noted over and over again, when the state does act it tends to do so hesitantly and therefore clumsily. Because state intervention is justified primarily by market failure, the domain of state action is severely cir-

[2] Richard N. Gardner, *Sterling-Dollar Diplomacy* (Oxford: Clarendon Press, 1956).

cumscribed, even arbitrary. We see this most clearly in the resort to law in order to control industrial relations, despite the preference of both employers and employees to reach agreements through "voluntary" methods. Even when statutes have existed enabling employers to sue for damages against unofficial strikers, employers have been reluctant to do so. But the government, even under the Labour Party, has readily imposed rather stringent incomes policies and even considered banning strikes to keep the economy on the course deemed necessary for strong currency and the balance of payments. These actions constraining the demands of the labor movement have become even stronger recently, as the British economy has worsened.

Before turning to the current conditions in Britain, I examine the background of labor/state relations, beginning with the roots of the development of unionism and the Labour Party.

Unionism and the Labour Party

The "making of the English working class" started earlier then elsewhere, and was a long, drawn-out process.[3] Industrialization in Britain was widespread and affected many categories of craftsmen and laborers, as well as farmers.[4] Understandably, the trade union movement also began early in Britain. Before the end of the eighteenth century, trade unions were organizing most branches of skilled workers and had already been made illegal by the Combination Acts (1799). This served only to fuel the flames of Jacobins and dissidents.[5] But the move toward organizing labor was fragmented, and the antagonism and sectionalism of the early trade union movement in Britain sank roots which have never fully dissolved, echoing the familiar adage about Britain concerning "the extraordinary tenacity of older atti-

[3] E. P. Thompson, *The Making of the English Working Class* (London: Penguin Books, 1963).
[4] Karl Polanyi, *The Great Transformation* (Boston: Beacon Press, 1944).
[5] Thompson, *The Making of the English Working Class*.

tudes."[6] The Trades Union Congress (TUC), founded in 1868, provided an umbrella for many of the separate craft and trade-based unions, but it has never provided a common voice for the particular battles which unions still wage in the pursuit of their interests. The Webbs' assessment of the trade union movement in 1894 remains valid even today:

> the basis of association of these million and a half wage-earners is primarily sectional in its nature. They come together, and contribute their pence, for the defence of their interests as Boilermakers, Miners, Cotton-spinners, and not directly for the advancement of the whole working class. . . . The vague general Collectivism [of the salaried officers of the unions] has hitherto got translated into practical proposals only in so far as it can be expressed in projects for the advantage of a particular trade.[7]

There was some question as to the effect such sectionalism would have on the development of a united parliamentary Labour Party. Although the TUC founded such a party in 1899, it was many years before individual unions affiliated with the TUC joined.[8]

The early Labour Party was very much a trades union party, seeking to advance the traditional interests of workers for better working conditions. It was not at first a socialist party, although some of its members and M.P.'s were socialist. Samuel Beer notes that the early party "studiously avoided commiting itself to Socialism and, although Socialists, especially from the I.L.P. [Independent Labour

---

[6] Andrew Shonfield, *Modern Capitalism* (London: Oxford University Press, 1965), p. 88.

[7] Quoted in Samuel H. Beer, *British Politics in the Collectivist Age* (New York: Alfred A. Knopf, 1965), p. 111.

[8] For example, the miners wondered "why we as a Federation should be called upon to join an Association to find money, time or intellect to focus the weaknesses of other Trade Unionists to do what you are doing for yourselves, and have done for the last fourteen years." Quoted in ibid., p. 114.

Party], occupied positions of power, they did so only on condition that, whatever their hopes might be, they accept the limited objects of trade union politics."[9]

The Party did become socialist, and strongly so, after World War I. The unity of the Party at that time was the greatest it has ever again achieved. There was a repeat performance immediately after World War II, but it did not last as long. In both cases, once the impetus to a united front that had been provided by the war wore off, the deeply rooted and institutionalized dissentions within the Party reappeared. These dissentions revolved less around the simple division between socialists and non-socialists, than around the division between the majority rank and file supporters of the former and the parliamentary representatives of the latter, a division, in short, between labor and the state. Let us examine first the nature of this division as it concerned differences in the idea of socialism.

Commitment to Socialism

All democratic political parties hold conferences to construct the party's platform and elect the party's leaders. In the case of the Labour Party, the first of these annual conferences, and even the latest, was gripped by a fundamental schism that has refused to be mended: that between the particular interests of trade unionists and the "national" interest of Party leaders. The conference is controlled by trade unionists who formulate specific demands which they seek to have placed on the parliamentary agenda. After the first few conferences, the National Executive Committee found it necessary to remind its constituents that conference resolutions are suggestive only and that the timing and methods of parliamentary actions are up to the "Party in the House" together with the National Executive.[10]

The early Parliamentary Labour Party did concern itself

---

[9] Ibid., p. 115. The ILP or Independent Labour Party was the early name of what later became the Labour Party.
[10] Ibid., p. 118.

largely with requirements for workers' protection, following the demands of its constituency. But as parliamentary leaders became more hopeful of holding power, their interests and methods diverged from the rank and file. As early as 1908, the Labour Party outside Parliament was described as "not a compact body . . . hardly a federation . . . but rather an instrument for combining the political action of many independent organizations for a single purpose, that of electing representatives of Labour to the House of Commons."[11] In contrast, the Parliamentary Labour Party was described as "a united party." This unity of the parliamentary group extended beyond its immediate party lines, for in 1906 Ramsay MacDonald negotiated a pact with Herbert Gladstone, the leader of the Liberal Party. The support of the Liberals by Labour M.P.'s was extensive, and no doubt contributed to the taste for parliamentarism of the elected group and the schism with its rank and file. Nevertheless, after World War I a common commitment to socialism developed and provided a temporary overarching concordance among the several elements of the Party.

The reasons behind the adoption of socialism by the Labour Party after World War I were at least once removed from the ideological fervor embedded in socialist doctrine. During the war, trade union membership tripled, standing at over three million by 1918. More than anything else, this tremendous growth in its constituent base gave the Labour Party the hope of achieving independent political power. What remained was to make the break with the Liberals, a move that came as easily to union leaders as to the Party leaders, both of whom had experienced the snub of "class" differences in the former Lib-Lab entente. Thus, in Samuel Beer's assessment, the commitment to socialism on the part of the Labour Party "can be regarded as a consequence of this breach" with Liberals, which itself was underpinned by the "divisive forces of the British class structure at the time."[12] This is not to say that the new faith was simply expedient.

[11] Ibid., pp. 120-21, quoting A. L. Lowell.
[12] Ibid., p. 145.

It acquired tremendous zeal, but it also required strong oppositional forces to sustain it.

The Labour Party claimed that its socialist program was based on the "interests of labour." During the war the working class came to acquire a positive attitude toward socialism. Mines, railways, and factories had all been under government control and, as a result of this wartime experience, "ordinary men and women understood that government control and intervention might mean a large weekly wage, a more secure employment, and a greater number of social benefits" after the war as well.[13] Thus, the working class and the trade unionists in particular, were attracted to the Labour Party's general identity with their class interests. But their loyalty was based less on a doctrinal affinity than on those particular features of the Party's program that related to their particular concerns. This is what gave meaning to any abstract ideas of socialism. To the trade unionists, socialism meant a "living wage" for a fair day's work, decent provisions for safety and health on the job, security from unfair dismissal or compensation for it. Summing up this central concern for job protection rather than socialism per se, one observer in 1928 said:

> The Unions as a whole will finance the Labour Party with its socialistic programme and socialistic leadership, and more than half of the membership will vote for its socialistic candidate. . . . But the heart of British unionism is still in these jealously revered organisations that stand guard over the collective economic opportunity of each group—the jobs and the working conditions that go with the jobs.[14]

The intellectual leaders of the Labour Party in the interwar years continued to advocate programs that had already been well developed, adding nothing new or creative.[15] During the interwar years the consensus of the Party

[13] Ibid., p. 139, quoting Stephen Graubard.
[14] Irving Richter, *Political Purpose in Trade Unions* (London: Allen and Unwin, 1973), p. 22, quoting Selig Perlman.
[15] Beer, *British Politics*, p. 150.

rested on a summation of particulars and on a general commitment to democratic politics. Except for a minority branch, which advocated revolutionary tactics, the Party as a whole was democratic and gradualist, oriented more to winning and retaining office as an independent force than to any great societal transformation. At the annual conferences the constituents continued to suggest specific courses of action but allowed parliamentary leaders to decide what could be done and when. There were times when the decisions of leaders ran counter to the particular interests of workers, though the leaders did not always win.[16] The occasional battle kept alive the fundamental cleavage between labor and the state. When union leaders and Party leaders met on common ground, it was often because the issue at hand combined workers' particular interests and experiences and the Party leaders' larger socialist orientation. Nationalization is a case in point. It could have put to the test much sooner the divisions within the Party. Trade union pressure for nationalization was confined to the situation in specific industries. Party leaders early on accepted the general idea of nationalization because it was "part and parcel" of the inherited socialist program "and not on the ground that [the specific industry] was in a special position in relation to the British economy."[17] While the two points of view were not contradictory, they were not identical either. For example, after the Miners Federation endorsed the Labour Party early in the century, a resolution on mines nationalization was adopted in the Party's 1918 platform. However, coal mines were not nationalized until 1946 and iron and steel not until 1949. In the long process of achieving their goals, the miners had to do what all unionists have had to do for recognition: plead, bargain, agitate, and strike, until it became neccessary for the Labour Party in power

---

[16] In 1931 Ramsay MacDonald wanted to accept a loan from New York City banks which carried the stipulation that unemployment benefits be cut by 10%. He did not receive sufficient support from either the cabinet or the Parliamentary Party. Discussed by Beer, ibid., pp. 160-61.

[17] Ibid., pp. 166-67, quoting R. Page Arnot.

to act.[18] Because the issue of the nationalization of mines was periodically readopted in the Party's platform, the miners were led to believe that they could rely on the parliamentary leaders to do what they could when they could. The miners also had strong traditional roots in Gladstonian Liberalism and all that this implied for non-violent, gradualist means of action.

In sum, it took unionists some time to realize that the Labour Party was not simply their legislative arm. Two situations in particular had kept the myth alive. One was the extent to which the first Labour M.P.'s, and especially the first majority Labour government, seemed to be working in the name of unionists' interests. The Labour government which was elected after World War II followed the Party's program to an extent "unprecedented in British political history."[19] In only a few matters did the government's legislation deviate from what had been laid down in the Party's Manifesto. This adherence to the Party program, however, was a unique instance, and stemmed from an unusual degree of consensus and cohesion following the war and the election. A second factor prevented unions from seeing that their position within the Party was declining. This was their own persistent fragmentation and sectionalism, which inhibited their capacity to appreciate their common interest and the power that could arise from collective mass action.[20] However, two issues finally brought out generalized rank-and-file disillusionment with the Party in power: economic planning and incomes policy.

Postwar Economic Planning

When the time came to put socialism into practice after World War II, not only did the former apparent unity of

[18] The demand for nationalization of mines became "so irresistible that no government, whatever its political convictions, could have allowed matters to continue as they were under private ownership." Ibid., p. 171, quoting William A. Robson.

[19] Ibid., p. 179.

[20] Such action has only been evident in occasional sympathy strikes.

the Party collapse under the weight of specifying what socialism meant but so too did the former apparent commitment to socialism. For the brand of socialism that emerged from the postwar years of Labour governments was odd indeed:

There had undoubtedly been important social reforms. But power had not shifted between classes. Qualitative social transformation had not come. Nor was it any nearer for the six years of office. In essence the Labour Government of 1945-52 had not created a socialist commonwealth, nor even taken a step in the direction. It had simply created a mixed economy in which the bulk of industry still lay in private hands, and the six years of its rule had only marginally altered the distribution of social power, privilege, wealth, income, opportunity and security.[21]

This outcome was, of course, conditioned by the economic constraints in which Britain found itself after World War II. As noted above, Britain was financially dependent on the United States, which in turn was adamant in its opposition to collectivism. The United States required that Britain return to convertibility, which it did, and it nearly drove Britain into bankruptcy.[22] Marshall Plan aid, a major devaluation, and more orthodox financial policy followed, all behind the shield of transitional arrangements, by means of which the European economies could return to postwar normalcy while discriminating against dollar goods. The most important consequence for present purposes was the impact of these developments on the power positions of dominant actors in Britain. Orthodox financial policy meant a greater role for the City of London, which wanted an early restoration of the international role of sterling, which in turn required further orthodox financial policy. Above

[21] David Coates, *The Labour Party and the Struggle for Socialism* (Cambridge: Cambridge University Press, 1975), p. 47.

[22] Since other west European nations did not return to convertibility, they quickly bought up sterling, creating a crisis situation in Britain. See Blank, "Britain: the Politics of . . ."; and Gardner, *Sterling-Dollar Diplomacy*.

all, wages had to be contained and a certain level of unemployment accepted. This reinforced the liberal remnants of British socialism, and led to the split between market-rationality in the realm of policies shaping the economy as a whole, and what I have elsewhere called "bureaucratic socialism" in certain compensatory social sectors like health and housing.[23]

This juxtaposition of market principles and bureaucratic socialism is evident in what happened to British economic planning, an attempt which ultimately and understandably failed. I focus specifically on the consequences for relations with labor. The term "planning" first entered the Labour Party's lexicon in the 1930s. It carried essentially the same meaning that Sidney Webb had suggested in 1918: "For the individualist system of capitalist production, based on the private ownership and competitive administration of land and capital [the Labour Party would build up a social order based on] a deliberately planned cooperation in production and distribution."[24] But when placed within the "liberal" framework of the postwar era, the meaning of who exactly ought to "cooperate" and for what purposes changed.

The orientation of the first postwar planning machinery was directed toward developing a close working relationship between government and the business leadership. As a PEP survey in 1950 observed: "Government Departments and Ministers, believing that an ounce of willing co-operation [with business] was worth a ton of compulsion, set themselves out to establish friendly contacts and consultations and to use their compulsive powers as little as possible."[25] Accordingly, the representatives of organized labor (who were also "producers") were not to be seen on any planning councils. Trained and competent managers, and not unversed union leaders, staffed and headed the development of "plans." That this was an application of the

[23] See the discussion in Chapter 5.
[24] Quoted by Beer, *British Politics*, p. 190.
[25] John Schmidman, *British Unions and Economic Planning* (University Park, Penn.: Pennsylvania State University, Studies No. 27, 1969), p. 11.

Fabian position on the role of the expert was obvious, and that planning would not be envisioned as an alternative to the imperatives of market forces should have been expected. As the 1947 Economic Survey said:

> controls cannot by themselves bring very rapid changes or make fine adjustments in the economic structure . . . under democracy the execution of the economic plan must be much more a matter of *co-operation* between the Government, industry and the people than of rigid application by the State of controls and compulsions.[26]

However, the application of this formula was confined to the managerial levels of government and industry. This was to change in the 1960s, when unions were represented on the National Economic Development Council. But by then the relations between labor and government were being defined by the issue of wages and the problem of inflation, as we will see.

The early type of planning consisted largely of gathering economic information and proposing detailed targets for production output and manpower use. No mechanisms for reaching those targets were specified. When the targets proved to have been badly miscalculated, the response was not to introduce and tighten existing controls but to tone down the aspirations and claims of economic planning. As the planners increased their demands to dismantle continuing wartime controls and return to the "free play of market forces," the Labour government gradually acquiesced. The net result of this first British effort at economic planning was to strengthen business. Of course, the same result came from the Conservative's form of planning when they were in office in the 1950s. Within this sort of liberal framework, the only type of planning that could be done was the very general level of accounting of resources.[27]

Public ownership had been an essential ingredient in La-

---

[26] Ibid., p. 10.
[27] Shonfield, *Modern Capitalism*, Chapter 6.

bour's attempt to plan the economy. It granted the state the authority to specify goals for the allocation of resources within sectors and industries, crucial decisions which had previously been determined by the market. During the war, the government had taken over such control; after the war the spirit of socialism was to have justified its continuation.[28] As it turned out, profit for the nation was not a sufficient justification. Nationalizing public utilities had caused no problem, but mining was another matter. Coal, iron, and steel were profit-making industries, and their nationalization brought strong protests as well as a "gentlemen's agreement" among the private sector industrialists not to assist the government in its management of mining boards. Sensing its uncomfortable position, the government responded by granting overly generous compensations to the former owners and left the internal structure of these industries basically intact. This made it easy for the next Conservative government to denationalize some mines with minimum disruption. For the remainder of Labour's term in office, the commitment to nationalization, which had never been especially strong except among a few Left-wingers, was limited to failing industries. This suited the private sector perfectly.

Incomes Policy

Incomes policy was another area in which the postwar Labour government acted in a manner one would not have expected of a socialist party based on the interests of labor. The two components of an incomes policy, concerning manpower and fiscal policies, tested the government's capacity to deal effectively with labor on the one hand and business on the other. The Attlee government had hoped to base economic recovery on the voluntary cooperation of workers and employers, using controls only where neces-

[28] It will be recalled that miners had been agitating for nationalization since early in the century.

sary and agreed upon. Its solution to the severe inflationary pressures plaguing Britain by 1947 was to have centered on building up manpower and production to the point of equilibrium while holding down prices and costs (including wages) by direct control. When voluntarism did not work, for reasons to be explored below, the government negotiated separately with labor leaders and business leaders to conclude an incomes policy in 1948. It amounted to little more than a wage restraint policy, with no manpower component, and was conditional on prices being held down. In a sense it was government's part of the bargain that failed, and not because of the government's doing. First, Britain's premature convertibility and later the liberalization of trade among the European countries which was required for Marshall Plan aid recipients severely drained Britain's reserves and caused a balance of payments crisis. Britain was forced to devalue the pound in 1949. There was a consequent rise in prices, since imports became more costly and exports were little helped. A relinquishing of wage restraint followed in early 1951. Since the whole experience set the pace and staging of later attempts at incomes policy, let us look more closely at what it reveals about the understanding that never developed between labor and the state, specifically as this involves manpower and voluntary collective bargaining.

Manpower.   During the war the distribution of manpower was achieved through a system of "industrial conscription," one of many direct controls of national resources.[29] After the war, continuing control of manpower distribution and redistribution through wages policies met with severe resistance from organized labor because it threatened traditional union prerogatives and domains of craftsmanship. Becoming a member of a craft or trade is not a simple matter in Britain, nor one that can be easily transferred in keeping with shifting macro "plans." The British system of

[29] Beer, *British Politics*, p. 191.

apprenticeship, which qualifies a worker as skilled in a particular trade, is "essentially pre-industrial in spirit."[30] It is based on the length of time spent with a master, the period (usually five years) being much longer than elsewhere. It serves to develop pride in one's work and preserves a romantic sense of craftsmanship. But it also tends to bind a worker to a trade, decreasing mobility. Manpower planning in Britain has not managed to overcome the rigidity of union requirements of apprenticeship either after the war or after the recent innovations described in Chapter 3. For example, a central element of manpower planning is to identify thriving industries where labor shortages exist and to use differential wage policies to draw workers to these jobs. Unions have never accepted major changes in their own prerogatives to determine trade-based wage differentials. And whenever labor shifts have been suggested or required, unions have adopted an attitude of protection for their workers. This is one reason why incomes policies have generally been reduced to wage restraint policies and have not included manpower components nor been effectively linked with economic recovery policies.

To be sure, much more than craftsmanship is involved. Adequate support for workers in transition has repeatedly been missing from government proposals. For example, individual, and not simply industry-based, differentials have not been systematically calculated to prevent a worker from losing pay when starting at a lower training scale in a new job. Nor has the government systematically assured immediate retraining or redeployment for job-changers. Redundancies in declining industries more often than not result in receipt of the "dole." Nor has rehousing assistance for workers changing jobs ever been included in the manpower policy nexus.[31] As long as government appeals for

---

[30] Shonfield, *Modern Capitalism*, p. 118.

[31] Public housing is in short supply and rents are heavily subsidized. Once a house is given up, the family moves to the bottom of the waiting list in a new area. The current Conservative government is responding less to the problem of mobility and more to a principle of ownership, by making it easier for tenants to buy their homes.

union cooperation in labor redirection are based on macro-level plans alone, without adequate support for workers in transition, there is little doubt that unions will take a defensive position.

Collective bargaining. Incomes policies also infringe, of course, on the sanctity of collective bargaining. However, incomes policies are thwarted less by the institution of collective bargaining than by the multiplicity of bargains and methods that characterize this tradition. Each trade union negotiates with its own employer or employer organization on matters related to working conditions and pay. In a single plant, this can result in any number of separate agreements, depending on the number of trades and sections of production involved. There are also wider, even industry-wide, agreements.[32] But there is an understanding that these are frameworks only, and that better agreements can be negotiated at the decentralized level. At any rate, no collective agreements are legally binding. The Industrial Labour Courts deal only with issues to which laws apply; except for the Sex Discrimination and Equal Pay Acts, these mostly concern protection and working conditions in particular industries.

The TUC is restricted in its capacity to conclude wide-ranging agreements. For one, unions prefer to speak for themselves. For another, only 23% of the 488 unions in Britain are affiliated with the TUC.[33] Nevertheless, governments always work directly with the TUC in their attempts to develop incomes policies, as we will see. The same diversity exists on the part of employers' organizations. In 1970, there were 1,350 employers' organizations in Britain, the majority outside the Confederation of British Industry (CBI), the main umbrella organization for employers.

What characterizes collective bargaining in Britain is the

[32] For a discussion of the variety and methods of agreements, see R. F. Banks, "The Pattern of Collective Bargaining" in B. C. Roberts (ed.), *Industrial Relations* (London: Methuen and Co., 1962).

[33] This is a 1975 figure. At the turn of the century there were 1,323 unions.

individuality with which separate unions and employers pursue their negotiations and seek to maintain their agreements and, at the same time, the "formal posture of intransigence" that prevails at all negotiating tables.[34] This posture stems from the principle of supply and demand that has always permeated collective bargaining.[35] It is a principle that both sides cling to, for it is the only way either has ever achieved any leverage. For example, unions made their gains during the wars, when labor shortages existed. The Depression of the interwar period favored employers, bringing progress in pay to a virtual standstill. The principle of supply and demand and the posture of intransigence which it fashioned are outmoded in an era of full employment policy. But since actual full employment existed only for such a short period of time in the 1960s, the traditional form of collective bargaining has reappeared on the British scene—with a vengence.

I refer to the resurgence of "shop-floor" activism. In the 1960s "rank-and-file disillusion with the slow pace of established procedures and the moderation of union officialdom" finally gave way to this new form of labor organization "largely outside and in part opposed to, the centralized order of accommodation between labour and capital."[36] The trend toward greater centralization, which many unions had participated in only grudgingly, has been halted by the accession of plant-level negotiations between occupation-based shop stewards and management. Governments continue to attempt to shore up the authority of the TUC to control shop stewards. Yet it is just this type of working relationship between the TUC and government, and the

[34] Shonfield, *Modern Capitalism*, p. 113.

[35] The Webbs had hoped the principle of supply and demand would be replaced by the spirit of collectivism and the principle of a living wage, making trade unions "professional organizations." See the discussion in Allen Flanders, *Trade Unions* (London: Hutchinson, 1968), p. 76.

[36] John Westergaard and Henrietta Resler, *Class in a Capitalist Society* (New York: Basic Books, 1975), p. 225.

incomes policies which have resulted from it, that led to the workers' reaction.

Unions and Governments

During the Second World War the standing of trade unions and of the TUC in particular rose tremendously. So too did the achievements of union leaders. This was due to the fact that unions were finally bargaining from a position of strength, stemming as much from the powerful personage of Ernest Bevin, head of the TUC, as from the wartime needs of the nation. Labor's entry into established government circles was greatly enhanced, union leaders acquired easy access to Ministers, and after the war labor was represented on many government committees and councils. In his authoritative study, Samuel Beer goes so far as to suggest that during this period labor finally achieved a position of equality with business in determining the pattern of industrial and governmental policy, regardless of which party was in power.[37] However, I would argue that whatever semblance of equality organized labor may have achieved was largely illusionary. Once again, the interests of labor were compromised for the sake of a particularistic conception of the national interest—wage restraints to achieve external balance.

It was the issue of an incomes policy that intervened to break the apparent accord in union-government relations. Every attempt to develop an incomes policy has been a painful process for the TUC, reminding it of the tension between its dual roles as a representative of labor and as an adjunct to government in its dealings with labor. By the time the Labour Party was back in power in 1964 and attempting again to manage the economy by means of an incomes policy, the TUC, its General Council, and its leader,

[37] Beer, *British Politics*, pp. 208-16. Relations with the Conservative government seemed to be comfortable until the late 1950s. See Flanders, *Trade Unions*, Chapter 8.

George Woodcock, were sorely concerned about the state of the economy and willing to cooperate as best they could with the government's efforts to do something about it. This meant working out an acceptable and meaningful incomes policy. The experience of past policies, which had either failed or had resulted in disruption or bad industrial relations, made it clear that:

> no policy could succeed unless it had substantial support from the trade unions, and that their support would not be forthcoming if "incomes policy" was no more than a euphemism for "wage restraint." This in turn implied two things: firstly, that price increases had to be examined at least as critically as pay increases, and both should be related to potential improvements in productivity in the firms or industries concerned; secondly, that incomes policy must be placed in a framework of national economic planning instead of being an improvised response to the latest balance-of-payments crisis.[38]

Incomes policies were negotiated in both 1965 and 1966. The unions had given the TUC an unprecedented degree of authority on their behalf, because of "their alarm at the growing scope of political intervention in wage determination and their desire to contain it by supporting a positive alternative."[39] The unions were compliant and fully cooperative with the "freeze," but only as long as prices also remained frozen. Sterling should have been devalued in 1964, but this was viewed as being incompatible with its reserve currency role. However, heavy borrowing failed to support the value of sterling against continued balance-of-payments difficulties and massive speculation. In 1967, the pound was at long last devalued and domestic austerity imposed. Unions rebelled at having to keep their part of the bargain alone. But even more than this familiar re-

---

[38] Flanders, *Trade Unions*, p. 116.
[39] Ibid., p. 169.

quirement that they must play the sacrificial lamb, unions were irked by government attempts to impose legislation restricting their traditional prerogatives and the principle of voluntarism.

The resort to additional legislation reveals the failure of the Labour government to establish a viable working relationship with both business and especially labor on economic policy. The TUC was, at first, more than willing to cooperate, having worked out with its affiliates an arrangement by which "unions were to notify the General Council of all claims under consideration relating to improvements in wages and working conditions."[40] And going somewhat too far beyond the call of duty, the General Council also reserved the right to tell the unions when their claims were not in the national interest. The government seems not to have fully trusted the TUC's ability to enforce its role in this "early warning" system, for within a few months the government was proposing various types of regulatory legislation: to delay the implementation of wage increases, to impose a more stringent wage and price freeze, to forestall a strike and require a pre-strike ballot, and finally, to quell the outbreak of wildcat strikes. To make matters worse, each legislative step came on top of an increasingly worsening economic situation. The TUC's faith was being tried, for it had engaged in joint efforts with government and business to control inflation with the understanding that such control would avoid the necessity of greater unemployment. But the government's priorities, even the Labour government's, placed devaluation of the pound as the act to be most avoided and allowed unemployment to rise.[41] In the event, each measure of "last resort" was tried, none managed to stave off the next, and all failed to reverse the downward direction of the economy. Britain got both inflation and unemployment. As a result of having a Labour

---

[40] John Schmidman, *British Unions*, p. 41.
[41] Andrew Martin, "Labor Market Policies and Inflation: Contrasting Responses in Britain and Sweden," *Polity*, 7 (1975).

government in power again after so many years, the stalemate in economic policy of the preceding years was broken, "but by *diminishing* the labor movement's power in the political economy rather than by increasing it."[42] Moreover, Labour's ill-fated attempts at incomes policy cleared the way for the next Conservative government to institute even harsher measures, fueling even more the reversion to shop-floor activism.

Conclusion

The Wilson government in the 1960s discredited the viability of the Labour Party as a close affiliate of the labor movement, particularly in the eyes of rank-and-file members. When the next Labour government, this time under James Callaghan, again tried to institute an incomes policy, it was cloaked in the slogan of a "Social Contract." The policy was successful for a time in holding down wages and prices, but more because of personal relationships than because of any renewed and lasting bonds in industrial relations. By the 1970s, shop-floor activism had come to be seen as the only way workers could achieve their demands— as always, through their own individual efforts, a lesson from the past that was once again proven correct.

The experience of incomes and prices policies is leading to a general conclusion in Britain that voluntary collective bargaining, even at the decentralized level, must be strengthened, and not weakened by further government intervention and legislation. Repeated commissions of inquiry, from the 1960s to the present, have come to this conclusion, and are suggesting various organizational forms and measures to enhance the principle of voluntarism.[43]

[42] Andrew Martin, "Is Democratic Control of Capitalist Economies Possible?" in Leon N. Lindberg (ed.), *Stress and Contradiction in Modern Capitalism* (Lexington, Mass.: Lexington Books, 1975), p. 36.

[43] *Trade Unions and Employers Associations* (London: HMSO, 1968) (the Donovan Report); *Industrial Democracy* (London: HMSO, 1977) (the Bullock Report).

Collective bargaining is considered to be the most appropriate democratic form of labor governance in a mixed economy. It is clear that this conclusion stems not simply from the failures of economic policies in Britain, but also the form that these failures took. We have seen again in this chapter, as in preceding ones, the basic hesitancy of state intervention in Britain, even on the part of a Labour government. When this predisposition not to intervene is overcome by the necessity for some form of action (to save the economy), that action invariably is overreaction—a series of clumsy measures that divide and antagonize more than they unite and conquer the problem. The imposition of incomes policies is a case in point. Why is this so?

The fundamental cleavage between labor and the state in Britain has a commonality with the various types of other social cleavages that have been discussed throughout this study—whether between categories of workers, between the Department of Health and Social Security and the Department of Education and Science, between the local and central government, and so on. All evoke a separation of domains, based on the particular interests of each. Lacking is a sense of mutual interests among strata, horizontally or vertically divided. In the case of labor and the state, government intervention has proved to be "always a second best alternative to trade union action,"[44] because the "national interest" under which governments act has been interpreted as distinct from (indeed, over and above) the "particular" self-interests of trade unions when, in fact, the interpretation of the national interest has itself been highly particularistic, particular, in essence, to capital. The Labour Party in power has responded to the unions in the same way as has any government, by requiring that wages be restrained so that the rest of the economy can progress. And when the size of the economic pie did grow somewhat, labor's share did not increase at all.[45] The failure of so-

[44] Schmidman, *British Unions*, p. 36.
[45] N. Robertson and J. L. Thomas, *Trade Unions and Industrial Relations* (London: Business Books Limited, 1968), pp. 94ff.

cialism to unite labor and the state has been the failure of the Labour Party to rise above the logic of a liberal economy, imposed by the imperatives of the international economic order and domestic competitive politics.[46]

LABOR AND THE STATE IN SWEDEN

Compared to Britain, industrialization in Sweden did not begin until quite late, around the 1850s. The date can be easily identified because industrialization follows such events as the breakup of the open field system, the abolition of guilds, and legislation to ease government controls on trade, all of which occurred in the 1840s.[47] Nevertheless, Sweden remained a predominantly agricultural country for decades. Not until 1910 was less than half of the population engaged in agricultural pursuits.[48] Besides its lateness, industrialization in Sweden is also characterized by a lack of diversity, especially compared to Britain. Iron and timber were Sweden's two principal exports until the turn of the century, when industrial production spread to paper and leather. These two factors of industrialization, lateness and relative uniformity, are critical to the evolution of the labor movement in Sweden. My argument is that they enabled the development of a coherent core, into which additional factors were readily absorbed. Moreover, it is of utmost significance that the core included not only organized labor

[46] For a discussion of the Labour Party's failure to "sustain its own class image and perspective," see Coates, *The Labour Party*, especially Chapter 6.

[47] M. Donald Hancock, *Sweden: The Politics of Postindustrial Change* (Hinsdale, Ill.: Dryden Press, 1972), p. 22. Hancock also notes the role of the reorganization of banking, credits from Germany and the U.S. and the creation of a national railway system.

[48] For comparison we can note that in 1870 almost 75% of Sweden's economically active population was engaged in the primary sector (mostly agriculture, some forestry) and 9% in manufacturing and crafts. In Britain at the same time, 15% of the population was engaged in agriculture, 43% in industry and crafts. Walter Korpi, *The Working Class in Welfare Capitalism* (London: Routledge and Kegan Paul, 1978), p. 55.

but the Social Democratic Party as well. Whereas in the case of Britain the fundamental cleavages between labor, capital, and the state continually unfold and deepen, in Sweden these cleavages barely had a chance to develop before they were assimilated into a common enterprise, namely national economic growth and productivity.

Unionism and the Social Democratic Party

Labor unions in Sweden began to form in the 1870s. These were at first mostly craft unions for skilled workers. By the end of the century, however, membership in unions for unskilled workers exceeded that in craft unions, attesting to the rapid growth of organized labor. At the same time, local unions, once formed, quickly coordinated their activities with other unions in the same occupational field or industrial sector. National organizations soon followed. By the turn of the century there were about 30 national unions combining about 300 local unions on the basis of occupation and, increasingly, on the basis of industry. In fact, within the first few decades of the twentieth century, industrial unionism exceeded both craft-based and "mixed" (that is, transport and commerce) unions.[49] One can immediately appreciate the significance this would have on the future course of collective bargaining, compared to Britain; having one union represent all the workers in a single place of work (and perhaps even at several plants) helps to reduce disparity among workers' conditions and pay, ease mobility, and establish consistency in negotiations. The diversity among unions in Britain maintains a sectionalism that became reinforced with time and events.

This period of rapid industrialization and unionization at the end of the nineteenth century also coincided with the introduction in Sweden of *both* liberalism and socialism. Extraparliamentary political parties based on these two perspectives were formed at the same time unions were form-

[49] Ibid., p. 64.

ing. The Social Democratic Party was founded in 1889 by a number of trade unions and by Social Democratic clubs convening in Stockholm for the purpose. The Party's first leader, Hjalmar Branting, was elected to Parliament in 1896. While liberalism took hold in Sweden earlier than socialism, and had influenced the institutionalization of free trade in the 1840s, a Liberal Party was not established until 1900. Very soon thereafter, however, the Liberal Party leader headed the lower house of Parliament (Riskdag), having formed a coalition with the Social Democratic Party. The basis of the coalition was a mutual concern with democratizing Parliament by extending the franchise and introducing parliamentary government. Once universal suffrage was achieved, the Liberal Party faded, for the mass of electoral sympathy augmented the strength of the Social Democrats.

The first Social Democratic clubs in Sweden were organized by a radical socialist, August Palm. By the time the Party was founded, however, the spirit of Palm's radicalism had already been tempered by the spirit of pragmatism that was to become the Party's essential quality. From its beginnings, the Social Democratic Party was reformist, not revolutionary, seeking gradual changes within the capitalist system. From its beginnings, too, the Party acquired the ability to steer a middle course, an ability acquired from experience within the Party organization as well as because of ties with the Liberals. The groups which founded the Party were divided on issues of priorities and means, but the Party's first program emphasized the one goal that all agreed on.[50] This was the achievement of universal suffrage as "the only way to a peaceful achievement of the social

[50] The program contained some vague revolutionary slogans but eschewed violence unless it became necessary and was fully supported by the masses. In the event, political power was achieved peacefully. By 1917 the radical minority faction of the Social Democratic Party broke off and formed the Left Social Democratic Party. See Dankwart A. Rustow, *The Politics of Compromise* (Princeton: Princeton University Press, 1955), pp. 48-54.

question."[51] The task necessitated cooperation and compromise with "bourgeois" political groups, which, in turn, provided the Party with its first lesson on effective political processes. Besides this common goal, the Party as a whole strongly identified with its largest internal faction, namely, the unions. The first program did not reflect the extreme sentiment of emphasizing primarily workers' concerns, but it designated these as the first order of social reforms to be sought once universal suffrage was achieved. True to their word, the Party's M.P.'s began in 1908 to introduce legislation for unemployment insurance and for public works projects at parity wages. Since then measures to combat unemployment have continued to be central features of the Party's proposals in each parliamentary session. The unity between the social democratic and labor movements was strengthened by growing unionization. The Party was always active in organizing unions. In turn, some national unions made support for the Social Democratic Party a condition of local union affiliation.[52] To this day, some unions still have "bloc voting" for the Social Democrats, with rights of reservation for persons who wish to vote as individuals.

Organized Labor and Organized Employers:
The Basic Agreement

In 1898 the Swedish Trade Union Confederation (LO) was formed, with strong support from the Social Demo-

---

[51] Quotes in Rustow, ibid., p. 49. Rustow also argues that the "simultaneous emergence of Liberalism and Socialism and their opportunity for cooperation in the suffrage question was one of the most important factors in fostering a moderate and pragmatic spirit within the Swedish Social Democratic movement," p. 53. Another significant factor was that the simultaneity meant that neither party had an established hold on power, requiring subordination by the other, as in the case of the Labour Party's support of the Liberals in Britain.

[52] The LO tried to institute this in 1898 but it was repealed within a few years.

cratic Party.[53] The coordinating function of the LO was put to use soon thereafter with a first national strike in 1902. The success of this strike made employers realize their need to organize themselves, which they did immediately as the Swedish Confederation of Employers' Organizations (SAF). As early as 1906 the LO and the SAF were engaged in negotiations. The first one concerned the right of organization for workers in a local dispute, and it led to the first of many "compromises," with the SAF recognizing the right to unionization and the LO accepting employers' prerogatives to "hire and fire workers, to manage and distribute the work, and to use workers belonging to any union or to no union."[54] This is not to suggest that relations between the two organizations were amiable from the start; in fact there were no further joint efforts until the 1930s. But, unlike the situation in Britain in which employers did not begin to organize until the 1930s, forcing labor to deal with management at the shop-floor level, in Sweden the early organization and collaboration provided a good basis for later developments.

The next general strike in Sweden, in 1909, was lost by labor. LO's membership was almost halved as a result, and both the organization and the labor movement were set back for some time. A long period of labor unrest set in. The depression period in the early 1920s, with its extremely high unemployment, further weakened the unions and their bargaining position. At about the same time the Social Democratic Party was also experiencing a "lost momentum," not unique to itself, for the whole decade of the 1920s was an era of stagnation in Sweden.[55] The economic policies that

[53] While we must not exaggerate it, this reversal of the British case (in which the TUC helped found the Labour Party) may have been significant as a basis for the future relationship of a more equal partnership between the LO and the Social Democratic Party than ever existed between the TUC and the Labour Party.

[54] Quoted in David Jenkins, *Sweden and the Price of Progress* (New York: Coward-McCann, 1968), p. 135. The clause remained in effect until 1976.

[55] Korpi, *The Working Class*, pp. 79-80.

were developed to overcome this stagnation are discussed below.

The road to economic recovery in the late 1920s necessitated first some quieting of the labor unrest that had characterized Sweden for decades. A long period of strikes and retaliatory lock-outs had achieved some industry-wide resolutions, but the overall atmosphere of labor relations was unstable. Moreover, a bitter ten-month strike in the building industry in 1933-1934 hurt the first Social Democratic government's public works program, and the government began to consider ways to intervene in labor relations. A parliamentary commission appointed in 1934 suggested that workers and employers be given one last chance to settle their differences before government legislation was proposed. Neither labor, employers, nor the Social Democratic government wanted to resort to legislation. Thus, in 1936 the LO and the SAF began a series of talks at Saltsjöbaden, in an atmosphere of earnest conciliation. The result was a Basic Agreement, which was marked less by its contents than by the spirit in which it was made and the institutionalization of collective bargaining to which it led. There are still few labor laws in Sweden (there are few in Britain too), but the results of collective bargaining are legally binding (after the Collective Agreements Act of 1928), unlike the situation in Britain. Collective bargaining has since evolved in Sweden into a three-tier system.[56] The top level consists of centralized negotiations between the LO and the SAF, a repetition of Saltsjöbaden every few years that leads to a "frame agreement." The second level consists of industry-wide negotiations on the basis of the frame agreement by member unions as well as by other centralized union organizations (such as TCO), which have granted the LO authority to include them within the frame agreement. The third level consists of workplace negotiations, in which the agreements are adapted to local conditions. The agreements include matters relating to wages and working con-

[56] Ibid., p. 97. See also my discussion in Chapter 4.

ditions, as well as rules on procedures of negotiations, settlement of disputes and of differences in interpretation. The Basic Agreement and the system of negotiations it led to continue to define relations between organized labor and employers. At the same time, the agreements became an integral component of government fiscal plans and policies. This contrasts with the more ad hoc relations between labor, employers, and the state in Britain.

The power that began to accrue to the LO during and after Saltsjöbaden has steadily increased ever since. This is not simply because the membership of LO is twice as large as that of all other unions combined. Nor is it simply because of the authority that LO exercises over its affiliates, an authority which includes refusing permission to strike when the national interest is adversely affected.[57] LO's power rests in large part on its special relationship with the Social Democratic government and on its role within the state apparatus. LO's role involves its contribution to economic policy. I turn now to an examination of the main economic strategy that unites the tripartite actors in Sweden.

Economic Strategy: Planning, Growth, and Full Employment

The ultimate goal of socialists is to effect an equitable distribution of wealth. Socialists differ primarily in their choice of means and in the priorities that are implicit in the choice of means. The strategy that many socialists (including the British) have traditionally emphasized is public ownership of the means of production. However, nationalization of key sectors of the economy never fully caught on in Sweden. In its early years, the Social Democratic Party did include traditional rhetoric about nationalization in its programs. And even years later, when the Social Demo-

---

[57] Anthony Carew, *Democracy and Government in European Trade Unions* (London: Allen and Unwin, 1976), p. 176. LO's authority amounts to a double veto power, since all unions affiliated with LO must also have the power to veto local strikes written into their constitutions. Korpi, *The Working Class*, p. 211.

cratic Party presented its first socialist program to Parliament, nationalization of natural resources, industrial firms, credit institutions, and means of transportation and communication were included among its 27 points.[58] But the parliamentary debate that followed in 1944 indicated intense opposition to nationalization so that the Social Democrats dropped this part of their program. At the same time, one of the Party's leading intellectuals, Ernst Wigforss, was developing ideas that downgraded nationalization and suggested instead a number of more viable alternatives, which were adopted.[59] Eventually, nationalization was eliminated from the Party's platform, as had been done with references to revolutions many years before.

In the event, neither proved necessary. Dropping both revolution and nationalization from the Party's platform may have led some to charge that the Social Democrats had so redefined socialism as to abandon it. But the Party's leaders believed they were moving society in a socialist direction, since "by carrying out a cautious, controlling policy we, so to say, prepare the form for another organization of production."[60]

Another strategy that socialists traditionally emphasize, which is closely related to public ownership of the means of production, is worker control of the production process. Swedish socialists also considered this strategy impractical to institutionalize in large-scale production. Industrial de-

[58] In its early years the Party did adhere to traditional nationalization principles. And in its 27-point Socialist Program presented to Parliament in 1944 there were proposals to "nationalize natural resources, industrial firms, credit institutions, and means of transportation and communication." Hancock, *Sweden: The Politics*, p. 210. But the parliamentary debate that followed was so intensely opposed to nationalization that the Social Democrats dropped this part of their program. At the same time, Ernst Wigforss, one of the Party's leading intellectuals, was developing ideas to replace nationalization with more viable alternatives.

[59] Timothy A. Tilton, "A Swedish Road to Socialism: Ernst Wigforss and the Ideological Foundations of Swedish Social Democracy," *American Political Science Review*, 73 (June 1979).

[60] Quoted in ibid., p. 516.

mocracy did eventually develop, to a fuller extent in Sweden than elsewhere (especially Britain). However, it came as a consequence of the economic strategy that was adopted rather than being its cause.

The unique Swedish strategy developed gradually. In the early 1930s Swedish socialists began to articulate policies based on the use of political power and the resources of government to affect a redistribution of wealth. Planning was of central importance. As Wigforss said in the 1944 program: "Whether an economic enterprise rests on private ownership or various forms of collective ownership, it must be coordinated in an overall economic plan, if labor and material resources are not to languish in idleness or inefficient production."[61] Wigforss's conception of planning included the useful functions that markets perform, especially in moderating inflation.[62] It amounted, in fact, to a special way of prodding the "invisible hand." This central element has been maintained to this day. Swedish planning emphasizes incentives, guidance, and assistance, not controls.

Swedish national economic management is noted less for the fact that planning was early adopted as a tool of management than for the goals which the plans have been intended to achieve. Planning organizes the economy, first, for a higher and more efficient level of production and therefore growth and, second, for full employment. The two goals are in no way mutually exclusive, nor is one given greater priority over the other. Proper use of resources, through planning, necessarily (in the Swedish perspective) contributed to both goals at the same time, and improvements in the one led to improvements in the other. Clearly, the impetus for this approach, which was first adopted in the 1930s, stemmed from the Depression. But by the time World War II erupted, certain key features of economic management had already been put into practice; others

[61] Ibid.
[62] Ibid.

were being discussed and elaborated. I look briefly at these key features through which plans were implemented and growth and full employment achieved.

The first feature involved the use of "Keynesian" measures of deficit financing, used in Sweden before Keynes fully developed his ideas. As soon as the Social Democrats were elected in 1932, public spending for public works increased.[63] Whatever the area of public employment, wages were paid at the rate normal for the occupation. This was one response to the unemployment problem. At the same time, it included a response to the problem of under-consumption. Increased employment at normal wages would increase demand, it was reasoned, setting in motion the spiral of feedback necessary for economic recovery. Sweden's rapid recovery seemed to confirm the effectiveness of these measures. There is considerable debate, however, as to what actually led to the recovery and its speed. It is becoming clear that public works and public spending were probably less significant than a much resisted devaluation of the kronor, which led first to increased exports and in turn to increased employment.[64] As in the case of Britain, international circumstances outside the control of the state created conditions within which domestic economic policies developed. However, whereas the conditions constrained the development of socialist policies in Britain, they led to economic prosperity in Sweden which, in turn, enabled the development of socialist policies. Once Sweden made the commitment to full employment using novel economic ideas, the commitment was reinforced by fortuitous circumstances.

In order to maintain the pace of economic recovery, public spending had to be complemented by increased investment in industry. This second key feature of Swedish economic management became increasingly refined over years

[63] Public spending increased in other areas too, such as for social programs for old age pensions, public health insurance, housing allowances, and support to families with children.

[64] Martin, "Is Democratic Control . . . Possible?" p. 39.

of experimentation.[65] In its early form, in the late 1930s, the system of industrial investment reflected the Swedish economy, which was still basically capitalist. At first, companies were simply given tax deductions for their investments. Later developments reveal a greater role of the state. By the 1950s, the deduction was granted for the allocation of investment funds to a reserve administered by the government. By the 1960s, companies were required to allocate up to 40% of their profits to the investment fund in the Bank of Sweden. Release of the funds is now determined by the state or must be authorized by the state or Labour Market Board. The role of this investment fund in national economic planning is clearly critical.

Two additional key features of Sweden's economic management are the industrial and labor market policies that were developed in the 1950s and 1960s. These policies have been discussed in detail in Chapter 4. Here I will review certain of their characteristics with the purpose of demonstrating how they further enhanced the already close relationship between the state and organized labor. These policies were developed through a process of deliberation and cooperation between the tripartite partners, with the state and labor playing superior roles, and the policies were adopted as an alternative to other measures, in particular incomes policies. An incomes policy had been negotiated and applied in the late 1940s, in much the same way, for similar reasons, and with similar consequences as in Britain. However, unlike Britain, its failure in Sweden marked the end of any more such ventures "because the LO refused to consent to any more and no Swedish Social Democratic Government ever tried to impose any form of wage restraint over the LO's objections."[66] Sweden turned instead to a "structural strategy of economic management."[67]

[65] "The Swedish System of Investment Funds," *Fact Sheets on Sweden* (March 1977).

[66] Martin, "Is Democratic Control . . . Possible?" p. 40. Martin notes further that LO was opposed to incomes policies because these by nature "threaten organizational and ideological interests of unions."

[67] Ibid.

Two LO economists, Gösta Rehn and Rudolf Meidner, are credited with having developed the model of economic management which LO proposed to the Social Democratic government in 1951 and which was implemented by the government in the 1960s.[68] The model related problems of aggregate demand to problems in productivity and employment. It placed solutions squarely on the structure of the economy and not only on countercyclical responses to the particular state of the business cycle. The model held that industries which are inefficient, have low productivity and low profits cannot afford to pay high wages and, therefore, they underemploy. If such industries are local or regional, those areas experience low demand, or depression-like situations. In contrast, industries at the other end of the scale on productivity and profits increase the wages they offer in order to attract labor. Since prices inevitably increase as a result of high wages, these industries potentially contribute to inflation. The LO model attacked the way industries with different levels of productivity push or pull the economy, either at the same time or in cycles. Their approach to demand management was guided by the twin goals of full employment and growth.

The first part of the model suggested that labor and capital be shifted from the less efficient to the more efficient industries. This would take care of problems of low productivity and growth, underemployment, and low demand. The second part of the model proposes various measures to facilitate and accelerate this structural change. The primary measure is the host of programs that go into the "active" manpower policy, including retraining, information about trends in the labor market, and financial support during job transition. Other measures involve rehousing assistance. Others still suggest a stronger state role in investment together with increased public savings to accumulate adequate funds for investment purposes.

[68] The Social Democrats did not have a sufficient majority in Parliament to put the plan into effect earlier. During the 1950s they had to form a coalition with the Agrarian-Center Party.

Clearly, if unemployment and inflation are considered a trade-off, the LO's model of economic management sought to overcome unemployment first. It proposed shifting labor to more productive sectors, increasing the productivity of those sectors, and thereby increasing demand for labor in those sectors. But the model did not overlook the problem of inflationary pressures, and it handled the problem in such a way as to maintain high wages. First, it proposed that the government take a stronger role in the use of fiscal policy to contain profits within acceptable limits relative to wages and prices. In particular, sales and other indirect taxes were proposed to prevent employers from reaping the benefit of higher prices and, therefore, to prevent them from raising their prices. Of course, these taxes also dampen demand. Second, LO included its wage agreements with SAF as a measure to control spiraling wages and inflationary pressures. These negotiations are conducted, of course, without government intervention. But overall, Sweden's economic strategy does tolerate a certain level of inflation as a price for no toleration of unemployment. Once again, this contrasts directly with the British calculation of the trade-off between inflation and unemployment.

The LO's model developed over time. Eventually, each feature became integral to the economic strategy framework. Certain features of the early "Rehn" model aroused considerable opposition, especially from business, and so were modified or discarded.[69] By the mid- to late-1960s, however, both the LO and the Social Democratic government were placing greater emphasis on labor market policies. While this emphasis is admirable in many ways, it cannot in and of itself be a predominant tool in demand management. For too much reliance on manpower policies to steer the economy, without strong complementary fiscal policies, gives too much rein to inflationary pressures. In-

---

[69] The industrial policy in particular is now given only lip-service, for declining industries rarely fold anymore, as plants in the textile industry once did. However, the manpower complement to industrial policy is strongly implemented.

deed, inflationary pressures did set in. These eventually led to a strain in the otherwise compatible partnership between labor and the state, as I indicate below.

Labor-State Partnership: Mixed Relations in a Mixed Economy

For our purpose, the significant points about this economic strategy concern the relationship between labor and the state that the strategy reveals. First, it is clear from the fact that the Social Democratic government adopted much of the LO model of economic structural change that the goals of the Party in office were the same as those of the labor movement. Full employment was given top priority. Taken together with the goals of productivity and growth, the consequences were certainly good for business too, that is, those businesses that could survive the competitiveness which the system embodied. Second, the compatibility of labor and Social Democratic goals is completely understandable in view of the close historical development of the two movements. From the beginning, the one movement needed the other to further its purposes. After the Social Democrats gained office in 1932 and had been there for some time, the security of stable tenure allowed them to develop and implement a socialist program which included, as always, workers' interests. Third, circumstances beyond the control of labor or the state were favorable to this collusion of interests. As we have seen, Sweden's economy was late in industrializing and highly specialized when it did. Sweden does not have the international burden of a declining international currency or overseas military pressure to contend with, and can therefore devote its full attention to national economic objectives, including effective national adaptations to changes in the international economy, on which Sweden is highly dependent. Fourth, good working relations developed among the leaders of both movements, as well as with business leaders, aided by the stability and longevity of leadership and the "solidarity" and increasing centralization in all three organizations. Finally, business did not pose a serious threat to the implementation of the economic strategy or to harmonious relations because the strategy ultimately made full use of competitive, capitalist free enterprise. Socialism was embodied in the distribution of society's wealth and less in its production.

The economic strategy did not, however, fully achieve its purposes. For a time, Sweden came as close to full employment as it is possible to come. But when the international economic situation worsened in the 1970s, Sweden was badly affected by payments difficulties and by inflationary pressures. The tendency of domestic policies did not help, of course. Sweden's heavy reliance on manpower policies for full employment already contained an inflationary bias; when it increased beyond tolerance, inflation created a strain in the relations between labor and the state. Rising inflation meant that the power of capital (to raise prices) was taking an upper hand in directing the economy. Indirect measures to handle rising prices, especially the sales tax to hold back demand, not only were insufficient but also began to hurt the lower income groups. As a final blow, it was becoming apparent that unemployment was beginning to rise. The LO, aware of the fact that income disparities had not decreased for years, became increasingly aggressive in seeking wage claims and in attempting to narrow wage differentials. Concerned about rising unemployment, LO began to press for legislation to improve employment security, breaking the tradition of collective bargaining as the sole means of arbitration in this field. LO's posture was necessitated by growing union militancy which finally broke out in wildcat strikes. Placed on the defensive, the government found it necessary to pass legislation controlling and restricting wildcat strikes.

These events have not led to a breach in relations or cooperation between labor and the state, but they have created a testiness, which became more acute with a nonsocialist coalition government in power. Labor's role as an equal tripartite partner had developed because of its alliance with the Social Democratic government. That role is no longer dependent on the alliance, but the degree of labor's cooperation is dependent on the state's commitment to labor's goals. This is true regardless of the party in power. Although the Social Democrats are able to elicit a greater degree of compliance from organized labor, the fact that labor did protest when necessary attests to its independence. Independence has enabled labor to maintain its identity as a class movement, one which has had common purposes with an essentially class-based political movement, but one which has been able to actively take politics to task when necessary.

Britain and Sweden Compared

The basic differences in the nature of the social coalitions that have developed between labor and the state in Britain and Sweden are differences in, first, timing and sequence of formation and events; second, the power, position, and role of labor; and third, the exogenous factors which have affected domestic policies.

In Britain, the development of the labor movement preceded by over a century the development of its representative political party, the Labour Party. This not only gave the labor movement time to acquire a firm sense of its special interests, it also retarded the consolidation of the labor movement as a political force, capable of achieving its aims democratically. The deep-rooted sectionalism of British labor, founded in the diversity of industrialization, the horizontal divisions among classes and occupations, and the organizational weakness of attempts at amalgamation, still prevail. In Sweden, industrialization and the development of labor and social democratic movements all took place within a few decades of each other. Right from the beginning, organized labor and the Social Democratic Party worked together to achieve a common goal: universal suffrage. That first experience of strength through unity continued to structure later cooperative efforts. Moreover, organized labor in Sweden was never as divided within itself as in Britain. For one, the homogeneity of industrialism in Sweden lent itself well to industry-based organization. For another, the speed of development and rapid affiliation with a political party encouraged early consolidation of labor's interests.

In Britain, the fragmentation of the labor movement at the time of the formation of the Labour Party weakened the initial link between organized labor as a whole and the Labour Party. Labour M.P.'s proposed a number of particular policies for workers in particular industries, but the Party as a whole did not develop a strong identification with a constituency of workers as a class. The early ties between the Labour Party and the Liberals contributed to this ambiguity in Labour's roots. When the Labour Party finally and fervently adopted socialism as its guiding philosophy in the 1920s, the Party's links with organized labor did not thereby become significantly tighter. For Labour's brand of socialism was intellectualized and abstract, whereas workers were concerned with the many specific objectives they wished to achieve. Through the Party Conference and its Manifesto, the Labour Party appeared to be the political arm of workers. However, the actual inclusion of organized labor in the political process was minimal, and eventually the already fragile link between the Party and unions was further strained by incomes policies. Organized labor has been an inferior actor in Britain's tripartite system. This has been due as much to factors structuring Britain's economic situation as to organizational factors in the labor and socialist movements.

In Sweden the early and strong ties between organized labor and the Social Democratic Party and the immediate testing of the political power of this coalition in the suffrage issue formed a core relationship upon which future endeavors could be built. Although the Social Democratic Party also had early ties with Sweden's Liberal Party, its identification with the working class was not thereby weakened, as it was in Britain. For one, the Social Democrats' ties with the Liberals were primarily expedient and issue-specific; that is, the two parties worked together in Parliament to pass legislation for universal suffrage, and at other times in other issues. While there was also an ideological link between the Social Democrats and the Liberals, it was not emphasized in any way. The Social Democratic Party looked instead essentially to the needs of the working class for its guiding philosophy, and the leaders of the unified organized labor movement were readily consulted and eventually were included in the political process of policy formation. The stronger role of organized labor in Sweden may well have stemmed from the success of the first Basic Agreement between unions and employers. From that time on, the stature of labor continued to grow exponentially. By the 1960s, LO economists had become more important in the government bureaucracy than most elected M.P.'s.

Lastly, the two countries occupy very different positions in the international economy. Great Britain has suffered from its imperial legacy in two ways. First, a continued international role for sterling has seemed to be inescapably seductive to successive governments, Labour and Conservative alike. But the attempt to maintain a declining reserve currency adds an enormous financial burden to the country as a whole, even though it may bring profits to some sectors. Moreover, choosing this policy option ipso facto strengthens the domestic sectors that support it and carry it out, and entails certain financial measures to sustain it. The critical set of decisions to pursue this option and thereby to subordinate domestic social policy to external financial orthodoxy was triggered by the United States, in the immediate postwar years. Once set in motion, it required no further exogenous push. Second, Britain has maintained a military presence abroad which, though repeatedly reduced, has always produced a drain on the balance of payments, thereby adding to the wage deflation required by international sterling. Sweden has had no such problems. It is extremely dependent on the international economy, but its instruments of economic management, including the value of its currency and its social policies, are ironically freer to pursue national objectives. Indeed, active domestic social policies are a means for Sweden, as for other small social democratic states, by which to adjust rapidly and effectively to changes in the international division of labor and thereby to compensate for international economic weakness.[70]

WOMEN AS WORKERS: UNIVERSALISM AND SOCIAL CHANGE

Perhaps the most significant development concerning women workers in Sweden is the tendency toward "universalization" of the category of worker. This means that the distinctions among workers based on class, occupation, and sex, are breaking down and becoming less determinant of workers' opportunities and rewards. Universalization can be seen both within the labor movement and in the state's relations with labor. It is absent in Britain. I discuss first how this tendency is manifest in Sweden and then present its significance for women workers.

The history of the labor movement in Sweden is marked by an ability to overcome sectional differences which remain divisive in Britain. As early as 1912, the LO made industrial unionism, rather than craft- or occupation-based unionism, its principle of organization. Having a single union responsible for all the workers in a single plant or industry, whatever their occupation, is conducive to greater unity in the labor movement. The LO is still predominantly a blue-collar or working-class organization. But by the 1970s its middle-class membership had risen to about 15%. Sweden's second largest labor organization is the Central Organization for Salaried Employees (TCO), formed in 1944 as an amalgamation of several white-collar organizations. Its principle of organization is also industrial unionism. About 75% of its membership is from the middle class. In all, about 80% of Sweden's workers are organized on the basis

[70] Peter Katzenstein, "Conclusion: Domestic Structures and Strategies of Foreign Economic Policy," *International Organization*, 31 (Autumn 1977).

of vertical or industrial unionism. These figures still "reflect the system of occupation stratification" in Sweden.[71] But they also indicate the tendency toward consolidation in the labor movement, and even toward greater homogeneity in its class basis. This tendency is further evident in the basic process of collective bargaining in Sweden. Although TCO has its own "Basic Agreement" with SAF, it has recently granted the LO authority to include it in LO's more frequent rounds of negotiations with SAF. In addition, the LO and TCO are beginning to cooperate in a number of other areas, one of which is the development of "wage earners' funds."[72] In sum, the labor movement in Sweden is beginning to show signs of becoming a more cohesive unit, based on a commonality of interests among all workers whatever their class or occupation. Although only a *tendency*, this development can be thought of as reflecting a conception of workers as a *general* category—not simply as manual laborers, but as *all persons who work*. This is unique to Sweden. In Britain, in contrast, workers are becoming more divided among themselves, as shop stewards seek more particularistic settlements with management and as the pressure for continued wage differentials heightens.

The tendency toward universalization of the category of worker is also becoming evident at the level of the state in Sweden. From its beginnings the Social Democratic Party was associated with the working class. Political organization developed at the same time as did working-class organization, and the two movements were mutually interdependent. Over time, however, the Social Democratic Party has become less a working-class party than a party *for the class of persons who work*. We can see this in two ways: the party's composition and the party's policies.

Well over half of Social Democratic voters have always been from the working class, but the class base of the Party's

[71] Korpi, *The Working Class*, p. 66.

[72] This is still in the formative stages of discussion. It involves "the idea that private firms, in proportion to their profits, emit shares to collectively controlled funds." Korpi, *The Working Class*, p. 332.

constituency is now becoming much more mixed. The proportion of Social Democratic voters with higher secondary education has been increasing steadily.[73] Moreover, while the size of the working class in Sweden had remained fairly stable for most of the century and their proportion of the vote for the Party has remained steady, the size of the middle class has grown considerably and the majority of *new* Social Democratic voters come from among the middle classes.[74] Among the Party's Members of Parliament now only half come from working-class backgrounds; among those who have served in Social Democratic governments as cabinet ministers or deputies, only about one-third come from working-class backgrounds and two-thirds have had a university education.

Voting patterns in Britain tend to follow class lines more closely. When affiliations change, they are likely to involve a greater working-class vote for the Conservatives than a middle-class or upper-class vote for Labour.

The tendency toward universalization of workers is most evident in the area of policies. Swedish labor market policies put into effect in the 1960s are particularly notable. These are explicitly intended to enlist all workers directly in the national goal of economic growth. For instance, the training service operated by the National Labor Market Board offers courses in every occupational field, but trainees are guided into those courses that are most likely to lead to good jobs. As a follow-up, the employment service, a public monopoly, keeps track of all job vacancies in the country and assists in speedy employment or redeployment. The operational premise of these programs is that all workers

[73] In 1961 25% of Social Democratic voters were in this category. Ibid., p. 105.

[74] Ulf Himmelstrand and Jan Lindhagen, "Status-Rejection, Ideological Conviction and Some Other Hypotheses about Social Democratic Loyalty in Sweden," in Richard Scase, (ed.), *Readings in the Swedish Class Structure* (Oxford: Pergamon Press, 1976). This does not mean that the Social Democratic Party has become more bourgeois. My use of the concept of universalization does not imply embourgeoisement.

can and must contribute to economic growth, but in order to do so labor must be efficiently allocated. British labor market programs, on the other hand, are victimized by their presumably unintended consequence of stratifying workers on the basis of class, occupation, and sex. The manpower program is especially flawed because of its heavy emphasis on skills training for blue-collar occupations or lower level white-collar jobs, and because class- and sex-based criteria are still strong determinants of occupational channeling. Training for most "middle-class" occupations in Britain is the responsibility of the educational system and is not connected with labor market policies (see Chapter 3). Moreover, the new state Training Services Agency in Britain is but one of many training programs, and it is probably less effective than the others, for privately operated programs offer greater certainty of jobs after their training courses while publicly operated job placement services are neither successful nor popular. In sum, Swedish programs treat all workers as potential contributors to economic growth. British programs are based on market determinations of labor allocation, and they stratify the labor force accordingly.

What do these developments mean for women as workers? This study has consistently shown that while economic imperatives for women's employment may exist, they are subject to interpretation and mediation by the state in a process that we might call the state's "construction of social reality." Specifically, not until labor market policies based on a *broader* conception of workers were adopted in Sweden did the state introduce policies facilitating the entry into the economy and the economic advance of *women as workers.* Special training programs for women re-entering the labor market, as well as day care programs for children, can be seen as part of this framework of policies making effective use of *all possible* workers in achieving productivity and economic growth. These policies attenuate those characteristics of workers that in the past might have affected their status in the economy, characteristics such as class, occupation, and sex.

In contrast, in Britain women have remained a particularistic claimant, one among many, draining government resources by requiring special programs. The conception of the place of women as workers differs from the Swedish, as does the attitude toward the necessity or desirability of doing something for women. When the state has developed measures to improve women's chances in the labor market, it has relied heavily on "selective" measures alone. A "universal framework" comparable to the Swedish labor market policy nexus for economic growth and full employment does not exist in Britain. Chapter 3 suggested that selective measures without a universal framework are limited in their potential contribution to social change. The case of the Sex Discrimination Act, for instance, showed that one kind of change (in employers' practices) can go no further in creating the conditions for a type of change (equality for women workers) that is multifaceted and enmeshed in a complex process of social transformation. The achievement of a universal framework for government policies in Britain rests on the capacity to overcome the forces of selectivity and particularism that fragment and divide the labor force within itself and from the economy and the state. As this chapter has shown, the possibility of achieving such a framework involves political and economic conditions which are unlikely to develop in Britain as long as the prevailing traditions of the British political economy remain in force. As long as the interests of labor remain largely subordinate to other concerns in economic management, women workers will be in a double bind—their position and role within the labor movement recapitulating that of labor within the governing coalition.[75] Thus, the tasks that confront women as workers in Britain are twofold: enhancing their position

[75] For the place of women in unions in Britain, see Chapter 3. Also see Ross Davies, *Women and Work* (London: Arrow Books, 1975), Chapters 4 and 5.

within labor and at the same time making labor a stronger social force.

One main task still remains for women in Sweden as well: it concerns the position and role of women within the labor movement. Thus far, women workers in Sweden have allowed their interests to be pursued by dominant coalitions speaking on their behalf. This has achieved the tendency toward universalization of the category of worker, a necessary aspect of progress for workers. But I have noted throughout this study an apparent halt in further progress for women in Sweden. What is required to achieve fuller equality for women workers in Sweden is greater use of selective measures to complement the well-developed universal framework of labor market policy. Specifically, progress for women workers in Sweden is constrained mainly by occupational segregation. Thus far, government measures to break down sex-based work assignments have met with limited success. These measures have not been sufficiently forceful because they impinge on the freedom of employers. Stronger measures or legislation requiring special considerations for women workers (perhaps including quotas) are called for. However, greater efforts by the state to institute selective measures are being stalled by unions' concerns about what this might mean for other categories of "special" workers, and concerns about the unity of the labor movement. Their concerns are well-founded. The unity of the labor movement may well be jeopardized if successive categories of workers make claims that require special consideration. The strength of unity in the labor movement in Sweden would be tested should this centrifugal pull increase in significance. Added to the emerging sources of dissatisfaction with the prevailing mode of organizing the Swedish welfare state that were discussed in Chapter 6, such a development could seriously affect the position of women, the place of labor, and the future of the welfare state.

In this chapter I have stressed the "workers" side of "women workers." I have attributed progress in the position of working women to progress in the position of workers within society. I have argued that the interests of women workers can be maximized only by their systematic incorporation into the broader framework of social coalitions. For the successful achievement of their employment pursuits, women must be incorporated into labor, and labor must be incorporated into the governing coalition. Otherwise, the condition of women workers is likely to remain separate and unequal.

INDEX

grants, government (*cont.*)
240, 255, 261n, 286, 288-289
Graubard, Stephen, 306n
Gregory, Jeanne, 123n
growth rate, *see* economic growth
guidance, vocational, *see* vocational guidance

Hadow Report, 186n
Hakim, Catherine, 66n, 67n
Hancock, M. Donald, 57n, 164n, 284n, 322n, 329n
handicapped persons, *see* workers, handicapped
Hart, Horst, 167n, 168n, 172n
Hartmann, Heidi, 23n
Hauser, Robert M., 65n
Hayward, Jack, 52n
Heady, Bruce W., 237n
health care, 182n, 299
Health Services and Public Health Act (Britain, 1968), 193-194
health-related occupations, *see* occupations, health-related
Heclo, Hugh, 182n, 206n, 240n
Heidenheimer, Arnold J., 206n
Henning, Margaret, 89n
Hewitt, Patricia, 122n, 127n
Himmelstrand, Ulf, 342n
housework, *see* Domestic labor, unpaid
housing policy, *see* policy, housing
Hunt, Audrey, 198n, 207n, 210n

Ideology, 4, 19, 57n, 62, 64, 305
ILP, *see* Independent Labour Party
immigration, 35-36, 58n, 162n-163n. *See also* migration, net
incomes policy, *see* policy, incomes
Independent Labour Party, 303-304
industrial expansion, 57, 59-60
industrial policy, *see* policy, industrial

industrial reserve army, *see* labor reserve
industrial sector, 27, 33, 48, 51, 71, 76, 148, 151-152, 158, 322n. *See also* manufacturing sector; occupations, craft
industrial societies, *see* societies, advanced industrial
Industrial Training Act (1964), 107
Industrial Training Boards, 107-109
industrial tribunal, 122-125, 127, 174
industrialization, 7, 9, 30, 38, 62, 185, 302, 322, 337
infant class, 215
infant school, 187n
inflation, 28, 54, 57-58, 97-98, 165, 311, 313, 319, 330, 334
interest groups, 16, 198, 250-252, 282, 292
International Labour Organisation Convention No. 100 on Equal Remuneration (1951), 70n, 125, 164
International Labour Organisation Convention No. 111 on Discrimination in Respect of Employment and Occupation (1958), 125n, 173
Intervention (state), 13-17, 29, 89-94, 99-101, 132, 295-298; ameliorative, 14, 90, 184; depth of, 11, 14, 88, 95-100, 132, 143-144, 182; design of, 183-184, 270-281; determinants of, 13-14, 183-184, 199-210, 261-270; form of, 14, 182, 245-247; institutionalization of, 15, 183-184, 233-247, 281-292; in private sector, 95-96, 183
Investment Reserve Fund, 59, 155-156, 331-332. *See also*, Public spending

18, 283-286, 297-298 (*see also*, corporatism)

Werneke, Diane, 79n

Westergaard, John, 316n

white-collar occupations, *see* occupations, white-collar

Wigforss, Ernst, 57n, 329-330

Wildavsky, Aaron, 240n

Wilensky, Harold L., 29n, 62n, 206n, 245n, 253n

Willmott, Peter, 208n

Wilson, Harold, 54n

Wilson government, 54n, 320

Winkler, J. T., 250n, 252n

Winston, Kathryn Teich, 3n, 162n-163n

Wolpe, AnnMarie, 22n, 23n

women-specific factors, as expla-

nation of policy responses, 9-11. *See also*, Discrimination, Stereotypes

Women's Advisory Committee of the TUC, *see* Unions, women's council in

women's movements, 3, 283

Woodcock, George, 318

Wootton, Graham, 125n, 235n

Workers, handicapped, 156; marginal, 9, 29, 53, 55, 61-62, 63-87, 118, 136, 150, 163, 248; permanent, 29, 84

Young, Michael, 208n

Zeliner, Harriet, 64n

Zetterberg, Hans, 292n

Library of Congress Cataloging in Publication Data

Ruggie, Mary, 1945-
  The state and working women.

  Includes index.
  1. Women—Employment—Great Britain. 2. Discrimination in
employment—Government policy—Great Britain. 3. Day
care centers—Government policy—Great Britain. 4. Women
—Employment—Sweden. 5. Discrimination in employment—
Government policy—Sweden. 6. Day care centers—Government
policy—Sweden. I. Title.
HD6135.R84 1984   331.4′12042′0941   84-42563
ISBN 0-691-09407-1 (alk. paper)
ISBN 0-691-10169-8 (pbk.)